FRIENDS NOT MASTERS

A Political Autobiography

The author

Friends Not Masters

A POLITICAL AUTOBIOGRAPHY

MOHAMMAD AYUB KHAN

PRESIDENT OF PAKISTAN

'*People in developing countries seek assistance,*
but on the basis of mutual respect; they want
to have friends not masters.'

1967
OXFORD UNIVERSITY PRESS
New York   London   Karachi

Oxford University Press, Ely House, London W. 1

GLASGOW NEW YORK TORONTO MELBOURNE WELLINGTON
CAPE TOWN SALISBURY IBADAN NAIROBI LUSAKA ADDIS ABABA
BOMBAY CALCUTTA MADRAS KARACHI LAHORE DACCA
KUALA LUMPUR HONG KONG TOKYO

DEDICATED

TO THOSE WHO HAVE WORKED FOR THE BUILDING OF

PAKISTAN

AS A PROGRESSIVE AND MODERN STATE

AND TO

THOSE WHO HAVE DEFENDED IT

WITH SUCH DISTINCTION

PREFACE

This is essentially a spoken book. After I had defined the broad scope and outlines of the book I asked some friends to prepare questions on the theme of different chapters. The question-and-answer sessions began in June 1964 and continued till the end of the year. The tape-recordings of these sessions came to nearly thirty hours and the transcript covered more than 900 pages. I got the transcript some time in 1965. Since then I have been going over it and revising it from time to time.

It is not customary for a man in office to write his life story. Apart from the limitations imposed by the consciousness of responsibility there is always the danger that any suggestion of success would be interpreted as an attempt at image-building. Let me say, therefore, that the credit for whatever may have been achieved in terms of political stability or economic development should go to those who were associated with me in the implementation of various reforms. I may have presented new ideas but these were refined and put into execution by my colleagues in Government and by able and dedicated men in the Services. Above all, the willing support and co-operation of the people of Pakistan helped to lift the nation from the social and political morass of the fifties to its present level of prosperity and growth.

The narrative covers events up to the Presidential Elections in 1965, though there are references to later events particularly in the chapter relating to Foreign Affairs. While revising the manuscript I made use of my notes and other documents but situations and conversations have been largely reconstructed from memory. There may be some errors in my recollection of chronological and other details but these should not affect the line of argument.

I undertook this exercise without quite realizing how long and arduous it was going to be. I also did not know that the people I had chosen for preparing and asking the questions would prove so persistent. Still, it has been a refreshing and rewarding job. I have tried, as dispassionately as possible, to revaluate the past and interpret significant developments which have influenced the history of Pakistan. This history is still in the making but I think it has taken a positive direction and a stage has been reached from where one can look back and see an integrated picture. I hope this account explains the process through which I evolved some of my ideas and will help towards a better under-

standing of what I have attempted to do since becoming the President
of Pakistan.

I have tried to keep the narrative candid and objective, concentrating on problems and events rather than on personalities. Here and
there I have had to give my impressions and assessment of certain people
who were at the helm of affairs before the Revolution. Whatever I have
said is intended to substantiate my interpretation of political situations
and not to hurt the feelings of any individual, and I hope it will be read
in that spirit.

It is a story of struggle—struggle to get new ideas accepted. Whoever presumes to act as a pioneer in the field of ideas must be prepared
to face criticism and resistance. I have had a good deal of both. But my
conviction of the need and validity of the changes which I have tried to
bring about in the social and political life of the country remains as
fervent and unfaltering as ever. We gained freedom after a long period
of domination which left in its wake a legacy of old attitudes and habits.
The problem was to change these attitudes and habits and to bring
about a more direct and intimate awareness of contemporary realities.
I venture to think we have made progress in many fields. I have not
hesitated to admit failures. Progress is a long and tortuous process, full
of trials and errors.

I have viewed problems as a Pakistani, a Muslim, and an Asian.
Pakistan is my passion, my life. A look of happiness on the faces of
people thrills and sustains me. Just as a shade of anxiety in their eyes
causes me anguish. I have woken up from sleep to see whether the
sound on the window panes is of the long-awaited rain. I feel parched
inside when I see a drought-stricken field. The soil of Pakistan fascinates
me, for it is my soil. I belong to it.

Every moment of my life I have dedicated to the service of my people,
never for a moment yielding to any pressure or disappointment.
Pakistan has to establish a distinct national identity of her own in
moral, social, intellectual, and political terms and all my endeavours
have been devoted to this objective. While we may learn from the experience of others, we have to work out our own solutions and our own
salvation. I have always pursued the possible in a pragmatic and
moderate manner, conscious of the limitations inherent in our situation.
And I have never introduced emotion in the presentation of problems
to my people. We have a weakness for the dramatic and the sensational
which I try to avoid. Too often we mistake the emotional for the ideal.
For us, the ideal should be to develop a rational approach to life. We
cannot allow our vision to be clouded by memories of past glory. It is
the present, with all its complexities, on which we must concentrate,

and it is the future, with all its promise, for which we must work. Our present destiny is to move from crisis to crisis. For us there can be no rest or relaxation.

Internally, the major problem for us has been to establish political institutions and stable instruments of government. These institutions and instruments had to be fashioned according to our own thinking, temperament, and needs. The process has not been easy. In the earlier years, the whole approach was on a personal basis and problems were rarely seen in the broad national perspective. This, inevitably, retarded progress. The political system which we inherited had no relevance to our conditions. The result was that the system was misused and exploited to serve limited interests. It needed a revolution to replace the system by one which reflected the traditions of the people and responded to their aspirations.

I cannot claim that the new system has found universal acceptance, but it has taken roots and people are beginning to recognize its advantages. We have yet to develop a strong sense of nationalism, which means rising above the personal and the parochial and evolving a mature mode of dealing with the problems of the country.

As a Muslim my sole anxiety has been to unite the people of Pakistan in the light of their faith and ideology. This ideology I understand in terms of certain immutable principles: the unity of God, equality and brotherhood of man, progress to higher levels of existence, and adherence to the fundamentals of Islam. Our society is torn by a number of schisms; the most fundamental is the one which separates the educated classes from the traditional groups. It is vital that understanding and communication between these two sections should be restored. This can come about through a proper interpretation of Islamic principles and their application to the present-day problems. Unless this happens the gulf will grow which may eventually isolate the traditional groups from the modern educated classes and alienate the latter from Islam.

In dealing with world affairs, I have viewed problems as an Asian. It is within the Asian community that we have to establish for ourselves a permanent place of respect and strength. This is what our national interests demand. And this is why we continue to work for peace and stability in this part of the world. We have been able to establish normal relations with our neighbours (with the unfortunate exception of India) while maintaining our traditional contacts with western powers, particularly with the United States of America. In this matter our thinking has been guided as much by our own interests as by the limitations of our political and economic resources. We are dedicated to peace because peace alone will give us the time which we need for our development. Our endeavour is to remain out of the orbit of major power conflicts. This we can achieve only through honest and straight-forward dealings with others.

A number of fateful events have taken place since 1965. I have not dealt with them in this volume because some of the events are too much a part of the present to permit a dispassionate interpretation at this time. I hope I shall be able to deal with them on some future occasion.

I am grateful for the assistance which I have received in the pre-paration of this book from various people. I must also acknowledge the kindness of the Government of Pakistan in the Ministry of Foreign Affairs and the Cabinet Division in permitting me to make use of official documents in order to complete some of the details.

FIELD MARSHAL MOHAMMAD AYUB KHAN

RAWALPINDI
28 February 1967

CONTENTS

ILLUSTRATIONS

MAPS
(at end)

FRIENDS NOT MASTERS

A Political Autobiography

بِسْمِ اللّٰهِ الرَّحْمٰنِ الرَّحِيمْ

In the name of Allah,
the Beneficent, the Merciful.

إِنَّ اللّٰهَ لَا يُغَيِّرُ مَا بِقَوْمٍ حَتّٰى يُغَيِّرُوْا وَاما بِأَنْفُسِهِمْ

Surely Allah changes not the condition of a people, until they change
their own condition.

1

Youth

People have often asked me to write about my life. How does one do that while in the thick of it? Then there is an element of demonstration in writing for public consumption, which is alien to my nature. All my life, whatever I have done in response to the call of duty, I have done silently and quietly, not even keeping a regular diary of my experiences.

I have been associated closely with the government since 1951 when I became Commander-in-Chief of the Pakistan Army and I have been responsible for running the government since the Revolution in October 1958. Many things have happened during this period, both good and bad, and it might be useful to re-state them. The problem has been to find time to revaluate the past. This was resolved by a period of forced leisure when I was convalescing in Murree after an operation in June 1964.

Life for me has always been busy, crowded with events. One of the few spells of inactivity that I can remember is an hour that I spent sitting, all by myself, one evening in the compound of a rest house in Cox's Bazar. I sat still, absorbing the silence around me. In the distance the sea-waves noiselessly rolled over the soft shores of the Bay of Bengal and for a moment the tumult of life subsided. Apart from a few such brief experiences, life has been a relentless pressure of duty.

I was born in the village of Rehana on 14 May 1907. It was the last day of the month of Ramadhan and the family was preparing to celebrate Eidul Fitr. My father had had four children by his first wife, who died, and I was the first child by his second wife. Rehana is a picturesque little village about fifty miles north of Rawalpindi in West Pakistan. It is surrounded by an undulating range of low hills, with the pine-covered slopes of the Himalayas in the distance. My forefathers settled in this area after emigrating from Afghanistan.

One of my earliest memories is of a bird which used to call at day-break. It was the signal to go to school, which meant getting pulled out of bed, a hurried wash, and a four-mile ride on the back of a mule. Even now, whenever I hear this bird I get restless.

My mother was a simple woman who spent all her life in the village. She continued to live in our modest ancestral home till her death, doing whatever she could do to help the village folk. She was a strong-willed person and remained mentally alert till the last. I remember the birth of my youngest brother. I was then about two and a half years old. I saw this child lying by the side of my mother. I seized a stick and wanted to beat him. I was taken away. It was a great torture seeing another child sleeping by the side of my mother and it took me a long time to get over that feeling. I remember it vividly to this day.

While I was deeply attached to my mother, it was my father who had the greatest influence of all on my character, outlook, and attitude towards life. He was a Risaldar Major in Hodson's Horse. Physically he was a powerful man; his presence in the village would inspire awe and respect. But I remember him as a friend, extremely gentle, pious, and affectionate. He had a sensitive and understanding mind and I always found great mental satisfaction in his company. He had a vague but strong sense of Muslim nationalism. I remember on one occasion in 1919 or 1920 an *a'lim* (religious scholar) from Mansehra came to him and said: 'India is *darul harb*. The rulers of this part of the world are *kafirs* (non-believers), we should therefore migrate from here.' My father said: 'Maulvi Sahib, my only desire is to die under the flag of Islam but where is that flag? There is no Muslim country today which is free. They are all dominated by colonial powers.'

My father was a deeply religious man. He never missed his prayers and would say his *tahajjud* regularly. I remember once waking up in the middle of the night. I could feel his tall figure standing by my bed, his head bowed in prayer. I knew he was praying for me but I did not stir in my bed lest I should disturb him.

It was from my father that I learnt most of my family history. We belong to the Tarin tribe which ruled over parts of Hazara and Camp-bellpur districts and was involved in a long and bitter struggle against the Sikhs and the British. The people of this tribe came from Pishin (now in Baluchistan) which was originally a part of the Afghan Empire.

I would be fascinated to know more about the life story of one of our ancestors, Sardar Mohammad Khan Tarin. He was a man of in-domitable courage and had great strength of character. He was the eldest son of Sardar Najibullah Khan Tarin and became ruler of the State and settled in Guldheri. The local tribes, Gujjars, Dalazaks, Jodoons, and Utmanzais, gave him a lot of trouble but he established his control over them by crushing their revolts. In the early decades of the nineteenth century he faced a number of Sikh invasions. In 1822 Hari Singh Nalva, the Sikh Governor of Kashmir, entered Hazara to

1 The author's father, Risaldar Major Mir Dad Khan

2   The author as second lieutenant after leaving Sandhurst, 1929

defeat the Tarin Sardar, but failed in his attempt. This failure infuri-
ated Maharaja Ranjit Singh who himself invaded Hazara with a large
force. Sardar Mohammad Khan was captured and taken to Lahore.
Hari Singh purchased him for fifty thousand rupees and brought him
to Rewat in Rawalpindi district. Hari Singh wanted him to accept the
Sikh rule in his area. This was not acceptable to Sardar Mohammad
Khan, so he was thrown into a dried-up well. He was fed on salted
bread and was given no water to drink: he died of thirst and starvation,
but refused to yield to the Sikhs.

Later, when the British tried to occupy Hazara district, our people
resisted them too. The head of the family and his associates were
arrested and taken to the Allahabad Fort. I saw their graves in 1926.
The head of the family, I was told, was blown off the mouth of a gun,
while the others were subjected to great torture.

My father had a large family, and the income from his army pension
and the land was limited. But he was determined that I should get a
proper education. More than that, he was anxious for me to have
a grounding in Islam and Muslim thought. He wanted me to become a
Hafiz-e-Qur'an. The village Maulvi was chosen for this purpose. There
was great excitement in the house the first day I was sent to the mosque
to learn the Qur'an. I was then four years four months and four days
old. Sweets were distributed and I was placed under the charge of the
Maulvi. The experiment was not much of a success. Whatever part of
the Qur'an I was able to memorize during the two or three months I
spent with the Maulvi was based on an incorrect pronunciation. The
Maulvi did not like me very much because I wanted to know the
meaning of what I was being taught. On one such occasion he slapped
me and I slapped him back. My response was not in the best of taste
and it brought our brief association to an abrupt end.

I was then sent off to another village called Koka about two miles
away. In Koka there was another Maulvi Sahib, a revered old man,
who inspired in me great respect and also great fear. I studied under
him for a while and managed to learn as much of the Qur'an as a child
of my age could do. By then my father had decided that whatever else
I might make I was unlikely to become a *Hafiz-e-Qur'an*.

The family decided that it was time for me to go to a regular school.
I was admitted to a school in Sarai Saleh which was four miles from
our house. It was a tough routine to be woken up day after day and to
be placed on the back of a mule early in the morning. My mother used
to put my primer and other school books, along with what she called
my 'ration', in a bag. It was a beautiful winding road but the pranks
of the mule gave me little opportunity to appreciate the vast stretching

fields and the soft clouds nestling in the hills. I would get back home by about three o'clock in the afternoon, hungry and tired. Fortunately my grandmother persuaded my father to move me to a school in Haripur and let me live with her in Darvesh, which was close to the school.

I was not a very bright student, nor did I find studies a particularly absorbing occupation. I loved outdoor life. A relative of mine kept hawks and dogs and that was excuse enough for me to slip away from school to look after his hawks. The result was that I failed in my tests in the sixth class when I was eleven years old. My father discovered what had been going on and gave me a sound thrashing, after which it became easier to attend to my studies. I managed to complete my schooling with a good second division and without much effort. I was not too good at mathematics or geometry; algebra was the thing I understood better, and I enjoyed geography, English, Persian, and Urdu. There was no provision for games at the school but I found enough diversion in *kabaddi, gulli danda,* and marbles. Later I learnt to play hockey.

Riding, however, was in my blood and the early morning mule rides provided all the training that I required. In those days the Army would buy young horses from *zamindars* and my father kept a string of them. One day when I was eight or nine years old I took a polo pony, without my father's permission, and rode it to a near-by village to see my sister. That part of the world is rather rugged along the foothills. As I was coming back downhill, all of a sudden a bird fluttered out of a bush. The horse took fright and reared. As I fell off my left foot was caught in the stirrup and I was dragged for quite a distance through thorny bushes. Luckily, the clip in the stirrup straightened, the stirrup came out, and my foot was freed. I lay on the ground unconscious for several hours. When the horse got home, riderless and with a stirrup missing, a search was organized and I was recovered from the bushes, still unconscious. Had I been dragged for a few more minutes I would have been killed. My bones were intact but my back was badly bruised and for the next six months I had to sleep on my chest.

On the whole I found school life quite enjoyable. The school was run by the Sikhs and the teachers were very kindly and considerate, except for Master Sujhan Singh who was a tartar. He did not need much excuse or provocation to beat up the whole class, including the monitor, a position to which I was often elevated. Whenever anything went wrong it was the monitor who was the first to be punished for it. I remember a cold rainy day when Master Sujhan Singh did not turn up. We hoped to God he was dead. I was deputed by the class to go and find out what had happened. I found the Master surveying the debris of his house, which had collapsed under the rain, looking as alive as ever but a trifle disconcerted. I conveyed to him the concern of the class and suggested that we should all come and help him rebuild the house. He brusquely turned down the offer and asked me to go back to school, which I did, anxious to communicate the good news to my companions without loss of time. He could not attend the school for a fortnight and we found that a great relief.

The Sikhs were large-hearted people. I found their rituals and their songs in Punjabi absorbing. I still remember a line which fascinated me at that time:

سو رنگ تماشے تکدے اکھیاں نہیں رجیاں

—life is a great spectacle of colours; one sees so much of it and yet one has an insatiable desire for more. I learnt something very important at school. It was that I should never judge a man by his locality, colour, or vintage. All my life I have been unconscious of these considerations. It has been an article of faith with me that a man should be judged on merit. On one occasion, much later, I had to tell one of my own brothers, who was a Major in the army and had committed a serious irregularity, that he must either resign or face a court martial. He resigned.

While I was still at school my father would ask me, 'Would you like to go to Aligarh?' I hardly knew what Aligarh meant or where it was. He explained to me that it was a famous Muslim college, in the United Provinces, beyond Delhi. It was an Islamic institution and it had been established by the Muslims at great cost. He wanted me to go to Aligarh so that I could learn to feel like a Muslim. As soon as he heard that I had passed my matriculation examination, in 1922, he told me to go to Aligarh. He was in such a hurry that he sent me a month before the university opened.

When I arrived in Aligarh, with a servant, I found a group of four empty hostels, called Minto Circle, set in a very isolated area. It was almost a jungle and for company, apart from some *chowkidars* (watchmen), we had only jackals, pye dogs, and wild animals. We inquired of a *chowkidar* where we could get a couple of *charpoys* (beds). The *chowkidar* opened one of the rooms and we found a lot of *charpoys*, none of which had any *advaans* (the string which holds the woven bed taut to the frame). The *chowkidar* explained that when the boys leave they take out the *advaans* to tie up their luggage. So we had to sleep on those *charpoys* with our legs hanging down. We lived there virtually alone and we had to travel quite a distance every day to get food. My servant suggested that we return home as the university was not due to open for another month. I would have liked to do that but I did not have the courage to face the old man and convince him that I had not run away from Aligarh. 'No, sir, I cannot go back!' So I stayed on till the university opened and, as time passed, I began to develop a great affection for the people and the institution.

Aligarh was unique in many respects. I found there boys from all parts of India, Iran, and the African countries. They were drawn from widely differing social backgrounds and they spoke different dialects and languages; but they all had to learn to adjust themselves to the atmosphere of Aligarh. Some of them found life too hard and exacting, and ran away. But for those who stayed, there was a great feeling of equality, brotherhood, and camaraderie. And there were some who never wanted to leave the place, like Aslam Sahib who was in the tenth class and had a son in the ninth. He sat for his examination regularly and when I saw him he had already failed nine times. He would say, 'I am the only one here who takes his examinations without any personal motive.' The place had a charm of its own. I suffered from one handicap, my pronunciation and accent in Urdu were a little odd and I would mix my genders. At home I used to speak Hindko, which is a variation of Punjabi. Some of the students were amused but I could never understand the cause of their amusement. I would feel quite unhappy at times, but gradually I improved my Urdu pronunciation and they got accustomed to it.

Discipline and behaviour in Aligarh was largely the concern of the students themselves. There was little real contact between the teachers and the younger students. The masters were kind and helpful but they concentrated on teaching. The routine duties, including the arrangements for food, as well as dress and behaviour, were the responsibility of the senior students. And they were hard task-masters and very severe on anyone who did not maintain the standards and traditions of Aligarh. Inevitably, there was a considerable amount of ragging. The popular mode was 'dove-tailing' which meant that in the middle of the night your bed was overturned and you were plastered with muck. I knew my turn would come and I was dreading it. I am a light sleeper. One night I heard some slight noise and woke up to find four or five fellows armed with buckets standing close to my bed. I made a lunge at one of them and hit him as hard as I could. I kicked the next one. They had not bargained for this, so they pacified me by declaring that I was one of them and there was no need to create trouble.

I don't know how much I learnt in the way of academic studies but I did learn how to live with people of differing origins and backgrounds and how to understand their points of view. Aligarh has always remained a place of pilgrimage for me.

Later in life I was able to help the university when I was aide-de-camp to the British Resident in Hyderabad, Deccan, in 1931. Sir Ross Masood was the Vice-Chancellor of Aligarh at that time and he came to Hyderabad to get a donation for the university from the Nizam. The Nizam was so much under British influence that he did not dare to do anything without the Resident's permission. Sir Ross came to see the Resident but did not find him sympathetic. After some time he came again and I had an opportunity to meet him. I was deeply impressed by his devotion to the cause of Aligarh. The Resident was getting a little impatient with Sir Ross so I found an occasion to put in a word for him. I told the Resident, 'You might think this man is making a nuisance of himself, but he is utterly dedicated to the institution. His grandfather established it and his father spent his life there. The Nizam will only waste his money. Why not let him do something for a good cause?' In the end the Resident agreed and Sir Ross Masood got his donation from the Nizam. In the process he became quite friendly with me; I would go and see him quite often and though he was a much older man he treated me with great consideration. I wrote to him once that there was excellent soldier-material among the Muslims and the university should encourage them to join the training corps. Indeed, I urged him to make the university responsible for training suitable young men for the army.

Toward the end of my stay at Aligarh a commission led by General Skeen, who was Adjutant-General of the Army, visited the university with two or three Indian officers. They were looking for suitable officer-material for the army. There was considerable complaint in the country at that time that Indians were not getting fair representation among officers in the army. General Skeen and his advisers held a general *darbar* in Strachey Hall. This was early in 1926 and I was a member of the University Training Corps. General Skeen asked me, 'Would you like to go into the army?' I said, 'Of course I would like to go into the army'. He asked me why, and when I explained my family background and my father's service record, he advised me to submit my application. Later, I was interviewed by the Deputy Commissioner and then by the Governor of the Province. The final examination and interviews took place at Simla, which used to be the General Headquarters of the army in summer.

Major Dane, who was Principal of the Intermediate College at Aligarh, coached me for the Sandhurst examination. This came about in a curious way. One day as I was coming out of the class-room, Major Dane accosted me in the corridor. 'Are you still here?' he shouted. 'Did I not tell you to leave at once?' I was taken aback. 'You did not tell me to leave. Why should I? What for?' It was now his turn to feel surprised. He called three or four other students to identify me and realized that he had made a mistake. Some other student who looked like me had been rusticated from the university. Major Dane was very upset and wanted to find some opportunity to make amends. One day he walked up to me in the middle of the theology class. Our Maulvi had a huge paunch and a big beard, which made him look like Santa Claus. He did not teach us much. Major Dane said to him: 'Maulana Sahib, will you kindly stop your lecture?' He then turned to me and said, 'I want to apologize to you for that silly mistake I made the other day'. So Major Dane offered to coach me for the Sandhurst examination. He gave me two or three hours of his time daily for about three or four months, took an immense amount of interest in my work and would come to my room or take me to his house.

Eventually, in June 1926, I was informed that I had been selected to go to Sandhurst and naturally I was excited at the prospect. I also had a sense of relief that I would not have to take my B.A. examination. But apart from my personal feelings and my interest in the army, I realized that there were too few Indians, and fewer Muslims, who held commissioned ranks. I knew that when Independence came it would have to be defended and that meant that my training at Sandhurst would be fully utilized by my country.

The decision to go to Sandhurst was my own. My father would have preferred me to finish my education and then choose a civilian profession. One factor which worried him was the large expenditure involved: I would need about 25,000 rupees for the Sandhurst course. My father worked his lands well but he had several children to educate and it was not easy to spare such a large sum of money for me. His answer to the problem was typical: he said he would sell all his land and property so that I could fulfil my ambition. Fortunately, I did well at Sandhurst and won several scholarships and the sacrifice was not necessary.

2

Early Days in the Army

I sailed for England in July 1926. I still remember how excited I was
when I boarded the S.S. *Rawalpindi* in Bombay en route to Sandhurst.
This was during the monsoon, and soon after leaving port the weather
became very stormy. Many of the passengers were sea-sick. I was too, but
I went on deck with my bedding and stayed there for three days and nights
until we reached Aden. After that everything changed dramatically,
the weather was good, the sea calm, and we had a very pleasant voyage.

There were six of us, selected for Sandhurst, travelling together from
India. When we arrived we found that the college had not opened and
we stayed for ten days in a little hotel called The Duke of York. In
charge was an old lady who was determined that we should behave
ourselves. She gave us long sermons on what we must and must not do
and every evening she would get us all together for another sermon. I
remember that we thought we would have to be very careful and very
correct in England.

I did not expect life to be easy at Sandhurst but it was much harder
and much tougher than any of us had suspected. At first I wondered
if I would be able to stand it, but I quickly adjusted myself to it. I was in
excellent physical condition and soon began to thrive on the demanding
Sandhurst life and even enjoyed the fifteen-mile run. During our first
fortnight the senior cadets gave us a demonstration of arms drill. We
were astonished at their skill and precision and yet within a month we
won a competition in arms drill against them. And although the life
was spartan, it had its lighter moments. I had an orderly named King
and he was very much the 'old soldier' in many ways. One day we had
been on parade until about nine o'clock at night, and after supper I lay
down on my bed still in my uniform. I was very tired and soon fell
asleep. Next morning King came along and found me lying there fully
dressed and sound asleep. In shocked tones he told me: 'Mr. Khan, you
are going to be no bloody good as an officer.' Then he pulled me out of
bed and helped me to get ready for our first parade.

There was a sizeable community of Indian cadets at Sandhurst at that time and we clung to one another. Somehow we all sensed that we were regarded as an inferior species. The British did not practise the colour bar in a blatant manner, as in some countries, but they were no less colour conscious. In those days anyone coming from a subject race was regarded as an inferior human being and this I found terribly galling. The tragedy of belonging to a subject race depressed us more poignantly in the free air of England. My relations with the British remained formal, by and large. I was reserved and aloof by nature and the sense of isolation which we all experienced at Sandhurst was not conducive to mixing with the British. Among my own age group we had a lot of fun, laughing and tumbling together, but there was never any close understanding.

At Sandhurst I was the first foreign cadet to be promoted Corporal and given two stripes. The Company Sergeant-Major said to me in his usual gruff voice, 'Mr. Khan, you will report to the Commandant's office at 10.30.' The Commandant was a Major-General and poor Mr. Khan a mere cadet. Still wondering what I had done and what my fate would be, I was marched into the Commandant's office. Facing me at a table and wearing full ceremonial dress was the Major-General, the Assistant Commandant, who was a full Colonel, and my Company Commander. I stood rigidly to attention, a bemused and worried cadet, until the Commandant addressed me very solemnly: 'Gentleman Cadet Ayub Khan, we are going to repose great trust in you. We hope you will justify the trust. We have today broken our tradition and decided to grant you two stripes and make you a Corporal. We are doing this as an experimental measure to see whether foreign cadets can discharge the heavy burden of this responsibility.' I was flabbergasted, not knowing what the responsibilities were going to be. I discovered that the trust so solemnly reposed in me meant that while the rifles of other cadets were inspected every day, mine was exempt from inspection. I had no command over anybody. I was an honorary corporal and not allowed to command any British cadets. That was the sum total of the trust placed in me. While I was busy discharging the obligations, my rifle suffered through neglect. The other cadets would keep constantly polishing their rifles, giving the barrels a high shine. One day our arms expert suddenly arrived to examine our rifles. He condemned most of them because constant cleaning and rubbing with metal polish had worn the rifling off the barrels; my rifle, even though a little dirty, was still serviceable.

On the whole we had an interesting though hard time at Sandhurst. We had plenty of leave, and a group of us, mostly Indian cadets, would travel on the Continent, usually in France and Switzerland. I made no close friends among the cadets. I used to know Nasir, Bhonsle, Nagar, and several others. Choudhry, who later became Commander-in-Chief of the Indian Army, was in the same platoon as I was. He was a good cadet, intelligent and hard-working.

I did fairly well in my examinations and passed about 60th in a class of 123 cadets. One is judged by one's overall performance and power of command. I was first among the Indian cadets: this may well have been due to the distinction of being a corporal.

While I was in Switzerland on leave, about a month before the results of our course were known, I received a letter from my mother, telling me that my father had died. It also revealed that he had died three months before I received the letter—in September 1927. This was terrible news and afterwards I found out what had happened. Just before his death he was almost blind with cataract and he would get someone to write his regular weekly letters to me. He had asked that in the event of his death I was not to be informed until I had finished my course at Sandhurst; letters were still to be sent to me each week.

I felt the loss of my father acutely. I was conscious of the responsibilities as head of the family, particularly in respect of my younger brothers and sisters. I went to the officer who used to act as a guardian for some of us overseas cadets and asked for his advice. He got in touch with the India Office, which in turn consulted the War Office. They confirmed that I had done well in my examinations and would be commissioned. I was given six weeks' leave and was able to return home. I travelled by a ship called the *Neuralia*. I remember the journey between Aden and Bombay: the sea was like an artificial lake, calm and serene. Throughout the day I used to see fish of all kinds and colours playfully jumping out of the water and diving back without a splash. At night I stood on the deck and it seemed that someone had magically arranged an illumination of the ocean. In the calm of the night and amidst the colours of the sea the thought of my father's death weighed heavily on me.

I spent my leave with the family. After that I was sent to a British regiment, the Royal Fusiliers, who were stationed in Ambala in the eastern Punjab. This was a trial period for junior officers before they joined the Indian Army, and for the British officers it was an opportunity to learn Urdu before their posting to an Indian unit. The Royal Fusiliers were largely recruited in and around London. Although they were townsmen, they were good soldiers. I was impressed by the high standard of their discipline and by their behaviour under very difficult conditions of climate and of terrain. The British officers were a lively crowd and we got along very well. They had able senior officers and I made some good friends among them. When I was posted to the Indian Army, my Commanding Officer reported that I would make a good officer in any army.

An interesting incident occurred early in my service. Every year a unit had to go through an exercise set by the Brigade Commander, the object of which was to test the Unit Commander. We were in Aurangabad in southern India and I must have been in the third year of my service. I was put in charge of the 'enemy' forces and there were to be two exercises. My Commanding Officer led the home forces. In both exercises I encircled him; I completely stymied him and frustrated his plans. At the end there was a conference in which the Brigade Commander commented on the exercise and the conduct of the Battalion Commander. He pointed out where things had been mishandled and where correct action was taken. He turned round to me and said, 'I have a real word of praise for the enemy Commander.' My Commanding Officer never forgave me after this; nothing I did seemed right to him. Instead of taking the whole thing in a sporting spirit, he chased me about and for a couple of years I had a difficult time.

In the Indian Army my first regiment was the 1st/14th Punjab which was raised from one of the Ranjit Singh units; the Sikhs used to call it the 'Sherdal' battalion. We called it 'Sherdil' (the lion-hearted) later. Like many other units of the British-Indian Army, it had four groups or classes: Pathans, Punjabi Mussalmans, Sikhs, and Dogras, all equally distributed. There were several Indian officers with me, including the late Colonel Khurshid who became the first Pakistani governor of the North-West Frontier Province. Among the others were Colonel A. S. B. Shah, and Dhillon, who later became a General in the Indian Army. I was soon aware of a certain amount of friction between the junior British officers and the senior Indian officers. Politically, events were moving gradually towards the granting of independence and not unnaturally there were suspicions and misunderstandings between the two groups. The Indian officers were all deeply interested in these developments and when the Indian National Congress stepped up its campaign for freedom, we Muslims began to wonder what would happen to us. Freedom, as far as we were concerned, meant freedom from both the British and the Hindus.

This political consciousness and the consequent strain was restricted to the officers; among the men there was great fellow feeling. Friction among the *jawans* was usually over questions of promotion, and right up to the time of partition the army remained a closely-knit force.

Even the earliest riots did not affect the rank and file until it became clear that two sovereign countries would emerge after the withdrawal of the British and that the army would be divided. When senseless killing started at the time of partition, communal feelings among the ranks did run high. It was feared at that time that the two factions might come to an open fight but fortunately this was avoided.

The ill feeling between the British and Indian officers before the war, in my experience, manifested itself in a number of ways and arose at times over seemingly trivial incidents. There was trouble in the Mess because the British officers would not let us have the food we wanted, particularly curry which was served only on Mondays, Thursdays, and Sundays. Then there was dissension over the question of music, when we wanted Indian records as well as western ones in the Mess. At one stage some Sikh and Hindu officers called a meeting to boycott certain British officers. I urged them not to quibble over little things, but these small arguments created a continual if slight strain.

II

Despite these differences, the Indian Army was a well-trained and disciplined fighting force which expanded swiftly after war was declared in September 1939. I was playing tennis with some friends at Bannu on the North-West Frontier when news came that Germany had invaded Poland and we realized that this meant a world war. Soon we were all separated.

The army started growing rapidly because of its commitments in the Middle and the Far East, and I was sent to New Delhi to raise a territorial battalion. Then I went to the Staff College at Quetta and, after completing my course, was posted to Army Headquarters in Delhi, as a staff officer. My next move was to the headquarters of 15 Corps at Barrackpore just outside Calcutta, where we worked in the office of the Governor's House drawing up plans for the defence of India against a Japanese invasion. As I moved around the area with its hot, humid climate I became increasingly depressed and disenchanted by that part of India, yet several years later when I went to East Pakistan as G.O.C. I developed a great liking for the area.

Around the time that 15 Corps entered the Arakan to fight the Japanese, I was made Second-in-Command of the 1st Assam Regiment. The Nagas, who had a hard time both during and after the war, were part of this regiment. We moved into Burma and were soon involved in heavy fighting as we crossed the Chindwin river and advanced to the Irrawaddy. After crossing the Irrawaddy river we fought our way to

Mandalay. It was hard, bitter, hand-to-hand fighting in the jungle. It used to rain incessantly and we found refuge in foxholes when the tents became too wet to provide any comfort. But even there we had no escape from the mosquitoes. We spent our time warding them off and nursing our blotches. The only thing that saved us was DDT and mepacrine. Rations used to be adequate but the frozen chickens from Australia which were dropped by three Dakotas one fine morning were specially welcome. It was only later that we discovered the supplies were intended for a British regiment as Christmas gift. There was hell to pay in the way of explanations but there was little we could do about it!

The Japanese attacked us day after day, night after night, and often I would see scores of dead bodies around me. One afternoon, while the guns were booming, I saw a peculiarly dressed man making his way towards me. He turned out to be an American G.I. who had received fifteen days' leave and was looking for a Japanese souvenir. He felt that without such a souvenir it would be no use going on leave. I had a small Japanese flag in my pocket which I gave him. He was so delighted that he left his jeep to supplement our transport!

I was in Burma for about eighteen months before I was transferred to the North-West Frontier of India, in the spring of 1945. There I was given command of a battalion of the 15th Punjab Regiment which was stationed at Landi Kotal in the Khyber Pass. While I was away my old battalion of the 1st/14th Punjab had been sent to Malaya and captured by the Japanese. I was stunned when I heard the news. Some of our officers who were captured joined the Indian National Army, a Japanese-inspired force.

When the war ended I was sent to the training centre of the regiment at Ferozepur to re-raise my old battalion. There some of these former war prisoners came back to join us and I found that they were still in a bad state, both physically and mentally. They had been reduced to skeletons and their faces showed marks of ill-treatment. I noticed, too, that they had become very cunning and suspicious, and were wary of everyone and very careful of what they said.

For them, as for the rest of us, the war had ended; yet, although we did not realize it at the time, another struggle, this time for our own independence, was approaching its climax. I was then President of the Army Selection Board at Dehra Dun where we selected officers for permanent commissions in the British-Indian Army. There was a large number of failures as the required qualifications and standards were very high. The political climate at that time was beginning to be reflected even in the army, and I was accused by certain Hindu and Sikh officers of deliberately failing their people as potential regular army officers. Of course, even as President, I had, like the other members on the Selection Board, only one vote, and so I could not by myself accept or reject any candidate for a permanent commission. In spite of this unpleasantness, I found my spell of service on the Selection Board extremely interesting and a great training and experience in assessing people.

But my service on the Selection Board was the lull before the storm. With almost no warning the horrors of communal rioting burst upon us. The communal situation in the Punjab deteriorated rapidly. After the Viceroy's announcement of the Partition Plan on 3 June 1947 there was some slight improvement. But the Sikhs soon started a vigorous agitation against the notional division of the Punjab described in the Plan. They were hoping to form a separate State of their own after driving out the Muslims from Sikh areas. On Tuesday 22 July 1947 members of the Partition Council decided to set up a Special Military Command from 1 August, to protect the population of Sialkot, Gujranwala, Sheikhupura, Lyallpur, Montgomery, Lahore, Amritsar, Gurdaspur, Hoshiarpur, Jullundur, Ferozepur, and Ludhiana— civil districts of the Punjab covering in all over 29,000 square miles. Major-General Rees was appointed Military Commander for this purpose. I was told that I had been attached to him in an advisory capacity on behalf of Pakistan, and that Brigadier Dhigambir Singh was to represent India. It was further decided by the Partition Council that after 15 August Major-General Rees 'will control operationally the forces of both the new States in this area'.

The Partition Council had hoped that the setting up of this Boundary Force would have a reassuring and stabilizing effect in the Punjab. They had not foreseen the holocaust which was to engulf the whole of the Punjab. The agitation launched by the Sikhs suddenly took a violent and dangerous turn according to a premeditated programme. The Sikhs had a well-trained organization which attacked the Muslims and drove them out towards Pakistan by moving flying columns of armed men from one district to another. The first clash occurred on 4 August 1947 at Majithia in Amritsar district. Two Muslim villages were surrounded and burnt to ashes and a large number of people were killed. From there the Sikhs moved to Taran-Taran where again there was a general massacre of the Muslims. On 14 August the Muslim police in East Punjab, particularly in Amritsar, were disarmed. This was a signal for a general conflagration and slaughter of the Muslims.

Understandably there was severe criticism of the Boundary Force and I also came in for a good deal of blame. But I was placed in a hopeless situation. I was an outsider whose role was purely advisory.

I had no staff and there was no one under my command. But that apart, the Boundary Force could not have prevented those massacres. Sir Francis Tuker has described the ineffectiveness of the Punjab Boundary Force in his book *While Memory Serves*:[1]

Our talk with General Rees at Ambala in early August showed that he had no doubts that the Eastern Punjab would blow sky high over the Boundary Commission's award when it came. On the 11th August we learnt that Amritsar had had a bad blood-letting the day before and that Calcutta had had rather more trouble than usual that night. Both police and army had had to open fire. While we knew that we could now hold Calcutta in check we were equally certain that Amritsar was but the spark to fire a train of horror in the north. The local administration was powerless to exercise authority against mob rule, for it had not been organised and strengthened to tackle the coming task as had the Army. Had it been so organised the task of the P.B.F. would have been far easier, for as much as anything it was the communal attitude of the local civil officials and police that made the task of the P.B.F. almost hopeless from the start. The administration of the whole of India was simply jogging along on the remains of the prestige that the British had built for it in the past hundred years: in the Eastern Punjab even that remnant died long before the 15th August, killed by communalism and mob rule.

There is another reference to the difficulties of the Boundary Force in Penderel Moon's *Divide and Quit*:[2]

There was, I found, a remarkable faith in the projected Boundary Force. I could not share it. The Sikhs, I thought, were bound to attack the Muslims when they saw the chance. If the Boundary Force was really powerful and effective they would wait till it was withdrawn. If it was ineffective they would disregard it. On my way back from Delhi to Bahawalpur I happened to hear some views about this force from a young Sikh major who shared my compartment for part of the journey. He was himself about to join it, but was utterly sceptical of its capacity to maintain order. He thought that a large proportion of the troops would be infected by the communal virus and prove unreliable. He was also doubtful whether mechanized infantry would be able to operate effectively in the rural areas during the monsoon. I fully agreed with him in this.

The Joint Defence Council which met in Lahore on Friday 29 August 1947 eventually decided to disband the Boundary Force. Describing this meeting of the Joint Defence Council, Alan Campbell-Johnson says in his book *Mission with Mountbatten*:[3]

Mountbatten was in Lahore yesterday to take the chair at the Joint Defence Council, which Jinnah, to everyone's surprise, attended as a member. After

[1] Cassell, 1950, p. 402.   [2] Chatto and Windus, 1961, p. 95.
[3] Robert Hale, 1951, p. 176.

prolonged discussion the decision was taken to disband the Boundary Force. Pete Rees received very few thanks from either side for his efforts to carry out a task of unparalleled difficulty. Without the whole-hearted backing of the Governments and Press on both sides, the position of the Boundary Force and its Commander became rapidly untenable, and otherwise steady and experienced troops began to feel the tug of communal loyalties deeper even than their military discipline.

I have quoted these authors to show that the Boundary Force was doomed to failure from the beginning. There was a great paucity of communications. The Force could only rush to a place that was being attacked, and by the time the troops arrived it was looted, burnt, and the Muslim inhabitants massacred. In the end all that this Force could do was to try and keep the roads clear for the refugees. This was done by patrolling the main thoroughfares and the railway lines.

This was the unhappiest period of my life. I had never before seen anything so terrible and brutal. Women and children were mutilated and innocent people butchered mercilessly. All human qualities seemed to have been snuffed out and the whole edifice of culture and civilization crumbled during these terrible weeks. My faith in human nature was shaken and I used to ask myself, 'what can one do to stop this madness?'

With great difficulty I managed to rescue a number of Muslims from Amritsar and elsewhere. There was a small area between the Grand Trunk Road and the railway line in Amritsar which was mainly inhabited by the Muslims. The colony was surrounded by the Sikhs, who had occupied positions of vantage in two-storeyed buildings from which they could snipe at anyone trying to leave the area. I was able to arrange a couple of trains and get some troops to escort the inhabitants of the colony. I remember a railway engineer who proved extremely helpful. We also moved a number of families from Simla, Dehra Dun, and Ambala. The whole operation lasted about three weeks. Altaf Qadir (later Lieutenant-General) was also there at that time and was associated with evacuation. I sent a message to the new Prime Minister of Pakistan, Liaquat Ali Khan, that we might have over a million refugees. I pleaded for the setting up of some central authority to organize refugee camps. No one realized at that time that the number of refugees would go up to eight or nine million.

III

From the horrors of Partition in the Punjab I returned to Waziristan to command a Brigade. I knew the area well. On my last posting there,

I had been stationed at Mir Ali in Waziristan. I had an untrained battalion at that time and had to cover about twenty miles of road so that the convoys could pass between Razmak and Bannu. This meant picketing the heights so that the tribesmen would not fire at the convoys. I put my troops through a very tough battle inoculation, firing over their heads with rifles and machine-guns, and inside a fortnight I had a well-trained battalion ready for active service in the very difficult terrain.

My most lasting impression, and it was a distressing one, of the various campaigns on the North-West Frontier was the sheer futility of it all. It was a great waste of time; and a great waste of men. Nothing was really achieved and when Pakistan was established there were several army divisions as well as Scouts and Levies all tied up on the Frontier. All they did was to provide a constant irritation to the tribesmen, and a target for them to fire at. Also no real progress would be possible in this part of Pakistan while this state of affairs continued.

There was only one sensible thing to do and that was to withdraw our troops from the North-West Frontier, and this in fact is what happened. A committee under that very fine officer, Lieut.-General Sir Francis Tuker, had studied the problem and recommended that the army be withdrawn from Waziristan. This bold and sensible proposal was made before Pakistan came into being and the new government of Pakistan accepted the findings and decided to implement them.

I was made responsible for a major part of the withdrawal. Now, troops had been in this area for over a hundred years and any withdrawal of this kind is always a difficult and potentially dangerous business. A few days before the evacuation a group of my men were fired upon by the tribesmen and several of them killed. I was extremely angry and decided to retaliate quickly and severely. As a result I was faced not only with angry tribesmen but also with a worried divisional commander and the political agent, who claimed that my action was irregular. I met the tribesmen and made my stand clear. I told them that they must never again kill our soldiers, who were good Muslims, like themselves, and that the killing was senseless. Also I stressed that these men were the defenders of Pakistan which was now their country as well as mine. Then I explained that we were going to pull out of Waziristan, but that if any of my men were harmed and if they opened fire on them I would turn back and attack. They knew I meant what I said and I was glad that when we pulled out, the tribesmen and their chiefs picketed the hills for us. They put up white flags on the strong points and all the leading *maliks* helped. We were able to arrange an orderly and successful withdrawal.

3   As Private Secretary to the British Resident in Hyderabad, 1931 (4th from right in front row). The occasion is the arrival of the marriage party of the Nawab of Loharu (7th from the left). To the left of the Nawab is the Resident, Sir Terence Keyes

4*a*   A distant view of the village of Rehana

4*b*   Rehana (in the background the top of the old family house can
be seen)

Today things have changed on the Frontier and we have made great progress there. Hundreds of schools have been opened, miles and miles of roads have been laid, and hospitals and colleges built. And the most encouraging sign of all is that the tribesmen are constantly asking for further development. My policy is clear: we will not intrude upon their areas unless they ask us, and when they do ask we will develop their territories, but not buy individuals. This approach has worked very well and there has been a great transformation on the North-West Frontier.

But in a way the North-West Frontier was one of the minor problems facing the new state of Pakistan. We had a long, hard road to travel, and right from the outset we met some terrible difficulties: millions of homeless and destitute refugees were flooding in; the sources of the rivers of the Punjab, which provided irrigation in our territory, were in India. These were but two of the many grave issues which confronted us.

For my part, the major problem I was called upon to solve was the formation and training of the army of Pakistan. I became deeply involved in this for several years, first as G.O.C. in East Pakistan, then as Adjutant-General, and finally as Commander-in-Chief of our army. Before describing in some detail my experiences in these posts I would like very briefly to mention the state of the army immediately before and after Partition.

In the British-Indian Army we Muslim officers had an instinctive sympathy for the great struggle in which the Quaid-e-Azam, Mahomed Ali Jinnah, was engaged to ensure the creation of the state of Pakistan. But we had no real knowledge of the personalities involved in this political struggle; and by training we had been taught that as army officers we should stay out of the political arena. So the politicians were largely an unknown quantity to us, as we were to them.

When independence was achieved we realized that we would have a separate homeland for the Muslims; and naturally the question of whether the army should also be divided became a major issue. Although I was not directly involved in the division of the armed forces, I was convinced from the outset that we had to have our own army for Pakistan; also that we had to create a first-class army to defend our country. General Cariappa, at that time the senior Indian officer in the army, approached me to support him in his efforts to keep the army undivided. He wanted to have one army for both India and Pakistan and thought that I would understand and appreciate his viewpoint. I told him that one army serving two independent countries was inconceivable. The army was the instrument of sovereignty and the shield of the people and it could have no entity outside the thinking and the will of the people.

'We must have our own army to carry out our policies and to preserve our independence', I said.

A Council was then set up to divide the armed forces. We had Raza, Akbar, and Latif on this Council representing Pakistan. I remember Akbar came to me in Dehra Dun, on one occasion, and said that there was a proposal to have common training institutions for the two armies. I told him that that would not work. It was true that the Pakistan Army would not have adequate training facilities in the beginning and that we might have to work under the trees, but we should be prepared to accept the initial handicaps and start our own institutions straight away. We must have a separate army and we must have separate training institutions and other supporting facilities to sustain the army. The future to me was clear. Two nations had emerged and each must have its own instruments of power. Sovereign States cannot share vital instruments of power. There was some thinking at that time that India and Pakistan, though divided, could live in a spirit of accommodation. Little did people realize that the Indian leaders had different designs. Far from co-operating with Pakistan in any sphere, they were determined to create problems for her.

Apart from this advice, I had little direct connection with the division of the armed forces. But, as I say, I had to face the problems created by the partition of the army. Let me state what they were. In the first place there was no complete Muslim unit of battalion size in the British-Indian Army, whereas there were complete and intact Hindu and Gurkha regiments. When the Japanese war ended and Partition came, our men from units in India began to trickle back to Pakistan in small groups. In some cases they were unarmed and in others they had to fight their way out. So we had to start our army with bits and pieces like a gigantic jig-saw puzzle with some of the bits missing. We had men untrained, half trained, and highly trained. They came from different units and different areas and they had all to be welded into fighting and ancillary units, divisions, and corps.

And that was not all. India had been the base for the projected invasion of Malaya and most of the military stores and installations were in South India, as was the bulk of the troops. Pakistan's share of the stores was there and we were entitled under the Partition agreements to 160 train-loads of military equipment and weapons. But very little of that ever arrived in Pakistan and when the wagons did arrive they were full of stones and wrecked equipment.

So our army was badly equipped and terribly disorganized. It was almost immediately engaged in escorting the refugees who streamed by the million into Pakistan; and not long after that it was also involved in the fighting in Kashmir. Throughout this period we had no properly organized units, no equipment, and hardly any ammunition. The position was so bad that for the first few years we could only allow five rounds of practice ammunition to each man a year. Our plight was indeed desperate. But from the moment Pakistan came into being I was certain of one thing: Pakistan's survival was vitally linked with the establishment of a well-trained, well-equipped, and well-led army. I was determined to create this type of military shield for my country and, with the help of dedicated men, I succeeded. Today I am convinced that without this army Pakistan could not have weathered the storms and attacks to which it was exposed; and the army behind the people of Pakistan is still a sure guarantee that our enemies will not be able to weaken us.

To fashion the army, to train it, to equip it, to find the right type of officers and soldiers, to create and maintain a high standard of morale, was a tremendously difficult task in the circumstances I have described. But it was also a challenging and absorbing one. And for me, as well as for many other Pakistanis, everything changed when our country gained freedom on 14 August 1947. We had a new reason for living and working, a compelling urge to work to the very limit of our capacity. Because I was striving for my own free country, no difficulty seemed insurmountable and no challenge or sacrifice seemed too great. It would be impossible to exaggerate the way my life and my whole outlook changed after the state of Pakistan came into existence.

3

The Army 1948–1950

I

I was commanding the Gardai Brigade in Waziristan in January 1948 when I was ordered to proceed to East Pakistan to serve as General Officer Commanding. I could not say that I was excited at the prospect. I had never liked the climate of that area, and there were certain personal problems such as finding accommodation for my family in Rawalpindi, so that the children might continue their studies. The Army could not help in the matter and I was forced to leave my family in the annexe of a building which was really used as servants' quarters. Having lodged them there, I packed a couple of suitcases and left for East Pakistan. It was a difficult and trying time for the country, and an exacting assignment. I spent nearly two years in East Pakistan.

The provincial government, with which I came in frequent contact, was newly formed and poorly staffed. But worse still, it was politically weak and unstable. There was no army. All we had in East Pakistan at the time of Independence were two infantry battalions; one of these had three Muslim companies, the fourth, a Hindu company, having been transferred to India. The other battalion had one Sikh company and one Dogra company, leaving us with only two more Muslim companies. We had very poor accommodation: at Headquarters there was no table, no chair, no stationery—we had virtually nothing at all; not even any maps of East Pakistan. Gradually we started to organize ourselves.

Around Tejgaon and Kurmitola airfields there were some thatched huts built during the Second World War. There was hardly any place for officers and we had to improvise some kind of accommodation for them. They lived in *bashas* (huts), which were often in a poor state and leaked almost incessantly during the heavy rains. It was not uncommon for men to keep shifting their *charpoys* at night to some dry spot under the roof. During the nor'-westers, the *basha* roof was sometimes blown off, leaving the man high but not dry. In the morning he had to go and look for his *basha* and bring it back in bits and pieces.

Gradually the position improved. Plans were laid for building permanent accommodation for a Brigade Group. It was necessary to locate some units near Dacca so that they might be available to act in support of the civil authority. Other sites were also planned. The difficulty was to find high ground which would not go under water during the monsoons. After much searching over the whole province I was able to locate two areas, and General Headquarters approved them. We built one cantonment near Dacca and the other on high ground near Comilla. Both these have since developed into established, picturesque sites.

The signs were far from propitious. Our borders were under a constant threat from India, and soon we were embroiled in fighting with her in Kashmir. As a result, it was difficult to get any reinforcements to strengthen our position in East Pakistan. The province was in an extremely under-developed state. Nothing had been done for it before Partition though there were great opportunities for industrialization and enterprise. The Muslims did not have the capital; and the jute trade, worth about 900 million rupees a year, was in the hands of Hindu Marwaris who repatriated all their profits to India. The only good stretch of surfaced road that existed, to my knowledge, was somewhere in Pabna district, covering a distance of about thirty miles. Then there was a bit of road going from Jessore to the north and a so-called road from the airfields around Dacca going to Narayanganj. Except for these, there were no roads in the province worth the name. River communication was, of course, available, but it was slow and inadequate. There was a good railway but it had taken such a beating during the war that the rolling stock was completely worn out and required immediate replacement.

I used to consider it a great pity that Calcutta should have been developed on the raw materials produced in East Pakistan and that no processing plant or factory should have been put up in any part of the province. The fault lay with us, since even before Independence the Muslims of the province had been fairly vocal in politics and had produced men like Fazlul Haq, Suhrawardy, and Khawaja Nazimuddin, who were associated with the government in one capacity or another. All of them had been Chief Ministers of undivided Bengal, but they had been unable to do anything for their people. It must be admitted that the task was stupendous.

Khawaja Nazimuddin was the Chief Minister of the province when I went there as G.O.C. He was a pious man, with a long political record.

But it was a torture for him to give a decision. I saw him in his office many times: I would see an impressive head behind a pile of papers which covered him up to the nose. It was commonly believed that the Chief Minister had a method of his own to deal with problems: any file requiring a decision was quietly pushed under the pile and there it remained till with the passage of time the problem solved itself. I also met Nurul Amin and Hamidul Haq Choudhry in those days. Choudhry was then Finance Minister in the provincial government. Nurul Amin impressed me as an intelligent man who observed things and had some idea of how the administration should be run. Hamidul Haq was known to be a clever man but there was a general impression that he was standing in the way of development as he was averse to any Muslim from outside East Pakistan coming into the province and setting up any industry. Discouraged, some who wanted to invest went back to India; others drifted to Karachi. Not, I should add, that it was easy to set up an industry: there was no power, no communications, and even land was difficult to get.

I could see that a mental barrier against outsiders was being erected. This proved a great deterrent to the movement of people and capital into East Pakistan. The attitude in West Pakistan was different: there was no emotional or political antipathy to the people coming from India. A large number of Muslim refugees from the United Provinces of India and from Bombay and other Indian cities came to West Pakistan after independence and played a major part in its industrialization. Similarly in the armed forces and in the civil services there were a number of refugees.

At the time of Independence there was only one East Pakistani officer in the Superior Civil Services. This necessitated posting officers from West Pakistan, or from amongst the refugees, to the provincial government. They came to be regarded as symbols of outside interference among the educated classes. The new middle class in the province began nursing a grievance against their West Pakistani compatriots. They found themselves lagging behind in respect of positions of authority, in jobs generally and in commercial fields in particular. The provincial leadership was faced with a difficult situation. They could face the problems squarely, identify the causes and work to create an adequate social and economic infra-structure, supported by corresponding educational and technical institutions, to prepare the youth of the province to compete with the rest of the country on merit. This required sober thinking and dedicated hard work, neither of which was forthcoming. The alternative was to build up political pressure and shift all the blame to West Pakistan. Some of the political agitators found this a much more convenient and popular course of action. Consequently, the political life of the province was given an agitational pattern and it worried and saddened me. I could see that some of the political demagogues were going to exploit the emotions of the people.

I had a revealing encounter with Suhrawardy at that time which gave me an insight into his mind. There was a function at Curzon Hall in Dacca. Someone introduced me to Suhrawardy and this was the first time I met him. 'General,' he addressed me with his characteristic flourish, 'they have issued an expulsion order. But they do not know that I can finish Nazimuddin in no time.' I said, 'Mr. Suhrawardy, why don't you leave East Pakistan alone? Haven't they got enough problems without your adding to them?' What he said in reply I cannot repeat because the man is dead, but it gave me sufficient indication of how he intended to exploit the situation in East Pakistan. Since he was a key-figure in politics, I knew then that the agitational pressures which were being built up in the province were not going to subside in a hurry. I made a large number of friends among East Pakistanis and I would talk to them quite frankly. I must say that individually they all agreed with me that little constructive work was being done by the government and that all energies were getting diverted into political channels.

The training of East Pakistani young men for the army was my direct concern. I found that the province was completely lacking in proper educational and training institutions at the higher levels. I was distressed that a population of such a large size should produce so few men of the requisite standard. I took up this matter with the provincial government and urged them to start good public schools where intelligent young men could be given the necessary training to build their mind, body, and character. I made repeated appeals to Khawaja Nazimuddin and argued at great length with Nurul Amin. They seemed to understand what I was talking about but were unwilling or unable to do anything about it. I never quite understood what they were afraid of. Perhaps they thought that general reaction to the establishment of public schools would not be favourable. I remember, for example, that an article was published in Maulana Akram Khan's newspaper *Azad* condemning the government for planning to start schools for the rich at the expense of the poor. Here were some forty million Muslims, the greatest Muslim concentration in the world in such a small area—and nothing was being done to create the talent which was required to run a free country. I kept harping on the need for establishing institutions for education and training but some of the politicians found that they

could get better and more immediate dividends by spreading distrust
and suspicion among the people.

The thing that surprised me was the lack of manpower with qualities
of leadership. The Army Selection Board would visit East Pakistan
every six months. In the beginning for the first one or two terms the
Board found four or five boys who could be accepted for the Army
Military College. But they were mainly boys who had come from refugee
families. When this material was exhausted they came to selection
from amongst the local boys. The Selection Board would then be lucky
to get even one or two borderline cases. I would advise the Board to
take them anyway because nobody would accept that the Board had
been fair and objective and that the rules and specifications had been
rigidly applied. Something was seriously wrong with the whole educational system: the younger people had to be got hold of and properly
educated and brought up.

Somehow I never got any response from the political leaders of
East Pakistan. I used to tell my friends, 'Ask your government to do
something or you will be left behind. Go and argue your case. Go and
quarrel with West Pakistanis if they are doing something against your
interests. Go and fight it out with the central government to get your
rights. Do so by all means, but also insist that your young men and
women should be properly educated and trained so that they can discharge their responsibilities as equal citizens as well as anyone else.
And do not take the argument too far. After all, human beings are
human beings, and if your brethren in West Pakistan start feeling
frustrated and unhappy at being constantly subjected to criticism and
pressure you will be doing a very great disservice to the unity of the
country. For God's sake keep your differences and your arguments
within the bounds of reason.'

I could not quite understand whether the agitational pressure in
East Pakistan was the result of a combination of little things, such as
personal complaints and grievances, or the manifestation of some
deeper malady. I often heard criticism of the conduct of West Pakistani
civil servants serving in East Pakistan. They were accused of being exclusive and aggressive and their attitude was regarded as patronizing. I
saw many of these officers at work in the province and I thought they
worked very hard and were deeply interested in the welfare of the
province. No doubt their manners and pattern of life were different;
an average East Pakistani was inclined to misjudge and misunderstand
them. It is quite common for a West Pakistani to answer a simple
question with a grunt and not realize that he is being impolite. An old
friend of mine, the late Raja Ghazanfar Ali Khan, was our Ambassador

in Iran for a long time. The Iranians are a very courteous people and Raja Sahib must have imbibed their tradition and culture. When he returned to Pakistan I asked him 'How are you, Raja Sahib?' He said, 'Well, I have come home and I expected a certain amount of warmth. But everybody I meet just grunts. You try to find out anything and the response you get is a surly "Huh".' 'Raja Sahib, you have certainly been denationalized a bit', I said; 'we don't seem to mind these things.'

It might well be that the mannerisms of the West Pakistani irritated the East Pakistani. I grew to like Bengali songs, though I have no real ear for music; they fascinate me. I told an East Pakistani friend once, 'You have such sweet music. I wish to God you were half as sweet yourself.' I found that once you got to know an East Pakistani he really accepted you without reservation. The trouble in the early days of independence was that there was very little social contact between East and West Pakistanis. The average West Pakistani found himself isolated and tended to form a group of his own. I would tell the West Pakistanis, 'Why don't you meet them? Ask them over and entertain them even if it is over a simple cup of tea. You will get to know each other at the human level and, from that, friendship and warmth and understanding will develop.'

The West Pakistanis were no angels or missionaries. Most of them were government servants who felt that they had been deprived of the comparative comforts of life available to them in West Pakistan. They all came from the middle class and had family commitments. Travel between the two wings of the country was difficult and expensive. Many used to be irritated by what they regarded as the general inefficiency of East Pakistan and never tried to make a secret of their unwillingness to serve there. It was a peculiar phenomenon that while an average East Pakistani in Dacca thought that the West Pakistan officials were a manifestation of some kind of colonialism, the West Pakistanis were the most unwilling and unhappy instruments of that imaginary 'domination'. I remember telling someone in fun, 'Why don't you start a little agitation against me and throw me out too? You know I will not resist a bit.' Now, many more amenities are available, both in the army and on the civil side, and for the people; today's life bears no comparison to what it was like at the time of Independence. For many then there were few arrangements for education, no accommodation, no sanitation. But eventually even those who went under compulsion developed a great fondness for East Pakistan and many of them look back on their service there with a feeling of nostalgia.

Returning to army life in those days, I kept myself very busy, touring every district and sub-division, identifying likely routes of invasion and preparing a defence plan for the province. I was also worried about the internal law and order situation. Very little was being done to redress the grievances of the police force and I knew that I did not have enough strength to deal with any large-scale disturbances. The police force—about 60,000 men—consisted of all kind of heterogeneous elements. Some had come from the Police Service in West Bengal. They were not very well disciplined and even the senior officers were not all that good. The politicians never took quick decisions about the requirements of the civil armed forces and the result was a feeling of acute discontent and inefficiency.

Trouble was brewing and finally broke out in Dacca on 13 July 1948. I was on tour with Zakir Hussain who was then Inspector-General of Police. We were staying at a rest house in Mymensingh when I was rung up from Dacca and told that the police had surrounded Government House and the Chief Minister's house. Some of them had been seen in front of the Civil Secretariat. They had removed arms and ammunition from a magazine in the police lines and had taken up defensive positions. It was a peculiar situation: on the one hand I had to pacify the head of the police whose guest I was—and on the other, deal with his mutineers. I told the Battalion Commander to give them a warning and prevent them from adopting a reckless course. The argument went on for hours but the police could not be persuaded to return to their lines. After some time the Battalion Commander rang me back to say that the mutineers were not responding to reason. Whenever an appeal was made to them, they would start abusing the army. We were left with no option but to take action. I told the Battalion Commander to take military action against the mutineers, using as little force as possible.

The defensive position which the police force had taken up was in the middle of the city and there was danger of members of the public getting injured by covering fire. We had no alternative but to attack the mutineers. A company of 3rd/8th Punjab Regiment was detailed to deal with the situation. They had to cover some three hundred yards of open ground to get on to the defensive position. They advanced quickly and occupied the position. One or two policemen, including the ringleader, were killed and ten or twelve persons were injured. Luckily the trouble was quelled, the situation brought under control, and the chances of its spreading to the rest of the province were eliminated.

On another occasion, too, I had to act in aid of the civil power. I was called by Khawaja Nazimuddin, the Chief Minister, who told me that he had a precarious majority of four in the Assembly. He was worried that he would soon lose support as Fazlul Haq had mobilized the students, who were intimidating his followers. He wanted me to prevent the students from attacking the Assembly Hall. I should have declined to intervene as it was essentially a task for the police, but I was worried that if there was a breakdown of the government it might lead to widespread agitation and lawlessness. So I deputed an Infantry Company under Major Peerzada to be available to the police force near the Assembly Hall should the need arise. The session opened and inside the House the Chief Minister embarked on his speech which he had described to me as 'very important'. Outside, the students were crying blue murder. Fazlul Haq knew his stuff: he would pop out of the hall every now and then and give a fresh slogan to the students which they would go on chanting. This went on till about five o'clock in the evening when I got a message that the students were getting very close to the troops and that there was danger of a clash.

It was winter and beginning to get dark. I was worried that if the students rushed the troops they would have to open fire, and this I wanted to avoid at all cost. I decided to go to the Assembly. I had never seen such confusion. The Chief Minister was haranguing an angry and violent House, while outside the students were having the time of their life. Obeidullah was the Superintendent of Police on duty. I asked him, 'Why don't you take some action and keep these boys away?' He said, 'Sir, if you order me I will take action. But I am not going to do anything for these politicians.' I was shocked and asked why. He explained that they would order him to disperse the students and the next day hold an inquiry and put the whole blame on him; they would never take responsibility. 'I want an order in writing', he insisted.

The morale of the police force was obviously pretty low. I went into the Assembly and got in touch with the Chief Minister. I told him that it was getting dark and the boys were already too close to my men. 'What shall I do?' he asked me. 'Disperse the House and go home', I advised. 'How can I do that?' he remonstrated quite seriously; 'I am right in the middle of a very important speech!' He must have seen the look of amusement on my face and decided: 'All right, give me five minutes.' He went into the House, spoke to someone and returned. 'Well, I am ready to go home, but how do I get out of here.' I asked Major Peerzada to bring the Chief Minister's car to the back of the Assembly Hall. Together we smuggled the Chief Minister out through the kitchen. Having accomplished that feat, I came out and told the boys, 'The bird has flown!' They roared with laughter and the whole scene which, a moment ago, had looked tense and pregnant with danger, assumed a jovial colour. Fazlul Haq came out along with Mohammad Ali of Bogra who was then in the Opposition, and they tried to work up the boys again. I tapped Mohammad Ali on the shoulder and said, 'Are you looking for a bullet?' He retorted, 'You are being rude.' I did not want the trouble to restart so I told him firmly to go home.

Mohammad Ali controlled five votes in the Assembly. He immediately went to the Chief Minister and threatened to withdraw his support. The Chief Minister summoned me and after thanking me for saving the situation told me that I had annoyed Mohammad Ali and this would cost him his government. I suggested that he might call him so that I could explain the position to him. When Mohammad Ali came, I embraced him and said, 'I was only pulling your leg. You should not have taken it seriously.' I was fed up and did not want to get involved any further in their internal wrangle. Mohammad Ali felt pacified and we parted as friends.

Meanwhile, I was looking for a place to set up the Divisional Headquarters. Dacca just did not have any suitable accommodation. I saw the High Court building but it was not easy to suggest to the High Court authorities that they should let us have a part of the building. The Chief Justice, Mr. Mohammad Akram, however, was a man of great understanding. Some of his Judges used to sit in tents, but they were kind enough to let us have the accommodation we required. I remember one day I was coming back to the High Court after an inspection. I found Fazlul Haq asking the students to lie flat on the ground to prevent the working of the Court. I looked out of my car and asked what it was all about. Fazlul Haq saw me and apparently decided that I looked dangerous. He quietly advised the boys to clear out. I must say life was not without its moments of excitement, and even amusement, in those days.

Before I left the province I was able to build up an adequate *Ansar* (civil armed guards) force. In this I received great support from Aziz Ahmed who was then Chief Secretary of the provincial government. He felt that such a force would bring discipline to the masses and persuaded the provincial government to spare resources for it. The East Bengal Regiment also came into existence in my time. It was the first time that people from this part had been enlisted in a combatant unit. I was also able to establish the East Pakistan Rifles, a police force, and initiate a system of giving all police officers battle-training. It did the force an immense amount of good and they developed tremendous confidence and pride in themselves.

I left East Pakistan toward the end of November 1949, with a heavy heart. I had grown very fond of the people and developed some understanding of the problems of the area which stood me in good stead later.

II

From East Pakistan I was recalled to General Headquarters at Rawalpindi. General Gracey was Commander-in-Chief at that time and General Ross Mackay was his Chief of Staff; I was appointed Adjutant-General. The Adjutant-General's Branch dealt with the maintenance of personnel, recruitment of officers and men, medical facilities, salaries and pensions, and discipline.

One of the first problems that I had to face was with regard to the Azad Kashmir forces. The fighting in Kashmir had ended in a cease-fire. The Azad forces needed to be put on a regular footing and brought under some military code of discipline. There were some 50,000 men under arms, of varying military quality, and no Army Act was applicable to them. A great deal of correspondence on this subject had been going on between G.H.Q. and the Azad Kashmir government. There was a gentleman called Shah who was head of the Azad Kashmir government and who had some connection with the State forces. He was deaf and used to carry with him an impressive hearing aid. He had been insisting that the Azad forces be governed by the British Army Act, and he based his argument on the fact that whenever State forces were employed by the British they came under the British Army Act and not the Indian Army Act. I was furious when I heard this and thought I should talk to the man. I told him that the British had gone and taken the code with them. We had only one code, the Pakistan Army Act, and it would be conducive to better discipline if this Act was applied to the Azad forces also. I noticed that whenever he did not want to hear anything, Shah would quietly disengage the hearing aid. I spent a long time with him but could not get any answer from him. Whenever I asked him whether he agreed, he would put up a blank appearance pretending not to have heard anything. However, in the end, the Azad forces agreed to be governed by the Pakistan Army code.

Gracey was a very kind man. He was extremely considerate and allowed me a great deal of freedom. Ross Mackay was a meticulous Staff Officer with a brilliant military record, and I found his advice in staff matters extremely helpful. He was a sound, sober, and stable officer. The army had no pay or pension code and all the perquisites available in the army for long and meritorious service had been taken away by the government. No honorary commissions could be given nor any monetary awards made to men in the ranks. I started an arduous battle with the Ministry of Finance and it took me nearly seven years to resolve some of these problems. I would take a proposal to Finance and my only request would be, 'Please, say yes or no, but please do say something.' It was like battering one's head against a wall of enigmatic silence. It was not always easy to get to the top people who were apparently busy building silent walls of their own. One had to be content with smaller walls like Deputy Financial Advisers. It seemed that everything had been left to people at that level and they were as impervious to reasoning as they were insensitive to the urgency of requirements. I thought Chaudhri Mohammad Ali, who was then the Secretary-General to the Government of Pakistan, would lend a hand in resolving our difficulties. He knew something about the army, having served as Financial Adviser, Military Finance, in pre-independence days. I did not come into direct contact with him much but, to the best of my knowledge, he never lifted his little finger to help resolve our problems.

The Pakistan Army was in truth being held together by precious little. We used to feel in G.H.Q. that in a situation of real crisis we would find ourselves hopelessly handicapped. I kept reminding the government at Karachi that it was not a healthy state of affairs. A man who one day might be called upon to give his life for the country must have some sense of security. At least his conditions of service should be settled. Unless this was done he could not devote himself wholeheartedly to his profession. Apart from this, there was need for clear-cut decisions in important policy matters affecting the future of the army without which we could not even begin to organize ourselves. We had inherited a war-time force comprising excellent fighting material but imperfectly trained. A large number of officers had been recruited against short-term emergency commissions and they were poorly trained and had no concept of serving in a peace-time army.

We had no complete Muslim unit: the British used to regard the Muslims as a dangerous element and had scattered them through different units. The result was that most of the men did not know one another and the units were still lacking in *esprit de corps*, thus adding to the general problem of indiscipline. I must confess that I adopted some rough and ready methods to deal with this problem. The news travelled fast through the army that I was inclined to deal with men at the physical level. It had a sobering effect. The indiscipline among officers required more drastic treatment, and I felt that I would not be able to carry the Commander-in-Chief with me. So I decided to postpone this operation till some more propitious occasion. I started an Officers' Training School and also went into the working of the Military Academy. The future of the army depended on our establishing sound training institutions which could produce regular officers with a sense of discipline and devotion according to peace-time requirements.

I served as Adjutant-General for about a year. The experience was most valuable because it brought me face to face with basic problems of overall army organization. It also gave me an opportunity to see the working of the central government, at least in the financial sphere, at first hand. Notwithstanding all the deficiencies and difficulties I had one satisfaction: we had a young army and first-class human material. God had given us a magnificent opportunity to organize an army of our own in the service of our country. And we did.

4

Commander-in-Chief

I

There was considerable speculation about the prospects of a Pakistani being appointed Commander-in-Chief at the end of General Gracey's term. Gracey would have liked to continue, but the feeling was growing that the army should be commanded by a Pakistani. At the back of this might have been Gracey's refusal to issue instructions to Pakistan troops to move into Kashmir, as desired by the Quaid-e-Azam in October 1947, without the approval of Lord Mountbatten who was the Supreme Commander. It is claimed that the Quaid-e-Azam had agreed to revise his orders at the intervention of Auchinleck, but in the process Gracey had not enhanced his reputation with the people.

I remember that long before the appointment of the new Commander-in-Chief, Prime Minister Liaquat Ali Khan came to Rawalpindi. There was a Divisional Commanders' Conference and I had come from East Pakistan to attend. The Prime Minister sent for senior Pakistani officers and addressed them at the Circuit House. Towards the end of his address he said that it had been decided to appoint a Pakistani as the next Commander-in-Chief of the Pakistan Army. He mentioned that the government had not yet selected the person but that it was possible that the appointment would not go to the most senior officer. He wanted to know the likely repercussions among senior officers in case a person lower in the order of seniority was chosen. He asked several officers and finally turned to me. I was sitting at the end. He said, 'General Ayub Khan, would you like to say something?' I said, 'Sir, may I say with great respect that this question should never have been asked. Our drill is simple and clear. As army officers we serve to the best of our ability and leave the judgement to our superiors. Whatever decision they take, whether we like it or not, we must accept it. And if somebody is not prepared to accept that decision, he should get the hell out of the army.'

I think General Raza and a few others were among the senior-most officers and they were frequently spoken of. There was also a great deal of talk about General Iftikhar, a good officer; there was an impression that the British were backing him. Unfortunately he and General Sher Khan were killed in an air crash at Jungshahi. General Iftikhar was a difficult man to get on with, and he was short-tempered. I do not know how he would have done as Commander-in-Chief but I am certain that he would have met with considerable difficulty.

By the time I came to Rawalpindi as Adjutant-General the talk about the identity of the next Commander-in-Chief had become very lively. Once or twice my wife also asked me who was likely to be appointed Commander-in-Chief. I remember telling her, 'Quite honestly, I do not know; but I do know that, whoever is appointed, I shall have to do a great deal of work for him.' People then started making direct inquiries of me. I thought the best way to avoid all the gossip was to take some leave. So I took my wife and children and retired to the cool heights of Changlagali for two months.

Finally, one September night in 1950, I was rung up by an officer of the Ministry of Defence and informed that I had been selected as the next Commander-in-Chief. I was deeply conscious of the great responsibilities lying ahead of me. I prayed to God that He grant me the courage and ability to prove myself equal to the task. It was an event of some significance for the country. After nearly two hundred years a Muslim army in the sub-continent would have a Muslim Commander-in-Chief. I knew that whatever traditions and standards were established would continue to guide the army for a long time. I was determined that I should establish the highest standards in professional work and in all my dealings with people. I was going to be entrusted with the job of organizing a young army. It was a great challenge and a great opportunity. My first concern would be to instil a sense of self-respect among members of the armed forces. They must learn to stand on their own feet and be judged on merit. I was soon to learn that this was going to prove far more difficult than I had visualized.

General Gracey took the announcement in very good part. I was appointed Deputy Commander-in-Chief so that I should be able to make myself familiar with the work. I went to Germany and England on a short visit to study military establishments.

I took over as Commander-in-Chief on 17 January 1951. General Gracey did not say very much to me when he was leaving. Not much can be done in handing over and taking over a job like this and the new man must start all on his own. But he did mention to me, somewhat vaguely, that there was a 'Young Turk' Party in the army. I wanted to know what he meant by that. He was not very explicit, but did say that there were some peculiar people, like Akbar Khan. Two or three months later the Akbar conspiracy, which came to be known as the Rawalpindi Conspiracy, was discovered.

I learnt of the conspiracy from Prime Minister Liaquat Ali Khan. He was on an electioneering tour at the time and sent for Iskander Mirza and me to meet him at Sargodha railway station. He had called me from Lahore and Iskander Mirza from Karachi. I arrived about an hour and a half earlier than Iskander Mirza. I noticed that the Prime Minister was a little restless. This was unusual because he normally maintained an impeccable calm and never showed any signs of ill-temper. He inquired about Iskander Mirza and said, 'What has happened to this damned fellow? Why has he not turned up so far?'

It was lunch time when Iskander Mirza arrived. The Prime Minister asked us to join him at lunch and throughout he continued to talk to us in a normal, almost casual, way. When lunch was over he leaned back and said, 'Gentlemen, I have bad news for you. It has come to my knowledge that a military coup to overthrow the government has been planned by certain army officers and it is going to be put into effect very soon.' I immediately asked for details. He gave me the full text of the report which he had received from I. I. Chundrigar who was then Governor of the North-West Frontier Province. I suggested we should check the facts before taking any action.

Iskander and I went to Peshawar to see the Governor and the police officer who had passed on the report to him, and also the informer. I spoke to the Governor and later met Kiani, the police officer. Kiani did not want to expose his informer but we finally got hold of him. While I questioned Kiani, Iskander Mirza interrogated the informer. It was soon clear that an uprising had been planned. One of the conspirators was Brigadier Siddique Khan who had served in my unit at one time and was then commanding a Brigade at Bannu. He was a rather unstable type, emotional and impulsive. I sent an aircraft for him and told him, 'Siddique, you tell me the truth or I shall string you upside down.' Siddique denied all knowledge and claimed that the report was completely false. We allowed him to go back to Bannu. On arrival there he rang up Colonel Arbab at Thal who, as it transpired later, was another of the conspirators. Siddique told him that the cat was out of the bag. This confirmed my fear that a serious plot to overthrow the government had been hatched.

By then we had enough material to go back and report to the Prime Minister and he decided that we should take immediate action. Inspector-General of Police Qurban Ali Khan was put in the picture and all the officers and civilians involved in the conspiracy were arrested in their houses the same night. My first idea was to hold a court martial to try the case but the difficulty was that certain civilians were also involved. The Prime Minister decided that a Special Civil Tribunal be set up and the trial held *in camera* to prevent exposure of State secrets. The trial was held in Hyderabad Jail and Suhrawardy was engaged by the accused as defence counsel.

Suhrawardy was a complex character, a man who loved the gay life of night-clubs and had tremendous energy and drive. He took great delight in attacking the army officers who appeared as witnesses and I felt he far overstepped the mark in his cross-examination. The Court, however, remained passive. There was nothing I could do about it at the time. The conspirators were convicted and sentenced. Some years later Suhrawardy and his supporters prevailed on the government to release them. That was the prerogative of the government and I could not object, but what I could not forgive was Suhrawardy's unnecessarily harsh and undignified cross-examination of the army officers.

Afterwards, when we were both Cabinet Ministers, in a Cabinet meeting when the subject of the conspiracy was raised and Suhrawardy made some comment, I rounded on him and said that he had done great harm to the army at the trial, and that he was no friend of Pakistan. He did not reply. Later, when he was to be appointed Prime Minister, I happened to be in Karachi, and Iskander Mirza called me and said, 'We are going to appoint Mr. Suhrawardy as the Prime Minister. In that capacity he will also be your Defence Minister and you know that he would like to settle his account with you.' He suggested that we meet. Suhrawardy came to President's House. I told him that I knew his feelings towards me and that, no doubt, he knew my feelings towards him. But as Commander-in-Chief I would obey and carry out whatever legitimate and lawful orders were given to me. At the same time I would expect that there would be no interference in the internal affairs of the army. Suhrawardy found that an acceptable arrangement and we shook hands on it. I must say that he never interfered with the affairs of the army and whenever I went to him I always found him ready to listen, and to give decisions.

II

The Rawalpindi Conspiracy had deep roots; it grew in the soil of discontent and distrust and it was able to develop for several reasons. There was considerable unrest among the officers caused by a spate of swift promotions from junior to senior ranks. This raised expectations to unwarranted heights. Every officer felt that unless he was made Commander-in-Chief no one would believe that he had done well in life. It was a curious phenomenon. Perfectly sensible people, Brigadiers and Generals, would go about bemoaning their lot. Each one of them was a Bonaparte, albeit an unhappy one. I used to tell myself that but for Independence I would have been lucky to have become a Brigadier. Even after Independence I would have considered myself eminently successful if I had retired as a Major-General. The most usual military expectation is the command of a unit, the rank of Lieutenant-Colonel, and then retirement from service. It was this sudden devaluation of the higher posts which produced fantastic ideas and ambitions in people.

Then there was the fighting in Kashmir. It started as an irregular campaign. Soldiers and officers were out on their own with little direction from headquarters and with considerable responsibility placed in the hands of junior officers.

But I think the main reason for this discontent was that we had a government which failed to discharge its functions properly. When Akbar Khan's papers were seized we found among them a thesis in which he had accused the Prime Minister and everybody else in the government of inefficiency and inability to give decisions. Akbar Khan's aim was to establish a tidier form of government. He was a brave officer enjoying considerable prestige in the service, but ambitious and a very persuasive talker. He knew how to influence people and he had cast his net widely and unobtrusively.

Although I never thought for a moment that he could be planning to overthrow the government, I had always been a little suspicious of him. I knew of his ambition, of his family background, and also of his political leanings. When, as Commander-in-Chief, I had to promote certain officers to the rank of Major-General, including Akbar Khan, I pondered for some time what I should do with him. I decided to post him to General Headquarters as Chief of General Staff. I did this to ensure that he remained under my eye and also not in direct command of troops. I noticed that as Chief of General Staff he was inclined to neglect his duties and spent a lot of time in Azad Kashmir in meeting the Sudhans and others. I gave him one or two tasks which he did not complete in time. I had told him, for example, that he should arrange the procurement of hard rations such as concentrates which were necessary for our men employed in enemy territory. He kept avoiding me. I said to myself, 'this man is either inefficient or has not got his heart in the job, or his mind is working on something else.' It was a kind of premonition.[1]

[1] Akbar Khan was tried by a special tribunal and convicted. After serving his sentence he was released and has become a private citizen.

The whole affair came as a great shock to me and to all right-thinking people in the army. The prestige of the army had received a grievous blow. People could legitimately ask what kind of a shield had they got. The army had inherited a great tradition of loyalty, sense of duty, patriotism, and complete subordination to civil authority. No one could imagine that when the country was in a difficult situation this great instrument of stability would prove so vulnerable. I shudder to think what would have happened to the army and the country if the conspiracy had succeeded. There were two possible ways of its succeeding: one, swift and complete success without any clash within the armed forces, because the conspirators would have placed people like myself and other loyal senior army officers under arrest, before we could take any counter-action. The army might or might not have accepted this change. In any case, there would have been a period of complete confusion. And then if Akbar Khan and his ilk had been clever enough, they might have been able to hold their positions and control the situation. On the other hand, the chances were that some of us might have got an inkling and moved troops to anticipate and counter the action of the conspirators. The result would have been a clash between units of the Pakistan Army. If that had happened, the Indian Army would have marched in. That was what I was really afraid of. I quickly recovered from the shock and set out to restore the dignity, efficiency, and self-confidence of the army. Once that was achieved I felt that it would regain its prestige in the eyes of the people of Pakistan.

We examined the antecedents of officers and got rid of the doubtful ones. We tightened up on discipline, embarked on extensive training exercises, and I kept moving around and visiting various units. I knew that the cancer had been removed but that there was still a tremendous amount of lost ground to be regained. Paradoxical as it might seem, I was, in a sense, grateful that I had so much to do and that I could lose myself in my work, for the malaise in the political and administrative life of Pakistan was becoming painful. Karachi was a hotbed of intrigues. It was providential that army headquarters were in Rawalpindi. I would come back from my occasional visits to Karachi depressed and distressed, wondering what was happening to the country. Why were people not attending to their work with some honesty of purpose and why could they not evolve some team spirit? Why all these factions, dissensions, and disputes? And why all this malice and distrust? They were all busy destroying one another. It used to take me three or four days to recover from a Karachi visit. I would then say to myself, 'Karachi is over there and we are here; let us run the army.' I found my escape in working harder and working the soldiers harder.

As Commander-in-Chief I had to take certain problems to Karachi. I would ask Iskander Mirza, who was Defence Secretary, whether he would like to take them up with the Prime Minister. He always wanted me to go and see the Prime Minister myself. It developed into a tedious routine: first, to get the Prime Minister's decisions, then to explain them to the Defence Secretary for follow-up action. Sometimes Iskander Mirza had to check on certain decisions with the Prime Minister. At one of my meetings with the Prime Minister I suggested that it would be convenient if the Defence Secretary could also be present. Liaquat Ali Khan said, 'You might bring him along, but you should know that I do not like him.' After that Iskander Mirza and I used to go to the Prime Minister together and their relationship improved.

In 1951 when the Indians built up heavy military concentrations against us all along the border, Liaquat Ali Khan seemed tempted by the prospect of war. He said, 'I am tired of these alarums and excursions. Let us fight it out.' I submitted to him that before making up his mind he should take into account the views of those whose profession it was to fight. We had only thirteen tanks with about forty to fifty hours' engine life in them to face the Indian Army at the time, and not only our politicians but our troops were itching to settle accounts with India. It was my job to hold them back which, thank Heavens, I did. The Prime Minister was a sound man basically, always prepared to consider the pros and cons of a situation dispassionately, and he never acted in a hurry.

I grew to admire Prime Minister Liaquat Ali Khan enormously. He had a stout heart and was a man of great courage. Nothing ever perturbed him. He had served as a loyal lieutenant of the Quaid-e-Azam, always content to work in the background. He was a lonely man—in a position like that you do become lonely—and sometimes I got the feeling that he was beginning to rely more and more on me. I would give him unbiased and honest opinion on problems when he consulted me. I noticed that he was very much under the influence of Chaudhri Mohammad Ali.

Towards the end Liaquat was being challenged from several quarters. Politics became regionalized, with the result that the Prime Minister was forced to depend more and more on the refugee group. The tension in the Punjab was growing because of the squabbles between the Nawab of Mamdot and Mian Mumtaz Daultana.

The affairs of the Muslim League, the governing party, were in a mess. The Muslim League High Command and the Working Committee were controlled by a small coterie of men and the party had no

organizational structure. Conflicts between the provinces were developing and demands from East Pakistan were becoming more insistent.
It looked as if Liaquat Ali Khan might prove too slow to regain the
initiative. His eye-sight was deteriorating: I noticed that he would
hold papers at a particular angle to read them. The people around him
were equally slow and indecisive. There was nobody who could
make up his mind about anything. It seems to me, however, that
this disintegration had started earlier, even in the Quaid-e-Azam's
time, with people like Choudhry Khaliquzzaman challenging his
authority.

A few months after the trial of the Rawalpindi conspirators the
Prime Minister was assassinated while delivering a public speech.
This happened in Rawalpindi on 16 October 1951. The motive of the
crime was never established. I was in a London clinic at that time
undergoing treatment for amoebic dysentery. For five or six years I had
been running a low temperature. I had an appendicitis operation in
1951 and thereafter something went wrong with my system. I remember
that Habib Ibrahim Rahimtoola, our High Commissioner in London,
rang me up in the hospital and gave me the tragic news. It came as a
great personal blow, for I had a high regard and liking for Liaquat Ali
Khan. And I knew, too, that his death was a terrible loss to the
country.

Before long it became apparent that none of the Prime Minister's
associates was capable of filling the gap created by his death. Conditions
throughout the country deteriorated rapidly and we witnessed the start
of a woeful chapter in our country's history and one which was to drag
on its unhappy course for several years.

When I returned to Pakistan I met several members of the new
Cabinet in Karachi—Prime Minister Khawaja Nazimuddin, Chaudhri
Mohammad Ali, Mushtaq Ahmad Gurmani and others. Not one of
them mentioned Liaquat Ali Khan's name, nor did I hear a word of
sympathy or regret from any one of them. Governor-General Ghulam
Mohammad seemed equally unaware of the fact that the country had
lost an eminent and capable Prime Minister through the fell act of an
assassin. I wondered at how callous, cold-blooded, and selfish people
could be. It seemed that every one of them had got himself promoted in
one way or another. The termination of the Prime Minister's life had
come as the beginning of a new career for them. It was disgusting and
revolting. It may be a harsh thing to say, but I got the distinct impression that they were all feeling relieved that the only person who
might have kept them under control had disappeared from the scene.
The political arena was now available to them for a free-for-all. The

assassination of the Prime Minister caused universal anguish. There were all kinds of wild rumours and some cabinet ministers and highly placed individuals were accused of having plotted the murder. I did not for a moment believe that any one of them was directly or indirectly involved in the assassination. I know that Begum Liaquat Ali Khan still thinks the government did not try hard enough to investigate the assassination and bring the culprits to book. I have seen the report of the expert who was called from Scotland Yard: he could find no evidence to show that the assassination was anything but the act of an individual. Had there been any complicity or involvement of any kind, I have no doubt that it would have been discovered. These things do not remain hidden.

It was my belief at that time that Liaquat Ali Khan could have blossomed into an active and positive leader of the nation. I hoped he would put his foot down and crush all the intrigues. Unfortunately he did not live long enough to give a clear lead and direction to the country.

III

Both these unfortunate events, the Rawalpindi Conspiracy and the assassination of the Prime Minister, occurred during the first few months of my assumption of office as Commander-in-Chief. I initiated certain schemes for the reorganization of the army immediately after the conspiracy was discovered. The political turmoil which appeared in the wake of the Prime Minister's death convinced me that we must not lose any time in building up the army which alone could hold the country together and defend it against any possible attack. India appeared to be watching these developments with satisfaction and I later learnt from Sheikh Abdullah that Pandit Nehru told him at the time that Pakistan would disintegrate in a couple of years. He wanted to come to some arrangement with Sheikh Abdullah on the assumption that Pakistan would soon cease to be a political entity.

Whatever institutions we had inherited at the time of Independence or had set up since then were crumbling one by one. People had fast lost their initial enthusiasm and found themselves surrounded by problems, with no one to attend to them. Everyone now joined in the political vaudeville. There was no organ of administration which was not pressed into service to promote individual political interests. All this hardened my determination to keep the army completely aloof from politics. Even though senior army officers were conscious of what was going on in the political sphere, I never permitted them to discuss political affairs.

One of the first things I did as Commander-in-Chief was to set up a Planning Board of which General Yahya, the Deputy Chief of General Staff, became the first Chairman. I would assign specific tasks to the Board for study. None of us spared himself and before one task was completed another would be there to engage our attention.

Our basic weapon was man. This was what I wanted my colleagues to realize. We must first solve all his problems and remove his difficulties, whether personal or professional, before this weapon could become fully effective. His conditions of service should be secure and he must have adequate incentives for work. The education of his children, his medical care, his food, his dress, and his accommodation should be our concern. The less he had to worry, the more active interest would he have in his work. While it took me some time to resolve the financial problems which I have already mentioned, we went ahead to set up agricultural and dairy farms and took steps to improve the breed of livestock. A number of horse-breeding centres were opened and we ensured the provision of a balanced and nutritious diet for everyone in the army. New medical centres and hospitals were set up, and trained and efficient doctors and nurses provided. The ex-soldier and his dependents were also taken care of through the investment of the pre-Partition post-war reconstruction fund. By 1964 about 2.6 million rupees per annum were being spent for the education and welfare of ex-soldiers and their dependents. To attract the right type of young men a number of cadet colleges and academies were established. To support these institutions a chain of public schools was started. All these reforms had an immediate impact on recruitment and morale.

My principal concern, however, was to train the army on appropriate lines. There was too much routine and drudgery and too little purpose in what we were asking the men to do. Most of the time they hardly knew what it meant; they just obeyed and followed. Was this the way to get the best out of them? Our organization and establishments were based on Second World War concepts which, apart from being cumbersome, had become completely obsolete. The army was organized not so much for the defence of the homeland as for an expeditionary force. This was understandable, as the primary role of the old Indian Army was to support the British forces in creating and policing British overseas interests.

We inherited six Infantry Divisions, one Armoured Brigade and a few training and static installations at the time of Independence. This looked quite impressive on paper. What we got, in fact, were truncated formations and units critically deficient in essential equipment. India's refusal to give us our share of armaments, equipment, and stores further added to our problems.

After the war, armies throughout the world carried out extensive research and modified their organizations in the light of new weapons and new requirements. We were unable to do so immediately after Independence because of our other pressing problems. Apart from following outmoded concepts, we suffered from serious shortcomings in logistic and training facilities. The country could not afford the extra expenditure required for making up deficiencies in essential units and equipment and for balancing and re-equipping the army. I started with a review of the organization and structure of field formations and units in order to achieve balance, with increased mobility and firepower. Manpower was reduced, wherever possible. Simultaneously, the operative procedures of our schools, training centres, depots, and other logistic installations were revised. It was here that the Planning Board proved particularly useful. The Board would analyse different problems and come to me directly with recommendations, thus eliminating the tedious routine of ministerial processes.

The first essential in reorganizing the army was to shift the emphasis from learning the technique of war to understanding the art of war. The important thing was to develop capability to apply the principles of war to areas of higher tactics and strategy.

In the system that we inherited there was little room for original thinking. Loyalty had become synonymous with blind obedience and there was little attempt at reflection or criticism. The whole system of training and promotion was directed to the production of stereotyped men and nothing new or unusual could emerge at any level. Worse still, we were completely dependent on foreign countries for our tactical doctrines and methods. It was a sad commentary on our methods of training that our men, who are natural hunters and stalkers, should become tactically clumsy after spending six months in the army. They lost all their resourcefulness, flexibility, and skill and became rigid, stereotyped, and inhibited. We were killing in them all that was natural. Clearly there was need for fundamental rethinking and drastic changes.

Our officers had spirit and intelligence but they were lacking in sympathy, with the result that their relationship with their men was governed by the rigid principle of command and obedience. I also thought that we might adopt a system of attaching outstanding officers to other professions so that they might be able to add a new dimension to their experience and acquire breadth of vision. I knew that whatever plans for reorganization we might evolve, they had to suit the likely operational role of the army and the geographic conditions and national characteristics and temperament of our people, apart from being sound in theory. Moreover, all new concepts and establishments should be within our means and the objective should be to achieve balance, increased firepower, and battle efficiency in as economical a manner as possible.

The operational and tactical background for reorganization was closely examined and comprehensive studies prepared to evolve new elements in strategy and organization. Each one of these elements was subjected to ground tests under exacting and realistic conditions. Every reform was developed in a pragmatic manner and given final shape on the basis of results obtained during actual trials.

The British Army had been backed by vast arsenals of ammunition and armaments. We must learn to do with limited resources. The Infantry Division was made considerably more mobile and effective though its basic structure remained unaltered in view of our reliance on conventional weapons. The firepower of the Division was increased by nine tons of metal per minute, all weapons firing at normal rate. Certain savings were made in administrative personnel, and mobility was increased by elimination of unnecessary equipment and introduction of more economical loading methods. These changes gave the Infantry more teeth and less tail. It took years of work, but I still remember the excitement with which I watched the new experimental Brigade under Gul Mawaz. This experiment determined the future organization of our units. The basic concept was to defend or attack a piece of ground with firepower and not with human bodies—introducing a seemingly irregular type of warfare on a large scale.

The design of our training centres was completely out of date, and the new techniques and concepts evolved after the last war had not been applied. The principal difficulty was that each separate training centre was designed to be self-sufficient in all trades required by the army. The result was uneven standards of output and dissipation of training effort. Centre Commanders were expected to supervise subjects of which they themselves had little knowledge and the existence of a chain of small centres inevitably added to overheads. I decided to centralize training. The smaller centres were amalgamated into more economical groups on the basis of common trades and common requirements. Where a trade required a high degree of technical skill and effort, the responsibility for training was entrusted to the agency most suited to the purpose.

From this emerged the idea of amalgamating regiments with common traditions, common class-composition, and common recruiting areas. The result was that the Baluch Regiment, the 8th Punjab Regiment, and the Bahawalpur Regiment became the new Baluch Regiment. The new Frontier Force Regiment absorbed the Frontier Force Rifles, the Pathan Regiment, and the old Frontier Force Regiment. And the 1st, 14th, 15th, and 16th Punjab Regiments became the new Punjab Regiment. The newly reorganized East Bengal Regiment retained its entity and composition. I knew all this would set up a howl. The old regiments which lost their identity were, understandably, unhappy. Slowly and patiently we succeeded in converting old officers to new ideas. I must say they responded magnificently after they got rid of their initial scepticism and the results were beyond expectations. The credit for this goes to the officers and men for their spirit of compromise and adjustment over such delicate issues as customs, traditions, and dress.

In the meantime, the whole training system was undergoing radical change. The syllabuses were being revised and the institutions were geared to the requirements of greater and more rapid turnover. The theoretical and practical aspects of training used to be treated in isolation. We combined trade training with military training. There was a tendency to forget that practical training and knowledge could be obtained only by actually serving with the troops and that experience gained the hard way as a cog in the larger tactical machinery of the army could not be replaced by purely theoretical study and separate academic training. We were gradually able to achieve the correct balance between academic instruction and practical work with the troops. The commanders, right down the chain, were given the responsibility for the training of their commands.

Another difficulty with our training system was in our attempt to train a young officer at all levels of command in addition to letting him specialize in the subject of his own arm or service. For every step forward in rank the officer had to go back to school. This reduced the unit to the status of a transit camp and the officer missed duty with the troops which was really the essential part of his training.

The logistic facilities available to the army at the time of Independence were practically non-existent. We succeeded in realigning our logistic concepts and doctrines, and, in consequence, our facilities, with the type and duration of any war in which the country might be involved. Greater reliance was placed on indigenous resources and latent potential was exploited in sectors common to defence and commerce. Efforts were made to achieve greater standardization in the requirements of armed forces and specifications were modified, where necessary, to accommodate indigenous capacity and workmanship. The organization and establishment of logistic installations and depots were revised to suit the current and anticipated needs of the reorganized field army.

All this work relating to the reorganization of the army was carried out in the light of certain fundamentals of defence. Our first concern was the defence of Pakistan against any possible aggression by India. We knew that war with India would be a national war in every sense of the word. India's aim is to expand, dominate, and spread her influence. In this she considers Pakistan as her enemy number one. Our strategic aim cannot be the conquest of India because that would be a negation of the very concept of separation. Our aim must be to make India realize that it is not worth her while to maintain a hostile attitude towards us.

India's military strength would always be greater than ours. Our aim should be to build up a military deterrent force with adequate offensive and defensive power; enough, at least, to neutralize the Indian Army. India can concentrate her forces against us without warning. We must, therefore, have a standing army ready to take the field at a moment's notice. In our circumstances a territorial army has hardly any place; it would take too much time to mobilize and train such an army.

It was a long and difficult struggle spread over several years, but in the end we were able to develop an agile and effective army capable of meeting any challenge. The new concept of fighting that we evolved, and the re-education of our officers and men, has made the Pakistan Army what it is today. It can take on an enemy several times its strength. And in spite of all the vicissitudes and pressures generated by political events, the army has been able to maintain its patriotic traditions and gradually develop into a powerful instrument of stability in the life of the country. My prayer and belief is that it will always remain so: a sharp and reliable instrument of peace and war.

This should not be taken to mean that while building the army I ignored the sister services: the Pakistan Navy and the Pakistan Air Force. I had a considerable hand in building them up into what they are today. The development of the air force has been my special concern as the defence of Pakistan is essentially a land–air problem, as is the case with all continental countries.

5

Politics 1948–1958

We crossed a river of blood to achieve Independence.

People were uprooted and driven like millions of dry leaves by a turbulent gust of fanaticism and blind passion. They were trampled and crushed under the feet of communal fury. Hundreds of thousands of men, women, and children were butchered and the sub-continent was engulfed in a bloody civil war. What sustained us was the abounding faith of our people in their destiny and their unfaltering devotion to the ideology for which they had secured a motherland of their own.

India's attitude to Pakistan continued to be one of unmitigated hostility. Her aim was to cripple us at birth. She denied us our share of financial resources and dishonoured solemn agreements for the supply of our share of stores and equipment. She then involved us in the struggle for Kashmir. When the cease-fire was called we had to hold and guard nearly 500 miles of the line along extremely difficult terrain. India maintained a constant posture of aggression which meant that we had to strain our limited resources almost to breaking-point to build up and equip an army which could contain Indian ambitions.

On the political front we were without a proper Constitution. We were working under the Indian Independence Act 1947; and since the Pakistan Muslim League had a majority in the Central Legislature, some kind of a government could manage to function. The Quaid-e-Azam, who had worked for the creation of Pakistan with supreme dedication, died in 1948 before he could give the country a Constitution which, coming from him, would have enjoyed popular support.

His successor, Liaquat Ali Khan, for some inexplicable reason, instead of first completing the process of constitution-making and consolidating the position of his party at the centre, started with general elections in the provinces. Perhaps he was discouraged by the reception accorded to the Report of the first Basic Principles Committee. I believe he was advised that if he could get a majority in the provinces he would then be able to establish a majority at the centre.

His position was considerably weakened by the political situation in the Punjab. Liaquat Ali Khan had decided to support Mian Mumtaz Daultana who was then the Chief Minister, as against the Nawab of Mamdot. A PRODA[1] case was filed against the Nawab of Mamdot for certain irregularities. All this was played up by the Press and a hostile atmosphere was built up against Liaquat Ali Khan. His opponents, backed by the Press, attacked his wife who, I know, is a very fine lady indeed. She was working for the amelioration of the conditions of women so that they might enjoy equal status with men and play their legitimate role in society. But attacks on her were essentially intended to embarrass the Prime Minister.

Those who followed Liaquat Ali Khan in political office proved unequal to the task. They did not understand the problems facing the country, nor did they have the courage to try to solve them. One after another they made a mess of things by trying to work an unworkable system of government, and the country started slipping very fast. The central government gradually lost its grip over the affairs of the state, being beset by the constant pressure tactics of parliamentarians and the growing relative strength of the provincial governments, who were virtually holding it to ransom. It was caught between the conflicting claims of the provinces, and any two provinces could gang up to brow-beat the central authority.

The period between Liaquat Ali Khan's death and 1958 was distressing. Not only was the central government at loggerheads with the provinces, but a great deal of intrigue and dog-fighting was going on within the central government itself. A civil servant who had become Finance Minister at the time of Independence elevated himself to the position of Governor-General. Another turned himself overnight from Secretary to Government (a civil service post) to Minister for Finance. All it required was rewriting the designation on the name-plates outside their offices. The politicians were naturally dependent on permanent services, but the more powerful among the services had developed political ambitions of their own. Everyone seemed to have a group of his own and his sole occupation was to grind his own axe regardless of whether the country was ground to pieces in the process.

One climax was reached in 1954 when Governor-General Ghulam Mohammad used the pretext of the worsening economic situation, near-famine conditions, and the Punjab disturbances to dismiss Khawaja Nazimuddin's Ministry. While the latter was busy making futile gestures, quoting his majority in the legislature and, some say, suppli-cating the Queen of England to come to his rescue, the Governor-

[1] Public and Representative Offices Disqualification Act of 1949.

General appointed Mohammad Ali Bogra Prime Minister and a number of Nazimuddin's colleagues in the Cabinet accepted office in the new Cabinet without demur, if without avidity. Mohammad Ali Bogra started as a protégé of Ghulam Mohammad. As he acquired confidence he thought he should disengage himself from the apron-strings of the Governor-General. People like Fazlur Rahman, Hashim Gazdar, and Abdus Sattar Pirzada encouraged him to assert himself. They would tell him that if he was not careful he would meet the fate of his predecessor. They thought the only answer was to curtail the powers of the Governor-General by amending the Indian Independence Act 1947.

I remember this very well as on that day I happened to be in Karachi, where I had gone to see the Prime Minister. I was aware of a great deal of coming and going and I found it very difficult to discuss any problem with the Prime Minister. Not that it was ever easy to discuss anything with him. In the midst of something quite serious he would pick up one's pen or something and ask, 'Where did you get this one?' He was like a child in these things. But apart from his usual childishness there was an atmosphere of peculiar hurry around the Prime Minister's house and I asked him what it was about. I had by then got to know these fellows: they were never in a hurry for any good purpose. He told me quietly that his colleagues wanted some amendment to be made in the Government of India Act by which the Governor-General's powers would be limited.

A Resolution was printed in the middle of the night and placed in the pigeon-holes of Members of the National Assembly. In the morning the Assembly met as a Constitution-making body, an hour before its scheduled time, and revoked Sections 9, 10, 10-A, 10-B, and 17 of the Government of India Act, thus stripping the Governor-General of the powers in exercise of which he had dismissed the Nazimuddin Cabinet. The Resolution was moved and passed within ten minutes. The Governor-General was convalescing in Abbottabad at that time.

I mentioned this once to the late Maulvi Tamizuddin Khan who was then Speaker of the Central Assembly. 'You talk about political morality. What about your changing the Constitution without even informing the Governor-General, who was in the country and had been appointed, presumably, by majority support of the House? If you did not want him you should have removed him. But you did not have the moral courage to do that. Instead a subterfuge was adopted. The change meant not only limiting the powers of an individual but destroying the focal point of authority.' Maulvi Tamizuddin replied that such things

5   The author's family house in Rehana

6 The Mosque at Rehana where the author studied the Holy Qur'an

were not unprecedented. 'Nor are murders', I said. 'But by that token you don't condone them.'

Ghulam Mohammad was not the kind of man to take things lying down. Whatever else he might have lacked he certainly did not lack courage. He could fight anybody and stand up to anyone; the man was absolutely fearless. He was a sick man at that time and his speech was quite unintelligible. He must have said to himself, 'All right, if this is how you have treated me, I shall pay you back in the same coin.'

I went to the United States soon after this, with Prime Minister Mohammad Ali Bogra, Sir Zafrullah Khan, and Chaudhri Mohammad Ali. The Prime Minister got a message from the Governor-General to return home at once. I sensed trouble and realized that the old man was on the war-path and was going to dismiss him. The Prime Minister was also worried and cancelled his visit to Canada. We decided to return as quickly as possible. When we reached London we found that there was no eastbound flight that day so we had to charter a plane to get back to Karachi.

At London Airport there was a telephone call for me from the Governor-General. I could not understand what he was saying and I gave the telephone to Iskander Mirza. All we could make out was that he wanted me to get back to Pakistan at once; he was not interested in the others. The Prime Minister was worried about what might happen to him on his return. It was with great difficulty that I persuaded him to accompany us back home. He kept asking me, 'Can you guarantee that I will not be put under arrest when I get back?' I could give him no guarantee but I assured him that such a thing could not possibly happen. He retorted, 'And supposing you are arrested too?' I replied, 'That will be fine. You will be in good company.'

On the way I told Iskander Mirza and Chaudhri Mohammad Ali that it would be extremely unwise if the Prime Minister was taken to the Governor-General immediately on our arrival in Karachi: such a confrontation could lead to an ugly situation. The decision was that some of us should go to the Governor-General's house and persuade the old man to act with reason and come to some understanding with the Prime Minister. The Prime Minister should go to his own house and wait for a signal from us. Mohammad Ali Bogra put up a brave front but, I think, inwardly he was quite frightened. He had sent a message from London that he should be provided with army protection on arrival. I was deeply perturbed myself. Knowing the Governor-General's temperament, I was worried that he might do something desperate. The prestige of the country was involved and if some extreme measure was taken it would bring her into disrepute. The only sensible

course was to bring about a *rapprochement* between the Governor-
General and the Prime Minister. Iskander Mirza, Chaudhri Mohammad
Ali and I went to the Governor-General's house while the Prime
Minister, with some others, went to his own house.

The Governor-General was lying in his bedroom upstairs. He had
very high blood pressure and an agonizing back-ache which compelled
him to lie flat on hardboard. He was bursting with rage, emitting
volleys of abuse, which, luckily, no one understood. Chaudhri Mohammad Ali ventured to say something and received a volley; then
Iskander Mirza said something and got another. We were pleading
with him to give another chance to Mohammad Ali. His only reply was
an angry growl, 'Go, off you go.' He kept on saying 'No, no'. All he
wanted was to shoo us off.

We marched out of the bedroom in single file, Iskander Mirza at
the head, Chaudhri Mohammad Ali following, and I bringing up the
rear. I was about to step out of the room when the nurse attending the
Governor-General tugged at my coat. I turned and found myself
facing a different man. There he was, the sick old Governor-General,
who a moment ago was insane with anger, now beaming with delight
and bubbling with laughter. I said in my heart, 'You wicked old man!'
He beckoned me with a peculiar glee in his eye. 'Sit down on the bed.'
He then pulled out two documents from under his pillow. On one was
written something to this effect: 'I, Ghulam Mohammad, so and so,
because of this, that, and the other hand over such and such authority
to General Ayub Khan and command him to produce a Constitution
within three months.' I looked at that paper and said to myself, 'Damn
your soul. For the last eight years you have done damn all, and you
expect me to produce a Constitution in three months.' The other
document was to the effect that I had accepted the offer, and for a
brief moment I had those historic documents in my hand.

As I looked at these pieces of paper, everything within me cried
'NO'. I said: 'You are being reckless and you will do the country
immense harm. I am engaged in building up the army. We have an
enemy, an implacable enemy in India. We may not want to be India's
enemy but she insists on treating us as one. I can serve this country
better in my profession. I believe I can do something useful, and in your
present frame of mind you are doing something which in the long run
will only damage the country.' His answer was another volley of
abuse. But he realized that I was not going to be a party to an act of
recklessness.

While I was going through this, Mohammad Ali Bogra was engaged
with his own advisers. They were telling him that the Governor-

General could not possibly touch him. We found some difficulty in persuading Mohammad Ali Bogra to come to the Governor-General's house. The Governor-General and the Prime Minister finally came to some understanding and a kind of truce was arranged between them. A serious crisis was thus averted for the time being. When I said 'No' to Ghulam Mohammad's offer it was Providence that helped me. Had I succumbed to the temptation the course of history might well have been different. We would certainly not have had an army worth the name and the one stabilizing element in the whole situation would have been neutralized.

The country still did not have a Constitution. The first Basic Principles Committee Report produced by Liaquat Ali Khan had proved unpopular. Nazimuddin took another sixteen months to produce the second Report which was equally unacceptable. Mohammad Ali Bogra tinkered with the problem for more than two years and yet there was no agreement on the basic principles of the new Constitution; and this seven years after Independence.

The demand for the dissolution of the Constituent Assembly, which had lost all prestige, was gaining support. At about that time Suhrawardy, who had led the United Front to a landslide victory in the provincial elections in East Pakistan, issued a statement from Zurich advising the Governor-General to dissolve the Constituent Assembly as it had become totally unrepresentative, at least in so far as its East Pakistan members were concerned. He further suggested that fresh elections be held from amongst the existing provincial legislatures.

The Constituent Assembly was finally dissolved on 24 October 1954, and I was asked by the Governor-General to join the new Cabinet, with Mohammad Ali Bogra as Prime Minister. Much against my inclination I had to agree to this, but I made it quite clear to the Governor-General that my chief interest was in the army. The one consideration which made me accept this offer was that I wanted to act as a buffer between the politicians and the armed forces. The government was utterly confused and almost leaderless and I knew that the politicians had their eyes on the army in which they wanted to create their own pockets of support. It was during this period that I presented my programme to the Cabinet contained in a document which I had drafted earlier. But about that I shall have more to say later.

The new Constituent Assembly was formed in June 1955. Suhrawardy had joined the Cabinet under Mohammad Ali Bogra in December 1954 and had been an ardent supporter of One Unit. In fact he drafted the One Unit Bill which he was to pilot through the Assembly. The intention of the Bill was to integrate the provinces of

North-West Frontier, the Punjab, Sind, Baluchistan, and States and Frontier regions into one united province of West Pakistan. The existence of different provinces organized on linguistic and racial lines facilitated political manoeuvring by unscrupulous elements to the serious detriment of the economic and strategic interests of the area. The One Unit Bill was intended to put an end to all this and to enable the whole of West Pakistan to develop and progress on a uniform pattern. But when Chaudhri Mohammad Ali was appointed Prime Minister in August 1955 with the support of the United Front he became lukewarm towards the One Unit proposal and suggested that the Bill be circulated to elicit public opinion.

Suhrawardy found himself outmanoeuvred and missed his chance of becoming Prime Minister. The Governor-General, who had brought him into the Cabinet, had gone on sick leave and Iskander Mirza had taken over as Acting Governor-General. To provide a counterpoise to Suhrawardy he started cultivating Fazlul Haq, forgetting that only a year before he had condemned him as a traitor. The whole situation was becoming curiouser and curiouser.

Chaudhri Mohammad Ali managed to produce a Constitution which was promulgated on 23 March 1956. It was a document of despair. The Prime Minister was so anxious to go down in history as the author of a Constitution that he was prepared to accommodate all points of view. What the country got was not a Constitution but a hotch-potch of alien concepts which had already brought enough confusion and chaos to the country. The Constitution, by distributing power between the President, the Prime Minister and his Cabinet, and the provinces, destroyed the focal point of power and left no one in a position of control.

Ironically enough the author of the Constitution became its first victim. During those days I saw him once in an almost helpless state in his office. He also held the Defence portfolio and I had gone to see him with some defence problem. He said to me, 'My party has deserted me. It is all over.' I uttered some words of encouragement but he would not be comforted. 'No, no, this is far too serious. Why don't you take over and save me from this business?' I said, 'Look, don't talk about these things to me. Talk to your President and try to find some sensible way out of this mess.'

Iskander Mirza had by then taken a firm control of affairs, having been unanimously elected first President of the Republic under the 1956 Constitution. Shrewd as he was, he could see how the Constitution could be used to promote political intrigues and bargaining. No one knew any longer who belonged to which political party; it was all a question of swapping labels: a Muslim Leaguer today, a Republican tomorrow; and yesterday's 'traitors' were tomorrow's Chief Ministers, indistinguishable as tweedledum and tweedledee!

In September 1956 Chaudhri Mohammad Ali yielded place to Suhrawardy who had by then managed to get into the good books of President Iskander Mirza. Once again Suhrawardy appeared on the political scene as a strong supporter of One Unit and blandly assured East Pakistan that on his assumption of office 98 per cent of provincial autonomy had already been given and that the slogan of provincial autonomy, which brought him to power, was a political stunt. After just over a year, in October 1957, Suhrawardy was supplanted by Chundrigar, who managed to complete a miserable 59 days in office and was replaced by Malik Firoz Khan Noon.

In West Pakistan, Dr. Khan Sahib became Chief Minister by the combined efforts of President Mirza, Prime Minister Chaudhri Mohammad Ali, and Governor Gurmani just before the One Unit scheme was actually put into operation. The elections to the West Pakistan Assembly in January 1956 gave the Muslim League a clear majority in the legislature and they wanted to oust the Chief Minister. To this the Governor of the Province did not agree and, the Muslim League Ministers in the Cabinet having resigned, their places were overnight filled by their political rivals within the Muslim League.

Dr. Khan Sahib went ahead and formed a new party in April 1956, called the Republican Party, comprising deserters from the Muslim League. Party indiscipline and lack of solidarity within the parties were manifested in the free use of threats and pressures. Members crossed the floor and changed parties freely and even charges of kidnapping and manhandling of Assembly members were made on both sides.

The Republican Party stand on the important issues in West Pakistan politics was in favour of separate electorates and in support of the One Unit scheme. However, Dr. Khan Sahib, under pressure from Iskander Mirza and Suhrawardy who wanted to maintain the political balance prevailing at the time at the centre and in East Pakistan, went back on their promise on the electorate issue. The Muslim League, in an effort to throw out the Republican government, joined hands with the National Awami Party on the pretext of undoing One Unit.

Many Republican Party members crossed the floor and joined the Muslim League which again became a majority party. But Iskander Mirza's reaction was to impose Section 193 in West Pakistan, by this means dismissing the ministry and asking the Governor to assume direct rule. The result was that after two months, when direct rule ended, the same Republican Party that had been defeated on the

floor of the House returned to power. Dr. Khan Sahib, however, resigned from the leadership and Sardar Abdur Rashid was appointed in
his place. Now the Republicans made the same promise to the National
Awami Party of undoing One Unit, to secure its support. One of the
results was a break in the Awami League–Republican alliance at the
centre and in West Pakistan Sardar Abdur Rashid had to resign both
from Chief Ministership and leadership of the Republican Party after
the N.A.P. had again withdrawn its support in favour of the Opposition
Muslim League on the basis of a vague programme of reforms. Rashid's
place was taken by Muzaffar Ali Khan Qazilbash, the third Republican
Chief Minister of West Pakistan.

In East Pakistan a serious crisis occurred on 31 March 1958, when
Fazlul Haq, the Governor, dismissed Ataur Rahman Khan's Cabinet.
Later that night Fazlul Haq was himself dismissed by Iskander Mirza.
Ataur Rahman was succeeded by Abu Hussain Sarkar who was in turn
dismissed within twelve hours of assuming office and the Ataur Rahman Cabinet was back again in power. As in West Pakistan, the N.A.P.
played its disruptive role of supporting and then opposing one ministry
after another in East Pakistan. Its withdrawal of support led to the fall
of the Awami League Ministry on 19 June and the United Front
Ministry succeeded it. The same day the N.A.P. switched support to
the Awami League and brought down the United Front Ministry. The
situation became so confused that the President declared Section 193
(President's rule) in the province on 24 June 1958. After two months
Ataur Rahman Khan was reinstated as Chief Minister. The provincial
assembly declared the Speaker 'of unsound mind' and a brawl in the
House on 21 September resulted in the death of its Deputy Speaker,
Shahed Ali.

By the middle of 1958 the whole country was in the grip of a serious
economic crisis. Reckless spending seemed to be the order of the day.
We were incurring foreign exchange liabilities to the extent of Rs.
30 to 40 million every month in excess of our earnings. The foreign
exchange reserves were down to Rs. 420 million, of which about
140 million were not negotiable. In another ten months or so the
currency would have lost all value and we might have had a complete
breakdown of the monetary and banking system in the country.

Throughout this confusion there was incessant talk of holding
general elections under the 1956 Constitution. These elections were
promised for November 1957. They were then postponed to 1958. The
President had thoroughly exploited the weaknesses in the Constitution
and had got everyone connected with the political life of the country
utterly exposed and discredited. I do not think that he ever seriously

wanted to hold general elections; he was looking for a suitable opportunity to abrogate the Constitution. Indeed, he was setting the stage for it.

To the politicians, particularly those who had been debarred from political life, the prospect of general elections was enough temptation to start a countrywide campaign, ostensibly for political support but, in fact, to intimidate their opponents. The leading personality was Khan Abdul Qayyum Khan who was going round the country spitting fire and preaching civil war. He went about saying openly that if his party did not win the elections, rivers of blood would flow. He found eloquent associates in my own brother Sardar Bahadur Khan and Raja Ghazanfar Ali Khan.

Khan Abdul Qayyum Khan built up the Muslim League National Guards, about 60,000 strong. They paraded in the streets, wearing uniforms and steel helmets and carrying rifles. On 20 September 1958 the government banned the wearing of military uniforms and the maintenance of military or para-military organizations by individuals or associations. Prime Minister Malik Firoz Khan Noon announced on 23 September that there would be little chance of free and fair elections if every political party had a private army of its own. Qayyum Khan was not to be deterred. He arrived in Karachi on the same day and thousands of his supporters defied the prohibitory orders issued by the government. The Working Committee of the Muslim League adopted a Resolution on 28 September that the government would be dislodged, 'if need be, by extra-constitutional methods'.

The situation was further complicated by the Khan of Kalat who, taking advantage of the general confusion, started conspiring to bring about the secession of Kalat from Pakistan. It was seriously suggested at the time that he was encouraged in this by Iskander Mirza, who was setting the stage for his final action. The Khan of Kalat was arrested on 6 October 1958 and deprived of all distinctions, privileges, and amenities.

What was more dangerous was that some of the politicians like Qayyum Khan had started making contacts with certain members of the armed forces. They were spreading all kinds of rumours to isolate senior officers and to create groups of army officers to support them in the pursuit of their ambitions.

From a soldier's position it was quite clear to me that the general elections were going to be stand-up fights. There would be large-scale disturbances all over the country, and civil authority, already groaning under the heels of the politicians, would be incapable of dealing with the situation. Whether the army liked it or not it would get embroiled, because in the final analysis it would become a question of maintaining some semblance of law and order in the country.

II

The army could not remain unaffected by the conditions around it;
nor was it conceivable that officers and men would not react to all the
political chicanery, intrigue, corruption, and inefficiency manifest in
every sphere of life. They had their relatives, they read newspapers, and
some had their contacts. Being a patriotic and national army, it was
bound to respond to the thinking of the people in the country. I could
see that many of the officers and men were feeling dejected and des-
pondent. Not infrequently they would be told, 'You *armywalas*, you
should be true to your salt. While the country is going to the dogs you
are enjoying yourselves.' Not only was I blamed: everybody in uniform
was being blamed. Perfectly respectable people would come to me and
say, 'You can save the situation but you are not prepared to take any
risk.' Some of my friends put it to me even more bluntly, and I said to
them, 'What can I do? After all, I am not responsible for all this. You
can only criticize me for the things that I am responsible for.'

As things deteriorated, more and more people came and talked
to me in the same strain. I could see a deep despair in their eyes.
Wherever I went—and I travelled a great deal, from one cantonment
to another, inspecting troops—and whenever people gathered, I was
aware of the same despair. The sense of demoralization had seeped
down to the masses and they started saying openly, 'Let somebody save
this country.' The implication was obvious: it was the army alone that
could step into the breach. That was the only disciplined organization
that could give the country the necessary covering fire, in order to
enable it to steady itself and extricate itself from the evils which had
surrounded it. Things did not look like improving. But I hoped that
someone might rise to the occasion. I would have been the first person
to welcome him and to give him all support. I kept hoping and praying.

Another worry I had was how, if the army once got drawn into
political life—and this seemed inevitable—it could withdraw itself
from the situation. The outside world was going to interpret the action
of the army in terms of the *coups d'état* which frequently occurred in
certain other countries. This would have had a damaging effect on the
image and reputation of Pakistan. A well-organized, trained, and
disciplined army would find it extremely distasteful to be turned into an
instrument for securing political power. But as conditions were, the
army alone could act as a corrective force and restore normalcy.

To me it was like exposing my own child to unpredictable hazards.
I used to counsel patience. Somewhere in the back of my mind was the
thought that Iskander Mirza might be able to evolve some pattern out

of the chaos which he had created. But he himself was feeling insecure and had lost credit with the people. He worked and thrived in an atmosphere of intrigue. He talked to me on several occasions during those days, and I could sense that he was feeling desperate and cornered. I would tell him that he would have to give a constructive lead if the country was to be saved.

I must have been under considerable stress at that time because I maintained some kind of a diary, a very unusual thing for me. The first entry is dated 2 May 1958 during a visit to the U.S.A., and the last one 6 September 1958. Selections from these entries give an idea of my thinking and preoccupations during that period.

2 May 1958

Played golf with General Nathan Twining and General Omar Bradley at the Burning Tree Golf Course. I was most impressed with the extreme dignity and humility of General Bradley—an old man of 67 still tough as a nut. He did a very difficult course in 80. Twining is also a very good player. During play Twining kept talking to Bradley about Pakistan and our armed forces in warm terms. He told me that he does not understand State Department's policy towards India. Twining told me that he is arranging a lunch for me on the 5th of May in which all the services chiefs would be present. This would give me an opportunity to talk to them informally about our problems. He said, 'I would like you to be as frank and forthright as possible.'

5 May

Met the services chiefs at lunch. Explained to them our security problems and also the problems connected with military aid.

In the evening met Allen Dulles and thanked him for putting his brother, who was the U.S. Foreign Secretary, in the picture regarding our problems.

6 May

Addressed the House Foreign Affairs Committee in the Congress buildings. In this talk I analysed the causes of the trouble in the Middle East and the danger of any aid to India unless she gives guarantee of good behaviour and solves disputes with us on a fair and honourable basis. I also tried to dispel the illusion that India's arms build-up was on account of the fear of China and that she had no aggressive intentions against Pakistan. They asked me some very searching questions.

At night flew all the way to El Paso (Fort Bliss). Saw anti-aircraft guided missile demonstration. It was very impressive. It is obvious that

the AA artillery is no longer of any use. The answer is to have these missiles which are 100% effective against anything that flies at any speed.
Left for New York at night.

8 May

Stayed with Prince Ali Khan. He had invited Cabot Lodge for lunch—Cabot is the man responsible for swinging America in favour of aid to India. I had a long discussion with him. I think, towards the end, he was feeling somewhat doubtful of the wisdom of his recommendations.

9 May

Left for England.

13 May

Went to The Hague to see Begum Liaquat Ali Khan. She seemed relaxed but was very worried about the political situation in the country. She thought that only solution was tight rule in the country for about ten years.

14 May

Went to Brussels to join Amjad Ali. Saw the Brussels World Fair. The Russians are making tremendous strides in the technical field and will be second to none in a few years.

18 May

Reached Karachi. Saw the judgement in Gurmani's case in the newspapers. The judges' remarks about Firoz Noon's part were most distressing. This will give us another setback in the world and demoralize our people further.

21 May

Left Karachi for Pindi by Tezgam on 20th May. I was to reach Pindi 21st evening. But I got down at Jhelum and met Azam. He mentioned to me something about a rumour emanating from Abbottabad that General ——— and Brigadier ——— had been arrested. I just laughed it off as being absurd. If there was any truth in it, Chief of Staff whom I rang up from Karachi would have mentioned it to me. In Pindi I heard some more rumours. I mentioned them to my wife and she said that she had been hearing all kinds of things. That has always been the way with her. Under adversity she has always shown tremendous courage and self-control and taken care that I should not be given any cause for anxiety. I feel that without such a wise and far-sighted companion I would never have been able to achieve in life what I have done. This freedom from home worries and lack of worry of bringing up a large family is the greatest blessing that a man can have and without which a man can never reach his creative ceiling. My wife told me the gist of the rumours, which was that a number of senior officers were accused of being Indian agents. It then occurred to me to what extent people were prepared to go to malign others for selfish ends or out of sheer jealousy. I was astounded at the credulity of some of our people. They seemed to be prepared to swallow anything, even against their most devoted servants. This surely is the sign of immaturity or some kind of decay. I am an optimist by nature but these rumours really shocked and depressed me. What if we were engaged in war and things started going badly and the enemy were to spread such rumours about the army in the back areas? The result would be disastrous. We would lose a war without firing a shot. A horrible thought!

22 May

Asked General Musa about the rumours. He told me that he had made inquiries and found that these rumours were started by some of the politicians in Abbottabad.

The elections, of course, are drawing near. The politicians . . . are trying to get back into power by hook or by crook. And having got there they know that they will have nothing to show for themselves except working for the disruption of the country further. In that case they will come face to face with the army and me. Hence I am regarded by them as enemy number one, for doing my duty. Their conscience is so dead that in order to obtain some political advantage they will not stop at destroying the army . . . which is the only shield they have.

I am one of those who have served democracy as I believe that there is nothing like it if we can work the system. I refused to take over power when offered by the late Ghulam Mohammad. Then I had the hope that some amongst the politicians would show patriotism, self-lessness, and the urge to get the country moving. But they have all been tried and found wanting. I am now certain that if the country is left to them we should expect nothing but ruin. It seems that we shall have to have a system of government for a generation or so which prepares the country for democracy and solves some of our major problems. Under the present Constitution no one seems to have any power except to destroy discipline and to do harm. A politician is lucky if he can hang on to his seat, let alone do any good. Even if he wants to do any good, his supporters demanding all kind of selfish things would ensure that he does not get a chance.

Meanwhile, certain actions have been put into operation to counter these rumours.

27 May

Addressed Station Officers on my visit to the U.S.A. and on the fundamentals of the defence of Pakistan.

1 June

Attended Conference on Kashmir Affairs presided over by Prime Minister Noon. There were three other ex-Prime Ministers. They could have collected two more if they had waited a little longer.

I thought the setting was made to enable them to score political points against each other, but instead they listened to me intently and with understanding. They asked me what we should do about Kashmir and stoppage of canal waters by India. Emotionally, of course, the answer is to go for India right away, but wisdom dictated a different course which I explained.

6 June

Had a meeting with Corps Commanders and Divisional Commanders.

7 June

Our new experimental Brigade has been formed. We are very excited about the future organization of our units. A host of new ideas are coming up. The underlying idea is to develop organizations on the concept of attacking or defending a piece of ground with firepower and not with bodies. The results should be interesting. Meanwhile, I have caused studies to be conducted in the manner in which we should use motorized infantry and armour in the Armoured Division.

9 June

Defence Secretary told me that I had been given two years' extension which will be announced mid-day. How it happened and my reaction to it are contained in the signals below.

Telegram dated 9 June 1958 from Mr. Firoz Khan Noon,
Prime Minister of Pakistan, to C-in-C Pakarmy

'I am very glad that you have agreed to stay on as Commander-in-Chief of our Armies for another two years STOP You are still very young being 51 years of age though very ripe in experience and ability STOP Pakistan at this juncture cannot afford to lose your services and I am confident that the defences of this country are safe in your hands as they have been in the past. Ends'

C-in-C's reply

'Grateful for your message of appreciation and encouragement on my extension of tenure STOP Personally I would have been just as happy to retire as I would be in further serving this magnificent army the building of which has been my life long ambition STOP In any case I have eaten its salt for thirtyone years and everything in me is due to it and belongs to it STOP So you can rest assured that I shall continue to give my best to the army and through it to the country.'

13 June

Went to Peshawar by air and inspected a Support Battalion and a Mortar Battalion. While both have a formidable amount of firepower especially anti-tank, it struck me that they had far too much transport. Some 150-odd vehicles. So much transport will require anything up to 30 miles of road space. So it is necessary to go into this aspect to see where the reduction can be made.

14 June

Left for Kaghan valley for some rest. Spent the night at Shogran, a beautiful place with lovely views. Went out for a walk. Climbed about 1,200 feet. Took it easy as it was my first day on heights.

15 June

Reached Naran and stayed there for four days. Did some fishing, but spent most of the time reading *The Men Who Ruled India.*

Climbed to Saiful Maluk Lake. It took me two hours and fifteen minutes to climb 2,500 feet and four miles. It was the stiffest thing I had known, but the art is to move on slowly. However, the grandeur of the scenery was well worth the trouble.

21 June

On return from Kaghan I was told that as a result of Ghulam Abbas's threat to breach the cease-fire line with large Jathas, a serious law and order situation had arisen. The President, who is nowadays resting in Nathiagali, had been authorized to interview Ghulam Abbas and recommend course of action. I found to my utter horror that he had recommended that no action should be taken against Abbas and his people until they reached the cease-fire line. Then the army was to arrest them without any use of force! I at once rang up the President and protested against this amateurish decision and demanded that if any action is to be taken it should be taken by the civil authorities in Pakistan territory or in Azad Kashmir territory. A Cabinet meeting was held on this and my recommendations were approved. The problem in my job is that I have not only to run the army but also keep a watch on so many other things concerning the security of the country. This would not be necessary if we had men of character and principles manning the government.

24 June

Attended a meeting of the Sub-Committee of the Cabinet on the future of P.O.F.[1] Wah at Karachi.

28 June

Went to see the President at Nathiagali. Also met Nawab Qazilbash, Chief Minister of West Pakistan. Had a long discussion with him on the future of the Border Police. They are some 58,000 men in East and West Pakistan worth about three Divisions. My contention is that they should remain a civil force but officered by army officers like the Scouts so that they can be trained tactically. In that case they will give a better service to the civil [power] in time of peace and be available for use by the army in time of war. This is the obvious solution in the higher interests of the country, but Qazilbash having once agreed had gone back on his promise. So I had to be quite blunt with him and told him a few home truths. His worry is the disposal of some 50-odd police officers who will become surplus. So to resolve this problem it was agreed that a Committee consisting of Defence Secretary, Chief Secretary, and a representative of G.H.Q. should go into this matter. Incidentally I am having similar difficulty with East Pakistan Government. However, I am determined to see that they do the right thing in the end. Pakistan cannot afford to lose the use of this manpower in time of war. In fact they may well prove to be a decisive factor.

30 June

Lately I have been doing some interesting reading. Apart from *The Men Who Ruled India*, I have read Gunther's *Inside Russia Today*, and Capt. Wynnes's articles on 'Pattern for Limited (Nuclear) War'; 'The Riddle of the Schlieffen Plan' published in RUSI *Journal*. These articles have set us thinking and re-examining some of our organizational concepts and tactical doctrines.

    I have to waste a lot of time in answering greeting messages on Eid

---

[1] Pakistan Ordnance Factory.

days[1] and other occasions but I do so not to hurt people's feelings. Some of these messages are touching. They seem to have blind faith in me. This makes me feel very humble and I pray to God to give me the strength to come up to their expectations.

4 July

Attended a meeting at Government House, Lahore, in which President, Prime Minister, Chief Minister and his West Pakistan Cabinet were present. The Chief Minister called this meeting to get clarification over Abbas's move to cross cease-fire line with volunteers, the mounting irresponsibility of the political parties [in stirring] up trouble in the country to do the government down and increasing sectarian tension. I was interested in the decisions about Abbas's move as that finally affected the army. It was decided that we should deal with Abbas and his men firmly and not allow them to create turmoil in the country.

13 July

Held a Joint Chiefs meeting. Several important things came up for discussion. Admiral Chaudhry raised the question of the concept of defence of Pakistan again, over which the decision had already been given by the Defence Committee of the Cabinet and he had agreed with the rest of us during the previous meetings. Heated discussion followed. Sent a message on this to Government.

14 July

Took off from Karachi at 0415 hours with the President in his Viscount for Teheran *en route* to Istanbul where the Conference of the Heads of the Baghdad Pact Muslim States was scheduled to be held. Had a meeting with General Hidayat, Chief of the Staff of the Iranian Armed Forces, to remove certain doubts about planning problems. During this meeting General Hidayat was called out by a Staff Officer and told that news had come through from their Commander in Khanikin that a *coup d'état* had taken place in Iraq. A Colonel supported by pro-Nasser and Communist elements had taken over. Prince Abdul Ala, the King's uncle, was murdered and his body dragged in the streets of Baghdad. The Palace was gutted and so was the British Embassy. The crowds were jubilant and Nasser's photographs were visible everywhere. News about the fate of the King and Nuri-es-Said [was] conflicting, but it looked as if Nuri had escaped though his house was burnt and that the King was held as prisoner.

This was very serious and sad news. With a heavy heart we took off

[1] Holidays, especially the Muslim festivals of Eidul Fitr and Eidul Azhar.

for Istanbul. As we were approaching Istanbul we were told to go and land in Ankara. There we were received by the President and Mr Menderes. The meeting was just like a mourning. The Turks were very upset by the news from Baghdad. They confirmed more or less what we had heard in Teheran. Their Ambassador in Baghdad had a transmitter and kept them well informed. But his reports were also vague as he and his staff could not go out to check details, there being so much confusion in the city.

Had dinner with President Bayar. It was a very informal affair in which the Shah of Iran, our President, Menderes and Zorlu were present. A meeting was arranged after dinner in which the situation in Lebanon, Iraq and the future of the Baghdad Pact was discussed.

I was impressed with the Shah's grasp of the situation and analysis.

15 July

Assembled at the Presidential Palace at 1200 hours in an atmosphere of gloom because of the Iraqi situation. News came there that Nuri-es-Said was murdered and that his body was dragged about in Baghdad. This is the way they have treated a man who had done so much for them.

16 July

The Heads of the three Muslim States decided that the Baghdad Pact meetings in London should be postponed though I was of the view that these meetings of the B.P. countries [should] take place to take stock of the changed situation.

19 and 20 July

The Turks are very sensitive about certain areas but they were good enough to let me tour the Gallipoli peninsula and visit the First World War battlefields. This trip was tiring—doing 800 miles in two days on bad road—but most interesting and instructive. In places the traces of opposing trenches are still visible.

1 August [back in Pakistan]

Visited Mitha's outfit in Attock Fort and Chirrat. The training of this unit, which will be of immense value in war, is coming on well and everybody looked very enthusiastic especially the young officers. They want to stay on there for ever.

To give this unit the ability to operate in considerable depth behind the enemy I am trying to obtain a certain type of aircraft which carry six passengers and can land and take off from limited space.

7 The author's present house at Rehana

8 With his mother at Rehana, 1963

Moved to Mardan in the afternoon to meet Commanding Officers of the new Punjab Regiment who had assembled for the annual conference of the [Regimental] Centre. They appeared to me to be alert and generally getting on well with one another. The new spirit of the enlarged regiment is emerging.

5 August

Attended 12 Div exercise at Murree. I was favourably impressed with the general level of professional knowledge. Our officers are now really getting to know their stuff.

11 August

A civil officer came to see me in connection with the organization of cadet corps. He was very depressed and painted a gloomy picture of the civil administration which was deteriorating rapidly through the perfidy of party politics. He felt that a majority of the civil servants also lend themselves to such misuse.

15 August

Went to Lahore to see a demonstration of an Infantry Company holding some 4,000 yards front on the new concept. We also discussed the organization of a Battalion on the new concept.

Also saw Qazilbash in his office. He agreed to give land to the recipients of gallantry awards and also for cattle-breeding.

19 August

Visited the Recce Battalion at Shinkiari. They seemed to be coming on except that they need additional 106 recoilless rifles per Platoon.

Later saw the Commando school. I was satisfied with the progress.

20 August

Inspected P.M.A. (Pakistan Military Academy, Kakul).

23 August

Flew to Nowshera and saw a very interesting demonstration of anti-tank defence taking on a regiment of tanks in attack. There is no doubt that this rifle[1] is a formidable anti-tank weapon but it requires great skill to use it to the fullest effect.

26 August

Recorded a message about Field-Marshal Montgomery for Radio Pakistan.

[1] 106 mm. recoilless rifle.

28 August

Secretary, Ministry of Defence, attended a meeting with Chief Secretary West Pakistan along with G.H.Q. representatives and representatives of the police to discuss militarization of the Border Police and the disposal of police officers who may be rendered surplus. The policeman is naturally trying to raise all sorts of objections and obstacles. The politician too is chary of making any hard decisions which may annoy the police as he probably expects a lot from the police during the forthcoming elections. I believe the policeman is regarded as the real election-winning factor. My instructions are to patiently keep relentless pressure until the right thing is done. It may take time but the security of the country demands that this force should be militarized.

I am receiving very depressing reports about economic distress, maladministration through political interference, frustration and complete loss of faith by the people in political leadership inclusive of the President. The general belief is that none of these men have any honesty of purpose, integrity or patriotism, to root out evils of the country which will require drastic action. The general belief is emerging that even I and the army are failing to do our duty by not saving the people from these tyrants. This dangerous belief is obviously based on the ignorance of the functions of the army, but when people become desperate they are apt to seek escape through any means. I wonder if they realize that if it was not for my keeping aloof from politics they would not have had this army and if this type of army was not there they would have lost their independence by now.

3 September

Disquieting news of massive economic aid to India by America and other western countries [is] coming in. This will further release India's resources for a reckless military build-up against us thus making our position far more difficult.

6 September

Visited Karachi. Discussed problems relating to evacuee property with Rehabilitation Ministry. Also discussed the charter of the D.G. [Director-General] Defence Purchases, with Defence Secretary. I impressed on him the necessity of speeding up procurement and disposal.

13 September

Attended passing-out parade of O.T.S.

14 September
Attended rally and recruitment *mela* [fair].

15 September
Flew off to Lahore at 0530 hours. Attended 10th Punjab Centenary. Returned after lunch.

18 September
Left for northern areas. Met the Political Agent and the Resident.

20 September
Did some fishing in Gupis river.

21 September
Returned to Gilgit.

22 September
Left for Hunza.

23 September
Halt [i.e. a day spent without travelling]. Received information about political flare-up in Karachi from the Chief of Staff.

24 September
Returned to Gilgit. Lunched with Mir of Nagar. Received a detailed message from the Chief of Staff about Muslim League's activity. I told the C.O.S. that no major commitment should be made without his prior approval.

25 September
Returned to Rawalpindi at 1015 hours.

6

The Revolution

The hour had struck. The moment so long delayed had finally arrived. The responsibility could no longer be put off. It was the 4th of October 1958, and as I settled down in my railway saloon I knew that an era was coming to an end. I was going to Karachi where an agonizingly prolonged political farce was drawing to a close. A few days earlier President Iskander Mirza had conveyed to me that the whole situation was becoming intolerable and that he had decided to act.

For years we had all hoped that the political leaders of the country would wake up to their grave responsibilities. Among them were patriotic men, men of talent and ability, some close associates of the Quaid-e-Azam who had guided the struggle for Pakistan with great vision, statesmanship, and unfaltering fervour and determination. Later they had seen the cool, courageous, and tenacious manner in which Liaquat Ali Khan was trying to steer the ship of state through turbulent water. Each for a time managed to grab the central trapeze caught in the beams of giant arc-lights, but the next moment hurtled down into a dark net of intrigue and incompetence.

I arrived in Karachi on 5 October. Yahya, Hamid, and one or two other officers had preceded me. I went to see General Iskander Mirza. He was sitting on the lawn, brooding, bitter and desperate. I asked him, 'Have you made up your mind, sir?' 'Yes', he replied. 'Do you think it is absolutely necessary?' 'It is absolutely necessary', he said firmly. My reaction was that it was very unfortunate that such a desperate stage had been reached, necessitating drastic action. And it was not pleasant to get involved in it, but there was no escape. It was the last bid to save the country.

A few days before this, three Ministers and four Ministers of State were sworn into the Central Cabinet, bringing the total to twenty-six, to bolster the tottering Republican–Awami League coalition government under Malik Firoz Khan Noon. There followed an unseemly wrangle over portfolios. On 7 October at 1.00 p.m. the portfolios were redistributed. Promptly the Awami League resigned from the government. A fresh allocation of portfolios was announced at 7.00 p.m., but by then the central authority had collapsed. The curtain was rung down at 8.00 p.m. when, in a dramatic sweep, Iskander Mirza abrogated the Constitution, proclaimed Martial Law throughout Pakistan, dismissed the central and provincial governments, the National Assembly and the Provincial Assemblies, and appointed me Chief Martial Law Administrator.

From that time onwards emotions had no place in the proceedings. Now that this job had to be done it must be done properly. A simple plan was formulated and put into operation. I advised General Iskander Mirza: 'You had better inform your Prime Minister about the situation.' He thought it was unnecessary, as he had no doubt about the legality of his action. I said: 'I want two things from you in writing: one, that I will administer Martial Law; and the other, a letter to the Prime Minister that you have taken this decision, that the government has been dissolved, that you have abrogated the Constitution and declared Martial Law, and that you have appointed me to administer the Martial Law.' He wrote the letter to Malik Firoz Khan Noon without any difficulty. But he did not seem particularly keen to give me the letter of authority to administer the Martial Law. I wanted him to write the letter to the Prime Minister so that he should assume full responsibility for his decision. He, as the constitutional head of government, had come to the conclusion that the country could not be run any more on a constitutional basis. I said, 'At least you have done something and I believe you have done the right thing. But I feel that I must have it from you in writing.' He hummed and hawed but finally agreed to give me the letter after two or three days.

Revolutions take long and painstaking preparation, detailed planning, clandestine meetings, and country-wide movement of troops. In our case there was very little preparation. It was handled as a military operation. What happened was that a Brigade was moved. Actually, two Brigades—an Infantry and an Artillery Brigade—are normally stationed in Karachi. We therefore had enough troops to deal with any situation that might arise on the promulgation of Martial Law. But, as a matter of precaution, we moved an extra Brigade from Quetta to Jungshahi outside Karachi. That was all the military preparation we made. The army always has something in hand for the unforeseen. In an operation like this you cannot accept failure. Had Martial Law been challenged, anywhere, even for a moment, a most dangerous situation would have arisen. Hence the precaution of moving a Brigade to Jungshahi. On the night of the Revolution we informed the Commanders-in-Chief and all local Commanders of what had happened and required them to ensure that law and order was maintained. That was all. We then proceeded to set up the normal hierarchy of Martial Law Administrators and their duties were defined. The relationship between the civil authorities and the army evolved gradually.

We had made sure that the operation would succeed: the question now was the extent to which one could go. My own feeling was that if there was any resistance it would be nominal and we should be able to deal with it very quickly. I did not think that there would be any occasion for the use of force at all. The people were completely fed up with the state of affairs and desperately wanted a change. And they had great respect for the army.

For a time there was talk of reviving a regulation which was operative during the first Martial Law period in Lahore in 1953 which provided for action against those responsible for the collapse of law and order. We considered this as the first regulation when revolution came, and it would have given us powers to deal with politicians who had brought the country to the brink of an abyss. But I said, 'No, we ought not to do that.' I was anxious that the people should settle down very quickly, and get on with the reconstruction of the country and the rehabilitation of society. I wanted to lower the temperature as fast as possible. When Martial Law came it was like pressing a button. Things started moving, and that was because our people were basically sound and we had a good civil service. That was also the reason why I did not operate Martial Law as a means of punishing people for their past misdeeds. Had we embarked on that, the whole effort would have assumed a negative complexion.

What the country needed was a positive effort to move forward, to build itself and the economy into a dynamic and progressive force. There could be little sense in wasting our limited manpower in creating an atmosphere of repression and intimidation instead of utilizing our resources for constructive work. It was also clear to me that for Martial Law to be of any use at all, it was necessary to reinstate and bring into operation the normal organs of the State.

The first thing I did on the morning after the declaration of Martial Law was to call a meeting of all the Secretaries to the central government. I explained to them what had happened and what they were required to do: I also gave them a general outline of policy. I noticed that one or two of them looked rather sulky, and I went for them; they all settled down after that fairly quickly. We started off with a Council of Secretaries and for a couple of months it continued to function.

As I have said, on the day of the take-over, certain troops were to move to some key positions in case there was any trouble. One or two units received very contradictory orders on the telephone; these orders were supposed to have been given to a Brigade Commander by the Defence Secretary. From that moment, men in the army began to get rather suspicious; they even started suspecting one another, for no one knew who might be trying to plant the seed of suspicion.

I think they came to the conclusion that Iskander Mirza had already got cold feet. We received information that his wife was quarrelling with him all the time: she kept telling him that he had made a great mistake but, now that it was done, he should finish off Ayub Khan. Iskander Mirza, through the Intelligence Bureau and others, tried to find out the disposition of troops at certain key points. He also tried to discover the army Order of Battle around Karachi.

One of my first acts was naturally to go to East Pakistan where the bulk of our people live, but Iskander Mirza appeared to be unhappy. He warned me, 'Be very careful because there are a lot of people after your blood.' I said, 'I am used to that.'

There was a big public meeting in Dacca which I addressed. I think after that Iskander Mirza became rather apprehensive. But I had told him myself beforehand, 'Look, circumstances have changed. A revolution has taken place. You have ushered it in and you have made me responsible for running the country. It is not just an ordinary routine revolution; there is going to be a real, basic change in this country. This is my policy. Now do not get frightened. It is my responsibility. I have to carry the load, but I am determined to carry out certain basic reforms, and please try not to get involved in any intrigue or anything like that. You've no reason to, since I am determined to uphold your authority and give you the fullest loyalty.' He said, 'Then it is all right', and I replied, 'Good'. But we kept on getting information that his wife was all the time nagging him, urging him to act quickly against me.

When I returned from East Pakistan and landed at Mauripur airport, Major-General Sher Bahadur came to me and said: 'Sir, in your absence, Air Commodore Rabb of the Pakistan Air Force was rung up by the President, General Iskander Mirza, and asked: "Are you loyal to this country?" Rabb said: "Yes, I am loyal." "Are you loyal to me as the President?" He said: "Yes, I am loyal." "Will you take orders from me even at the risk of your life?" To which Rabb replied, "Sir, let me know what the orders are." Iskander Mirza said, "I want you to go and arrest three army Generals. They are General Yahya, General Sher Bahadur, and General Hamid." Air Commodore Rabb hesitated and played for time. He suggested "Sir, may I come over? Would you put it in writing?" '

I told General Sher Bahadur: 'Do not take it seriously.' I did not want the thing to boil up. At the same time, I knew that Iskander Mirza was capable of doing such a stupid thing. It was stupid because it would at once have led to trouble between the Services, and God knows what would have happened. What Iskander Mirza did not realize was that if he had moved against the army and its leadership, the first thing the army would have done would have been to finish him. So I went to him and said, 'Look, what are you up to? I hear you have been ordering arrests of army officers.' He tried to reassure me: 'You have been misinformed. There is no truth in it.' I warned him, 'No monkeying and no tricks. Be very careful. You are playing with fire and in any case there is no need for it. We are all prepared to give you our highest loyalty. Why then are you indulging in this mischief?'

Meanwhile, the army's legal experts came up with the opinion that since the Constitution had been abrogated and Martial Law declared, and a Chief Martial Law Administrator appointed, the office of President was redundant. That, according to their light, was the legal position. I said, 'Now, don't you chaps start creating more problems for me. Why do you bother me? It will serve no useful purpose.'

Chief Justice Munir was there, I think, when this point came up for discussion. He had been advising Iskander Mirza about certain matters before the revolution. I called him and thought that I would see Iskander Mirza too. I asked Colonel Qazi to state his point of view. His position was that the President no longer had any place in the new arrangement. Munir disagreed. I told Qazi, 'I agree with Munir. This is final. Accept this as a decision.' I then asked him to leave. I had hoped that Iskander Mirza would settle down to the new situation. We had been good friends. I told myself that unless he did anything overtly wrong, it would be disloyal on my part to act against him. A few days later my military commanders came to me and said: 'This man is no longer bearable.' I said, 'Why do you say that?' Then they cited instances of his ringing up various people to involve them in some deal.

In the meantime the feeling was growing among the people that so long as Iskander Mirza remained on the scene, intrigues would continue and nothing worth while or constructive would be done. My associates said: 'Your difficulty seems to be that you don't want to go and tell a friend that he is being thoroughly disloyal. But this is something bigger than your personal friendship and we sincerely advise you, we beg of you, to understand that we cannot carry him with us any longer.' I said, 'All right, give me a couple of days to think it over.' I hoped that he would settle down and my own associates would settle down too. But the clamour became louder from headquarters and from the army officers. They all said, 'Whatever you may be doing, this man is going to nullify it all.' They feared that the people would have no faith in our policies and there would be no peace in the country. All efforts at improvement would come to naught. I said finally, 'If you feel like that, I shall go and tell him so.' They said, 'No. You should not go. We will tell him on your behalf.'

Three Generals went to him—General Burki, General Azam, and General Khalid Shaikh—and conveyed to Mirza from me that I was very sorry but he had not been very wise in the way he had been going about things. He was told it was also quite clear that the people did not like him, and that they were not prepared to put up with him. Now what was to be done? The interests of Pakistan were involved, and he must rise to the occasion. It seems that he realized the gravity of the situation and agreed to surrender power.

Major-General Cawthorn, Australian High Commissioner and an old friend of Iskander Mirza, asked where Iskander Mirza was going. I told him that he wanted to go to England. The question was to find him accommodation and a suitable aircraft. For four or five days we could not find one and we were afraid that if he remained in Karachi, the people might flare up and the situation deteriorate. So we asked him to go to Quetta. He agreed and we flew him there. Cawthorn said, 'I would like to go and see him.' I said, 'You can go and see him. You can go with him if you like. He is not a prisoner or anything like that.' I think he went to the Karachi airport and met him. When Iskander Mirza finally left for England he had to wait for a few hours at Mauripur airport. Most of his friends met him and bade him farewell.

I was most unhappy making this decision. I was unhappy for him too. How unfortunate that he could not be loyal to anybody! There are some who believe that my faith in Iskander Mirza was misplaced and people often wonder why I did not realize that he was not the man who could have served the objectives of the revolution. But during the period when he was Secretary to the Ministry of Defence one could get decisions from him and, where his personal interest was not involved, he was quick and efficient. It was not entirely unjustified to hope that, with our support, he would be able to operate as an effective head of government. After all, he had more experience than any other politician one could think of. All the politicians had been tried and found wanting; there was no one else left on the civil side.

So I continued to have faith in Iskander Mirza even when everyone else appeared to have lost it. But that is part of my make-up: I can face very hard things in life, but I dislike being rude or discourteous. I only act when my patience is exhausted, which is why my actions in such matters are at times delayed. Of one thing I am certain now. Even if Iskander Mirza had wanted to play straight he would not have had the courage to stand up and face the consequences of the reforms which were being introduced. I do not think his remaining in office would have done any good. He could not have identified himself with the change.

During the Martial Law period I once told the Pressmen: 'I am a man in a hurry. There are so many things to do and there is so little time in which to do them.' My aim was that instead of my doing everything, equipped with absolute powers, people should do things for themselves. The quicker they learnt to act on their own the better. The sooner we made them face up to their problems the better it would be for the country. That was why I wanted Martial Law to end quickly and the Constitution to come in. There was a crying need for certain major reforms. Martial Law was just a base from which to carry out those reforms. True, if anyone had resisted them, severe action would have followed; but luckily there was no need for such action.

Take the example of how readily people declared their untaxed hidden wealth: they declared Rs. 1,700 million. I asked a businessman: 'Why did you do it?' He said, 'In one of your photographs, I saw you with your finger pointed like this, and your mouth screwed up like this. I said to myself: "This man will not leave us alone. He will go for us if we don't respond." So we all sat together and decided to play the game. In any case we were paying 33 per cent income tax, as against 75 per cent, so we thought we were getting away rather lightly. Why not take advantage of it?' He added: 'Although you never lifted your little finger, that photograph did the trick.'

7

Martial Law

I

The revolution had immediate as well as long-term objectives.

The immediate objective was to rehabilitate the civil and constitutional organs of the State. They had become ineffective and oppressive through misuse and exploitation and needed the protection of Martial Law to recover their original sense of purpose so as to be able to operate within a constitutional framework. During this phase the army was positioned in certain key places whence it could be moved into action. People were a little surprised that the army was not visible during the early days of the revolution. The very word 'revolution' implies a replacement of existing civil authority by military, or at least a 'special' authority. Now this replacement had in fact taken place but I was anxious not to make a demonstration of it. It was vital that the army be kept in the background because that was where it belonged in the normal life of the country. Had it too got directly involved in the civil administration, the effect would have been a further demoralization and disintegration of the civil authority. It would have also made the withdrawal of the army from civilian life to their normal sphere of work more difficult. I did not have any doubt that the army would be destroyed if it got too mixed up in running the civil administration or too involved with the economic, social, and political affairs of the country.

Among the long-term objectives of the revolution was the introduction of major reforms designed to remove the confusion and imbalance in the social and economic life of the country. These reforms were to culminate in the introduction of a proper Constitution and restoration of constitutional life. There was a suggestion made to me at one time that along with the reforms I should introduce an interim Constitution, a rough working arrangement, before the final Constitution was adopted. Now, this I regarded as dangerous. The Martial Law represented the working Constitution and before Martial Law was lifted the country should have a permanent constitutional framework.

I said to myself: 'When the Constitution comes, it must be the final thing.'

It did not take me more than six months to achieve the immediate and short-term objectives. The basic structure of the civil administration was sound: all that it needed was a sense of confidence and freedom to operate without having to worry about extraneous considerations. The civil institutions responded to the situation admirably and started functioning efficiently and independently within a very short time. But there was a feeling in the army that things were not moving fast enough; that civilians were not reacting as quickly as they should and that people were beginning to feel frustrated.

I told them, 'Look, you are used to running a system on which the country spends its last rupee. You are given all possible equipment and weapons so that when the time comes you do your job a hundred per cent well because on that would depend the survival of the country. With all the facilities, training, and equipment, look at the amount of criticism that takes place at the end of every exercise. One has to be patient in these things. Your life is a regulated life. A civilian officer, once he gets the command, will do a good job, but he has to work within the limitations of the law and in the full gaze of public opinion. A person may have suffered wrongfully and even if a civilian officer wanted to act immediately to remove the cause of his suffering he would come up against the law of the land. He must act in full consciousness of the requirements and limitations of the law. And the civil administration is running at seventy per cent of its normal strength: one cannot put too much pressure on it. Also some people are not above false complaints or wanting more than their due.'

All this would silence the army officers, but they were not really convinced. What they did not understand was that civil action was subject to the limitations of the law and had to take into account currents and cross-currents of public opinion. I would tell them of the results of two quick actions which were taken by us during the first days of the revolution. We produced two Martial Law regulations: one made the adulteration of foodstuffs a criminal offence, and the other made black-marketing subject to heavy punishment. The result was that sweet-meats started selling at Rs. 1·50 a seer and adulteration of foodstuffs was completely checked. But within a fortnight all the stocks were exhausted and business came to a standstill. There was great initial enthusiasm for price controls, too, and everybody started buying crockery, cutlery, and watches at very reasonable prices. But once the stocks were sold there was nothing to replace them. The businessman had no incentive to re-invest.

I remember on one occasion we had a meeting of senior army officers and they submitted to me a paper which explained how everything was going wrong in the country. The Commander-in-Chief, General Musa, was also there at the meeting. I asked him: 'Does this paper represent your views too?' He answered, 'Yes, all of us feel like that.' I said, 'You know, this paper was given to me this morning when I was having a cup of tea. I read it and it gave me the feeling that Pakistan must be coming to an end. Then I took up the morning paper in which some Italian had predicted that tomorrow would be Doomsday. I do not know about Doomsday, but so far as Pakistan is concerned it is there and it will stay and no one will be able to thwart its progress.'

That was a little hard on them but I wanted to show the army officers that they should not expect miracles. They were deeply impressed by the initial enthusiasm of the people for the change and were getting disturbed when the enthusiasm began to ebb. People always want immediate results. When Pakistan was established they thought that they would have no more problems in life. Similarly, when the revolution came they hoped that everything would change overnight. Now, the revolution was a logical culmination of events in the country; it did not mean the end of all problems; it only meant a fresh opportunity to deal with the problems in an earnest, realistic manner. This opportunity had to be utilized by the people. What was required was hard work, dedication, and patience. And patience is not an easy virtue to acquire; nor, for that matter, is the habit of working hard cultivated without effort.

I was not looking for dramatic results. The enthusiasm of the people could have been easily maintained at a high pitch by adopting sensational and extreme measures. I think there was some expectation that the revolutionary régime would provide dramatic openings and sequences. Had I succumbed to the temptation of pandering to public taste I should have diverted national energy into negative channels. So I was quite prepared to face a certain amount of dissatisfaction among the people and a measure of pessimism within the army itself. I was determined to go about my work in a moderate and rational manner, not for a moment forgetting the real and long-term objectives of the revolution.

This consciousness of public reaction also set a limit on my timetable for the introduction of the reforms. I felt that I must launch my full programme within a period of about two years and by then the stage should be set for the introduction of the Constitution. My first anxiety was to introduce land reforms and to settle the refugee problem. Then there were reforms to be brought about in the administration and in the sphere of education. The legal system of the country needed revision and there was need to regulate the *auqafs* (trusts). The whole pattern of social and political life in the country had to be reorganized on democratic principles so as to ensure the participation of the people in the affairs of the country in a constructive and meaningful way.

I knew that the objectives of the revolution could not be achieved through force. Of course, we do need disciplinary arrangements to deal with those who cross the line, but people must have freedom to think and act independently and sensibly. You cannot change social attitudes by stringent measures: stringency begets resistance and every now and then you are forced to tighten the screw. The result is an extreme form of oppression and constant application of force to which there is no limit. Social attitudes can be changed and given a positive direction only through persuasion and education. We were able to set certain standards during the early months of Martial Law and show how affairs should be run, but people had to learn to do things themselves.

I was told at that time that I was dealing with the politicians, who had been responsible for the ills of the country, in too moderate a fashion. Merely keeping them out of politics for a certain number of years was not the answer; the moment they got an opportunity they would hit back. Now I was not dealing with individuals. It would have been possible to liquidate a certain number of people in the customary fashion, but that would not have meant the end of those inherent weaknesses or the social and political conditions of which individual politicians were only a manifestation. So long as those conditions continued, the place vacated by the politicians would be occupied by others who would behave in the same way.

Harsh and violent methods of dealing with individuals only establish harsh and violent precedents and lead to an unending political vendetta. My target was problems and not individuals. Whenever terrorism, particularly political terrorism, starts in a country you can never eradicate it from the bones of the people. It stays there. Once this phenomenon appears, it rubs off the thin veneer of civilization and provides an outlet for man's most primitive and animal instincts. Political victimization leaves a lasting scar.

The revolution could easily have turned into a blind alley where there would be no going forward and no return. My ambition was not to prove to the world how well I could run the show: my anxiety was to establish conditions and set up institutions to prove how well the country could run itself. The vital thing was to help people to identify themselves with the objectives of the revolution so that things should move on their own momentum. People must recognize the advantages of the revolution and acquire a sense of participation in their own affairs.

II

Soon after the promulgation of Martial Law, I defined the relationship between the civil and Martial Law authorities to prevent misunderstanding and parallel actions which might create confusion and frustration. I made it clear that the running of the civil administration was the responsibility of the provincial governors. It was for them to see that their officers discharged their duties in a sympathetic, efficient, honest, and expeditious manner. The basic administrative structure remained the same. I selected a Cabinet, and through the Martial Law Regulations and the normal administrative processes of the two provinces, we put our programme into action.

The primary role of Martial Law was to give support to the civil authority so that it should be able to rehabilitate itself and cope with the new problems which would arise with the introduction of reforms. This support should take the form of producing Martial Law Regulations to fill any deficiencies in the normal law, and of providing assistance in carrying out the inspection of administration and by patrolling trouble spots. Special and summary courts should also be set up where required. As a general rule cases against Martial Law and cases involving anti-State and anti-social activities should be tried by military courts. There should be frequent meetings between the governors and the Martial Law Administrators to exchange views and seek guidance and assistance. Military officers were told that the best help they could give was to appreciate the conditions under which the civilians had to work; to recognize the limitations of economic and other factors and respect the attitudes and opinions of the public.

The first years of the revolution were, in many ways, the most rewarding years. The régime enjoyed widespread public support throughout the country and was sustained and inspired by popular enthusiasm. Every measure we took evoked immediate response. I took full advantage of the situation and introduced my full programme of reforms without losing time.

We used to meet frequently in the Cabinet in those days. I remember our first meeting on Monday 27 October 1958. It was midday when the meeting started. I gave my colleagues an assessment of the situation prevailing in the country prior to 7 October 1958. I then outlined the problems that we were facing. The first requirement was to bring about stability in the economic life of the country. In the past, economic matters had been dealt with more on the basis of political or parochial considerations than on economic and financial considerations.

The second problem was food shortage. We had enough land and manpower to become self-sufficient in food: what was needed was leadership and direction. A Land Reforms Commission had been set up and we ought to be able to evolve a more equitable system of land tenure. The educational system of the country also required attention. Our aim should be to provide a system designed to meet the needs of the people and to produce better and more useful citizens. It would be necessary to give it a more practical bias and set up some mode of selection whereby students might qualify for higher studies.

The resettlement of displaced persons, refugees from the time of Partition, had been delayed too long. It was essential to solve this problem quickly in the interests of the displaced persons as well as the economy of the country.

I thought that the civil services were overstaffed and underpaid. A complete reorganization of the federal and provincial services was necessary. A Pay and Services Commission and a Reorganization Commission should go into these questions. We should take steps to weed out inefficient government servants. This might require some drastic measures, but we would have to adopt them in the interests of sound administration.

I then explained to the Cabinet the nature of Martial Law: it was not an instrument of tyranny or punishment; it was an arrangement under which government had acquired certain unusual powers to implement a programme of basic reforms. What the country needed was sound administration, a stable economy, and a reasonable standard of living. The new régime was determined to achieve these objectives. Normal trade and business must be re-established. There was a sense of fear in business circles and it was important to restore business confidence.

I was informed in this meeting that a number of businessmen had surrendered smuggled goods within the time-limit of our amnesty. It was decided that those who had acted within the time-limit should not be punished and goods surrendered by them should be returned after charging customs duty. In certain areas Martial Law authorities had asked people to pay their income-tax arrears within fifteen days. I was told that some people might have to sell their business premises in order to comply with these orders. That I thought would be harsh, and the time-limit was extended to three months.

We examined the question of the repatriation of unauthorized foreign exchange holdings abroad by Pakistani nationals. I wanted a system

9 With Quaid-e-Azam Mohammad Ali Jinnah, as G.O.C. East
Pakistan in Dacca, 20 March 1948

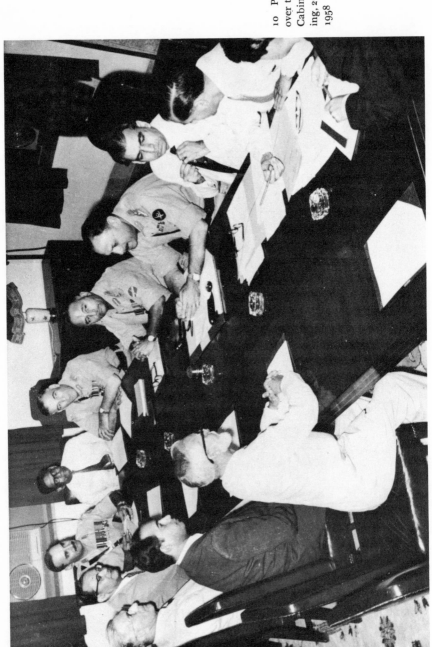

10 Presiding over the first Cabinet meeting, 27 October 1958

to be worked out under which we could get these holdings. Screening committees in the various ministries and in the provincial governments were to look into cases of inefficient and corrupt officials. I wanted machinery set up to reward good and efficient civil servants. I advised my Cabinet colleagues not to make tall promises to the public in order to win cheap popularity: people should be told that we were facing a difficult period and that they should not expect miracles. Miracles could happen only if everybody worked hard and did his utmost in the service of the country.

Too much publicity was being given to the arrests made by Martial Law authorities and was creating a scare in the country. Our effort should be to restore normal conditions and not to create an impression that we were going to deal with every little lapse in a harsh manner. We should devise some machinery to review the cases of all persons who had been arrested under the preventive provisions of the law after the imposition of Martial Law.

Our preoccupations at that time can be shown by extracts from the memoranda I kept of some of the discussions at Cabinet meetings.

1 November

I emphasized the need for exercising greater control in financial matters. The investment policy of the Pakistan Industrial Development Corporation was discussed. It was decided that P.I.D.C. should not enter into any future commitments for capital expenditure without obtaining prior approval from government. In line with my ideas contained in the 1954 document, I was working on the future pattern of autonomous organizations. The normal working of government departments is severely restrictive; there is too much red tape. The needs of agricultural and industrial development called for the setting up of special institutions with sufficient authority and autonomy to regulate their own working. These autonomous institutions should be assigned specific tasks and given the resources to accomplish them, and there should be as little interference in their working as possible. That would be the only way to maintain the momentum of development. These institutions should be functioning before the Constitution was introduced; that would ensure that development activities would go on unhindered by politics.

6 November

I mentioned in the Cabinet that we should take up the construction of the Quaid-e-Azam's mausoleum. I asked Miss Fatima Jinnah to associate herself with the committee set up for the purpose.

The previous governments had been lax in giving people permission to start daily and weekly newspapers. In certain cases permission had been granted to those who did not have adequate funds to run the paper, with the result that they were earning their livelihood by resorting to blackmail. It was important that we build a healthy and responsible Press.

There was need for civil and military officers to get to know each other. Young civilians after training in their respective academies could be profitably attached to the army for a period of two to three months. This would give them a chance to acquaint themselves with its working and benefit from army discipline.

4 December

I mentioned in the Cabinet that we should clarify our future policy with regard to the problem of Jammu and Kashmir. We should also consider what further steps must be taken to bring about a just and honourable settlement of this dispute. Once it was resolved according to the wishes of the people we would have peace in this region.

People should be prepared for land reforms. There was no reason for unnecessary fear because the reforms would be scientific and realistic and government would act justly towards all concerned.

I mentioned in the meeting that I was working on my broadcast to the nation on the Quaid-e-Azam's birthday on 25 December. I wanted to use this occasion to remind the people of their responsibilities. We were making a fresh start in life. It should be clear to everyone that the régime had not come to power for personal gain. Its achievements would depend on the amount of hard work which was put in, individually and collectively. As individuals we should undertake an exercise in self-analysis and purification and collectively we should observe the principle of avoiding all that might harm the interests of the country. We should defend our country not only in physical terms but also by combating anti-Pakistan ideas.

I would also give the people some idea of the future Constitution. The new régime was anxious to introduce a fully representative form of government based on a democratic system capable of being understood and worked by our people. We must avoid political instability. As soon as the major problems were solved and basic reforms introduced, the best constitutional brains of the country would be asked to frame a Constitution. In doing so, the wishes and desires of the people would be fully respected consistent with the interests of the country.

We should immediately prepare a paper spelling out our foreign policy and objectives. Our relations with other countries would be determined by our requirements of national defence and development and must reflect the geo-political compulsions of our location. We would hold fast to those who were our friends but would continue to seek new friends, particularly among our neighbours.

24 December

I asked for an objective study of the future shape of the Baghdad Pact.

31 December

I mentioned in the Cabinet that the introduction of Roman script for all the languages of Pakistan would help increase literacy and could result also in the creation of a common language. I wanted my colleagues to consider this problem dispassionately.

There were a number of *waqfs* (religious endowments). These could be administered by the government and their income utilized for the welfare of the people. Similarly income from *zakat* (money reserved for the poor) could also be centralized under the government.

I wanted the commission which had been set up for siting the Federal Capital to complete its work quickly. The capital must be moved out of Karachi; the place was humid and unhealthy. Also, it was dominated by business which had a corrupting influence on the services.

10 January 1959

There were persistent complaints of neglect from certain areas. The reason was that provincial administration had not been separated from local administration. We must have further decentralization of authority and administrative powers.

Administrative and political reforms must be woven into the future pattern of our Constitution. We should start giving thought to the matter. We must first decide whether the country could be best governed under a Parliamentary system or a Presidential system. What kind of legislature should the country have and what should be its size? While the principle of universal adult franchise was accepted, we should evolve a system in which people would be able to exercise their right of vote with understanding and judgement.

And so the days rolled by. The civil organs of the administration were revived. The army went back to barracks. One by one the reforms were launched and we came to grips with the basic political problems of the country.

8

The Basic Measures 1958–1960

I

In the 1954 document[1] I had said: 'Nothing much will be gained unless we carry out land reforms in a scientific fashion. Possession of vast areas of land by a few is no longer defensible nor is acquisition of land without compensation.' So when Martial Law was proclaimed in October 1958 I had the priorities worked out in my mind and I knew how I should proceed when introducing the various reforms. I had told Iskander Mirza that now that the Revolution had come there were going to be some basic changes and that no one would be allowed to obstruct the logical course of the Revolution.

On 17 October 1958 I issued a statement in which I said: 'There seems to be a fear in the minds of people that if Martial Law is lifted soon the old order will return with its attendant wickedness and evils, and all the good that has been done will be lost. Let me assure everyone that, while Martial Law will not be retained a minute longer than is necessary, it will not be lifted a minute before the purpose for which it has been imposed is fulfilled. That purpose is the clearing-up of the political, social, economic, and administrative mess that has been created in the past. The country has to be brought back to convalescence, if not complete health. In addition, certain major reforms have to be introduced. All these things will need the cover of Martial Law.'

I made out a list of reforms and asked my colleagues which one, according to them, would be the hardest to implement. The unanimous view was land reforms. 'Well, then, let us have the land reforms first!' I decided. A Land Reforms Commission was set up on 31 October 1958. Seven to eight thousand powerful families were involved and, knowing how attached our people were to land, I had no illusions about the extent of the resistance I should have to face. I knew that if I could get this through, other reforms would have comparatively smooth passages.

The situation in West Pakistan at the time was that more than

[1] See Chapter 11, pp. 186 ff.

50 per cent of the available land in the Punjab, a little less than 50 per cent in the North-West Frontier, and over 80 per cent in Sind was in the possession of a few thousand absentee landowners. The information available for the whole province showed that o·1 per cent of owners held between them 15 per cent of the land in properties of over 500 acres each. At the other end of the scale were 65 per cent of the owners together holding just as much land in holdings of less than five acres each. Out of a total geographic area of 198,600,000 acres, the area reported as usable was only about 62,000,000 acres, the 'unreported' areas comprising desert land and the 'special areas'. It was estimated that 'unreported' areas included about 23,000,000 acres of cultivable land which would bring the total cultivable area in West Pakistan to 85,000,000 acres. Little progress had been made in agricultural development through the kind of legislation enacted by the former provinces of the Punjab, the North-West Frontier, and Sind.

Now, the laws and institutions which govern the ownership and use of land have a direct effect on production and determine the social attitudes of those engaged in agriculture. There is thus a direct link between land reforms and economic and social development. The low agricultural production and the general apathy of the rural mass of the population arose principally from institutional defects in our agrarian structure and maladjustments in the terms on which land was being used for agricultural purposes.

Ever since Independence, politicians had been tinkering with the problem but nothing effective had been done. The main purpose of the so-called reforms introduced in West Pakistan before the Revolution was to preserve the privileges of the *zamindars* and not to secure the rights of the tenants. The landlords subverted all attempts at a more rational distribution of land through the influence they exercised over the political parties. Even the very mild land reforms enacted in the Punjab in 1952 were annulled by Malik Firoz Khan Noon, the Republican Chief Minister, in 1953. Apart from its social and economic consequences, such concentration of power naturally hampered the free exercise of political institutions. Democracy could never have a chance so long as the big landlords enjoyed protected constituencies immune to any pressure of public opinion.

The extravagant promises which the politicians used to make only raised false hopes and unfounded fears. This had the effect of further embittering landlord–tenant relations and creating uncertainties regarding future rights and obligations on both sides. All this contributed to stagnation in agricultural production.

I told Akhtar Hussain, Governor of West Pakistan, who was to be

Chairman of the Land Reforms Commission, that I was not thinking of land reforms as a punitive measure. The object I had in mind was to remove social imbalance. I wanted a rational land-tenure policy which would satisfy, on the one hand, the need for greater equality of opportunities and social status and, on the other hand, the economic need for increasing agricultural production and improving the standard of living through a more equitable distribution of income from land.

Land reforms represented a vital link in the chain of measures that I proposed. We could not have a democratic system if a vast majority of people in the countryside were living the life of serfs. Voting, in such a situation, had no meaning as whole constituencies were controlled and dominated by a few landlords. Experience had shown that even under the so-called direct elections the trend of voting was dictated by four or five people in each area. The power of landlords could be curtailed, by breaking up large estates and fixing a ceiling on the maximum area each person could own. But it was also important that the class which would emerge as a result of the redistribution of land should have sufficient interest to invest in land and to treat it as a whole-time occupation. In this way we would also help in the building up of a strong middle class.

I tried to ascertain the income which would enable a family to live reasonably well on the land by working hard. I wanted to fix the maximum land holding at a level which would provide adequate income to a family to work whole-time on land and to invest in its modernization and development. I knew from experience that in a large number of families the widows and unmarried women were forced to give away their shares to the male members of the family. If the landholding of a male member was reduced too drastically he would just drive the women out. That meant that some provision would be necessary to allow landlords to bequeath land, subject to a maximum limit, to dependents and widows. We adopted a ceiling of 18,000 units for this purpose, a unit being based on the productivity of the land and thus varying from area to area. This measure, too, contributed towards a wider distribution of land. These were the ideas according to which the ceilings of the land-holding were fixed. We also bore in mind the fact that the unit of holding should be large enough to enable mechanized agriculture to be introduced and better fertilizers and seeds to be used.

The requirements of social justice and the interests of economic development are not always identical. It was thus a difficult task that I had set for the Commission. I had also required it to submit its recommendations with all possible speed. Despite the complexity of the task, it was able to produce a comprehensive report within three months.

The main findings of the Commission were that in relation to the size of the rural population, land offered limited economic opportunity. The ownership of land in many areas was also inequitably distributed. Employment opportunities outside agriculture being relatively few, there was growing congestion on the land. The pressure of population and the laws of inheritance were creating uneconomic and highly fragmented holdings. Despite the availability of the necessary man-power, the development of large estates was often very slow and a considerable portion of the cultivable land was not being utilized to full capacity. Tenants suffered from a general sense of insecurity. They were denied rewards commensurate with their efforts. Initiative and enterprise were utterly lacking and there was no productive investment in agriculture.

To remedy these defects the Commission recommended certain specific measures as the minimum programme of land reform and the government, after a careful consideration of the recommendations, announced its decisions on 24 January 1959.

The following, in outline, were some of the major decisions: no person was to own more than 500 acres of irrigated or 1,000 acres of unirrigated land, with minor exceptions relating to existing land-owners, and the land thus released would be distributed to tenants and other deserving claimants; landlords would be paid compensation for resumed land in the form of heritable and transferable 4 per cent bonds, redeemable in twenty-five years, on a fixed scale according to the number of units owned; existing tenants on such land would be given the opportunity to buy it on instalments spread over twenty-five years, and special consideration would be given to tenants in congested areas. All tenants would have security of tenure: compensation would be paid for legal ejectment and an embargo placed on rent increases and illegal exactions in the shape of fees, free labour or services. The division of holdings below an economic level would be forbidden and provision made for the compulsory consolidation of already fragmented holdings.

The most important of these measures was the imposition of a low ceiling on individual ownership. This served to break the concentration of landed wealth in the hands of some 6,000 landlords throughout West Pakistan. It reduced the area of inequality and encouraged more intensive use of land and productive investment in agriculture by the actual tiller of the soil.

These reforms helped substantially in eliminating social and economic injustice and contributed to the establishment of a progressive agricultural economy. Apart from the dictates of social justice to which we subscribed, I considered the introduction of these reforms an absolute necessity for the survival of the system and values that we cherished and that brought Pakistan into being as a free State.

My approach to the problem was not emotional. My idea was that even after the reforms, farming as a profession should remain sufficiently respectable and profitable to attract and engage suitable talent on a whole-time basis. It should provide a standard of living which would compare favourably with that obtaining in other professions. My anxiety was not to destroy the existing system but to improve upon it so that it should provide opportunities for enterprise and produce leadership capable of influencing rural life. The landlords were guaranteed a fair and equitable deal and, with the compensation they received, they were able to adjust themselves, without undue hardship, to the changed situation.

For the peasants it was a Magna Carta of rights. We had done all that could possibly be done for them in the prevailing circumstances. For the first time, their role as a crucial factor in production in West Pakistan had been fully recognized. From now on they would have adequate security and all the incentives necessary for good husbandry and increased agricultural production.

I have done a lot of bird-shooting in Sind. At one time you could get many birds because the area used to provide ample cover; you would find bushes in the middle of fields. The farmer just went round them, never bothering to pull them out. Today, because the farmer has a stake in the land, you do not see a single bush in any field; every inch of land is being brought under the plough.

The disappearance of the class of absentee landlords, who exercised great political influence under the previous land-holding system, marked the beginning of a new era in West Pakistan. A strong new middle class would surely emerge which would be able to make its influence felt in future elections as well as in other aspects of community life. The disintegration of large land-holdings would tend to consolidate the smaller holdings of the new middle class and this would be an incentive to better farming and higher production.

But the most revolutionary effect of the reforms has been in terms of political and social leadership. Since the bulk of our population is settled on the land, it is these people who should provide political initiative and guidance, once they are relieved of the oppressive legacy of the past. The urban areas used to exercise dominance over the rest of the country quite out of proportion to their numbers, experience, or talent. These reforms should eventually bring about a wholesome balance between the urban and the rural populations.

The data available showed that out of the 2·7 million acres of land surrendered by landlords, about 2 million acres were land held in excess of the ceiling by over 6,000 people, while another half a million became available through the abolition of *jagirs*. Some 9 million acres of land have been consolidated under the scheme for doing away with fragmented holdings and this process is continuing.

In East Pakistan, the politicians had introduced land reforms on the basis that everybody should be given a piece of land. They divided the country into bits and pieces, and by adopting punitive and extreme types of so-called reforms destroyed the entire middle class. The result is that today nobody has any real interest in land.

The Muslim League ministry in East Pakistan had brought in these reforms and had also promised some compensation to the landlords. But when the Awami League came to power they passed a law that all estates stood resumed as from that day. In East Pakistan there was no land record because of the Permanent Settlement during the British régime and nobody knew who owned what. So no compensation was paid.

A Land Revenue Commission set up for East Pakistan in 1958 led to an amendment of the East Bengal State Acquisition and Tenancy Act 1950 by which I was able to raise the ceiling of *khas* (self-cultivated) land from 33 acres to about 120 acres or so. With 120 acres in East Pakistan, one can have adequate production if one is prepared to work. The land is fertile and responsive. Under the same amendment, the limits of 'subsistence' and 'economic' holdings in East Pakistan were fixed at three acres and eight acres, respectively.

Meanwhile, I had been pressing the East Pakistan Government to get the land records made as quickly as possible and start giving compensation to the landlords from whom land was resumed. They had to have something with which to start life afresh and become useful members of society.

Some people have asked me whether mechanization of agriculture and use of improved fertilizers and better seeds could not have been achieved through co-operative farming. We have found from experience that co-operative farming does not work in our social system; it can succeed only under a Communist system. The Indians are experimenting with co-operatives. They have split up the holdings to 30 acres each: the results have been dismal. You cannot get results through co-operatives in conditions comparable to ours unless there is a measure of compulsion.

And this notion that everybody must own land just does not make sense. We do not have enough land to give to everybody. You can broaden the base of ownership but you must have a class of people interested in investing in land and working on it on a sound economic and progressive basis. If you destroy this class you are just killing the goose. About 60 per cent of Pakistan's income comes from land. Under our land reforms, landlords, by tradition a lazy people, are working harder on the land and are getting far more out of it. They have introduced mechanization, fertilizers, and better seeds. A whole class of young people after finishing college are going back to the land. All this makes for a healthy agricultural community.

It is not easy to encourage investment in agriculture. In the dry areas land revenue is fixed, but in the canal areas in Sind, the amount of revenue fluctuates with the type of crop and the prices. In other words, a man who works harder and produces more has to pay more taxes to the government! The West Pakistan government is now considering a system under which it can have a fixed land revenue. Once that is done the farmer will be encouraged to get the maximum out of his land.

Co-operatives can be useful in Pakistan, but in the field of common credit facilities. I should like to see finance co-operatives started in every Union Council, to take the place of the village moneylender who has, fortunately, disappeared; but the void left by him has not been filled. Rural credit facilities are a problem. The answer really is that the Union Councils should establish their own savings accounts and co-operative arrangements.

The democratic content of the new Constitution would have been a sham without the land reforms. Ask a farmer whose family has been tilling a plot of land for generations how these reforms have changed his whole attitude towards life. He sweated and toiled, as did his fore-fathers, but neither they nor he could claim that plot of land as his own. The land reforms have changed his destiny: he is now likely to be the proud owner of his land.

The pattern of our social and political life is being transformed. Governments who manoeuvred themselves into power on the strength of their vast estates will no longer be able to stage a come-back. Leadership will now be judged not in terms of acres of land but by social and human values. The curtain has been rung down on the dismal inter-play of extreme poverty and excessive wealth which had long dominated the rural scene.

A good deal of what I planned to do was going to affect the lives of powerful people in the country as well as the masses. They all had to be clear in their minds about the necessity for the change, so that once it was made, although it might prove distasteful in the beginning, it would have their support and they would try to sustain it in future. In that, I think, I succeeded to a large extent.

All reforms hurt vested interests and most of my reforms were directed against vested interests. Six thousand powerful landlords in West Pakistan lost through the land reforms about 2·7 million acres of land. Murders are committed over an inch of land: here were nearly three million acres given up without a squeak.

II

I have described the holocaust of Partition. At that time I had made a rough guess that about a million Muslims would seek refuge in Pakistan, and even that prospect worried me because I was extremely doubtful of the administration's capacity to deal with a problem of such dimensions. In actual fact about nine million refugees poured into Pakistan. The continuing animosity of Hindus and Sikhs, the economic and social boycott, the political persecution of Muslims, and the harsh application of evacuee laws in independent India brought about one of history's most tragic and politically-motivated migrations. Every sixth man in Pakistan was a refugee from India. The previous political régimes were interested in keeping this problem alive and refugees became a pawn in the game of party politics.

In 1954 the government decided to launch a scheme for the payment of compensation for properties left by displaced persons in India. From 1955 to 1958 no action was taken and the only tangible progress was the enactment of legislation for the registration and verification of claims and the setting up of a claims organization. In February 1958 an Act was passed by Parliament for the permanent settlement of claims on agricultural lands, but, as on previous occasions, no concrete steps were taken to put its provisions into effect.

The basic mistake made by previous governments, and even by us in the beginning, was to have worked on the assumption that even though a major calamity had occurred and a massive shift of population had taken place under chaotic conditions, it should still be possible to determine how much property each man had left in India and what he should therefore receive in Pakistan as its equivalent. It was a futile exercise. We soon realized that it would be impossible to determine what a man was entitled to in the absence of documents, especially from those areas in India which were not covered by the formal agreement on evacuee property between the two countries. The only solution to my mind was to give the refugees a new start in life and not talk loosely about compensation. After all, who can compensate when a major tragedy overcomes some nine million people who are forced to flee their homes? And look at the strain on the administrative machinery of the country that gave them refuge in trying to 'compensate' them. The West Pakistan administrative machinery almost ground to a halt and remained neutralized for a long time because of their approach to the problem. The politicians ended up by adopting a perfectly ridiculous formula: it meant that if a person could produce two witnesses who deposed that he had owned half of India, then the government of Pakistan would have to accept this! He could, in return, testify that the other half of India belonged to those who had testified in his favour. And the government must accept this also! It opened the floodgates to dishonesty and immorality.

I am not blaming the poor refugees. But the net result of this formula was that it corrupted them and it corrupted the society in which they were seeking assimilation. On one occasion, with some difficulty, we managed to get records from India relating to those who had migrated to Pakistan. On a sample check, we found that the claims registered with us were true only to the extent of about $7\frac{1}{2}$ per cent. The Rehabilitation Ministry was naturally alarmed. It was obvious that we must give the refugees a fresh start in life. Their resettlement had been hanging fire for several years owing to incompetence, corruption, and party politics. Here I was bringing in land reforms and reducing the number of Nawabs and landlords; yet if we had followed the refugee rehabilitation policy of the previous régimes we should have created a new class of Nawabs. I certainly did not want this to happen.

Within three months of the proclamation of Martial Law we had set the stage by promulgating an Ordinance on 4 January 1959 and following it up with further Ordinances, the most important of which was Regulation 89, in September 1961. The entitlement in agricultural land determined under this Regulation followed a graduated system for the preparation of fresh entitlements relating to the claims already made. An entitlement not exceeding 1,500 produce index units would be met in full, whereas for example an entitlement exceeding 4,000 units would be met by 2,150 units plus 10 per cent of the entitlement in excess of 4,000 units.

This formula meant that a heavy cut was imposed on people with large claims. True, it was an arbitrary law, but it was merciful and more than just under the circumstances. I checked up with a large number of people affected. Many confessed, now that the matter was over, that

they had got three times more than they were entitled to on the basis
of what they had actually left behind in India. But the people in the
top slab did suffer, and to give them relief we allowed them to buy up
to 36,000 produce index units, which was the maximum holding
allowed under the land reforms. The price charged was nominal,
Rs. 10 per produce index unit, and payable in easy instalments. This was
how we dealt with the refugee problem as it existed at the time of our
assumption of power. Compare this with what they would have got
left with if they had stayed in India: 25 to 50 acres.

Along with this compensation programme, we took immediate
steps to accelerate the establishment of new refugee 'colonies' in the
towns, to provide basic housing and sanitation for as many of the homeless refugees as possible. I laid the foundation stone of the Korangi
Colony outside Karachi in December 1958; and 15,000 quarters were
completed there in five months. Similar new townships were built in
North Karachi and at Mohammadpur Colony in Dacca.

All this, however, was by no means the end of the story. India
continued a calculated policy of driving wave after wave of Muslims
from their homes and pushing them into Pakistan, particularly in our
eastern wing, and there was a lot of talk in India about exchange of
population. I still wonder what the Indians have in mind and what is
really behind this irresponsible action. I wish and pray that Indian
leadership would realize the barbarity of their action and put an end
to this inhuman treatment of their own nationals.

III

The British Government announced their plan for the emergence of
India and Pakistan as two sovereign independent States on 3 June
1947. The plan was to come into effect from 14 August of the same year.
While the Government of India inherited a well-developed capital in
New Delhi, Pakistan had to find a place to house its central government. There was hardly any time to select a permanent site: the
immediate requirement was to find some place where accommodation
was available. Looking around, no one could think of a place better
than Karachi. I believe Rawalpindi was also mentioned at the time but
it had few facilities to offer, and in any case it was to be the Headquarters of the Pakistan Army.

The Provincial Government of Sind vacated their secretariat in
Karachi where a rudimentary central secretariat was set up, but the
accommodation proved grossly inadequate. Temporary hutments

were put up in various parts of the city to house Central Government offices. The position regarding residential accommodation was still more unsatisfactory because no houses were released by the Sind government. A large number of army barracks were converted into temporary residences. Naturally there was considerable resentment among government servants because they could not give of their best in those conditions.

Karachi is the only port for West Pakistan. It is situated on international air routes and even before Independence was a centre for foreign commercial firms. After Independence a large number of men with money and business acumen migrated from Bombay, Kathiawar, and other places in India to Karachi, and the town soon developed into the principal commercial and industrial complex of the country. With the influx of refugees and industrialization, its population began to grow rapidly and civic facilities began to deteriorate. A city of some 250,000 in 1941 had grown to over a million by 1951—and the census of 1961 showed a population just short of two million. As it is, the place has an enervating climate which saps one's energy and efficiency. This, along with unhygienic conditions prevailing throughout the city, had a serious effect on the health of the government servants. The whole administration looked worn out after the first few years.

The town also became a centre of agitational politics: politicians found that they could collect mobs with the help of industrialists and businessmen and bring all kinds of pressures to bear on the government. A time came when one large public meeting attended by a riotous mob could determine the fate of the government. Constant contact with businessmen had a corrupting influence on government servants and many of them succumbed to temptation. Also the Central Government ministers got embroiled with the affairs of Karachi's local administration.

Even before the revolution the Central Government was thinking of moving to a healthier place, and Gadap near Karachi was mentioned in this connection. No decision was taken because government at that time was not strong enough to resist vested interests in Karachi who would have lost control over the Central Government if the capital had been shifted.

In January 1959 I appointed a Commission under General Yahya to examine the suitability of Karachi as the permanent capital of Pakistan from the point of view of geographical location, communications, defence, climate, and availability of a productive hinterland; and if Karachi was considered unsuitable, to recommend an alternative site. The Commission carried out a thorough and painstaking examination of the problem and came to the unanimous conclusion that Karachi was not suitable. They studied alternative sites in both wings of Pakistan and finally recommended that the capital should be located in the Potwar Plateau near Rawalpindi. I agreed to this and the new capital was named Islamabad.

The capital is about seven miles from Rawalpindi under the lee of the Margalla Hills. Spread over 350 square miles of the Potwar Plateau, the site is a panoramic expanse of natural terraces and meadows, rising from 1,700 to 2,000 feet above sea level with a back-drop of mountain ranges. The place has a rich history. It was one of man's earliest homes, dating back four hundred thousand years, as shown by the Stone Age relics of the Sohan Culture found in the Potwar Plateau by Sir Mortimer Wheeler. Later, inhabitants of this part of the world built a centre of their power at Taxila, on the other side of the Margalla Range. The reason these Buddhists (who were followed by the Greeks) chose the other side of the hills was because only on that side did they have an assured water supply. The first thing I did was to order the building of the Rawal Dam, to re-create the conditions that existed for Taxila some two and a half thousand years ago. We thus went back to Taxila which was a notable seat of civilization and learning long before the dawn of the Christian era. It was the cradle of Gandhara art.

After considering all the basic factors, including geographic and climatic suitability, development potential, communications and defence, the Commission observed: 'The capital of a country is not merely another city, it is a leader amongst cities. To this city come leaders of administration and politics, of commerce and trade, of literature and art, of religion and science. From this city flows the inspiration which pulsates life into the nation. It is a symbol of our hopes. It is a mirror of our desires. It is the heart and soul of the nation. It is, therefore, essential that the environments of the capital should be such as to ensure continued vitality in the Nation.'

My own thinking was also that capitals are not built, nor do they exist, just for the sake of, shall we say, utility. Utility is important, but at the same time the capital of a country has to encompass much bigger vistas, and provide light and direction to the efforts of the people. It must, therefore, be located in the best possible surroundings. With the two provinces of Pakistan separated as they are, there is greater need to bring the people to a common platform. The thing to do was to take them to a new place altogether.

So it was not just the building of a city: it was an opportunity to unite the people of Pakistan, and to give them the right environment in which to produce the best results. The Central Government represents all the thinking and policy-making organs of administration. The best talent has to be there in order to be able to work for the betterment of the people. I have noticed the difference in the health of the officers and staff ever since they came to Islamabad. They look a different people although they have to work much harder.

It gives me great satisfaction to see the new capital growing up. The new secretariat buildings are almost completed; residential areas are being developed and already the city has become a symbol of the unity of the country and reflects the hopes and aspirations of the people.

IV

At my first Press conference, two days after the promulgation of Martial Law, I had defined three immediate tasks that would have to be undertaken: namely, land reforms, refugee resettlement, and educational reforms.

We needed an educational system which could produce competent leadership in different shapes and yet be within our means. I set up a Commission on National Education on 30 December 1958, and asked them to get on with the job. They wanted to make a basic study of the educational system and educational theory and talked in terms of years; but I told them that I wanted the report quickly. They worked hard and produced a comprehensive report within about eight months.

Our foremost need was to have a large body of trained and disciplined men and women who could provide leadership and direction. To my mind, this was the hard core of our national requirements. All reforms in the sphere of land and agriculture, law and administration, and all attempts to produce a greater measure of political, constitutional, social, and economic stability and well-being were intended to provide the conditions necessary for the growth of the right type of men and women.

The object of all our endeavour was the young people, at school or college today, but who tomorrow would be called upon to assume the leadership of the country in all spheres of life. When I talked about leadership, I did not for a moment accept the time-worn concept which confined it to the realm of high public offices; to me leadership meant a universal trait which operated at all levels. The mother in the nursery, the wife in the home, the teacher in some remote primary school, the doctor in a rural dispensary, the clerk in a small municipal office, the tiller of the soil, and the worker in a factory, each one of them had to be a leader in his or her own line, able to do the job adequately and constructively. What we needed was a sound and sensible system of

11   With the Indian Prime Minister Jawaharlal Nehru at Murree,
26 September 1960

12 With Mr. and Mrs. Eisenhower and President Kennedy at a state dinner given by President Ayub at the Mayflower Hotel, Washington, 13 July 1961

education to liberate the talent for leadership in every sphere of national life. At the same time, I was clear in my mind that the purpose of educational reform should not be to demolish unnecessarily any good or valuable traditions built up over long years. Proud legacies and treasures of the past have to be protected, but old laurels do not stay fresh unless nurtured by an urge for new achievements.

The Commission started by identifying the basic weaknesses in the educational system we had inherited from the past. These were 'passivity and non-cooperation; indiscipline and non-acceptance of public authority; placing of self before the community; and the disruptive forces of regionalism and provincialism'.[1] The Commission reached these conclusions after making a careful study of political developments in Pakistan and analysing the causes which had contributed to the breakdown of the whole political system. I cannot do better than reproduce the findings of the Commission: 'During the early period of foreign rule, the attitude of the government to the people was one of paternalism, while that of the people towards government was one of passive submission. . . . Initiative was seldom expected or encouraged and the relationship between the government and the people was the impersonal one between ruler and subject.'[2] The Commission felt that this passive attitude had been changed into one of active resistance to government during the struggle for independence, but that after the creation of Pakistan some of the worst of the old attitudes, both passivity and suspicion of government organization, had reappeared.

Having summed up the basic weaknesses of the system, the Education Commission went on to devise remedial measures. It recommended that the basic necessity was nothing less than a 'revolution in attitudes' so that the characteristics in our society which they had pointed out could 'give way to a spirit of individual initiative, personal integrity, pride in accomplishment, trust in one's fellow men', and 'a private sense of public duty'.[3]

The Commission formulated a plan which was aimed at raising academic standards, at encouraging the bright, and not only the rich, child, and at solving, through education, the problems of mutual ignorance and suspicion between the two wings of the country and between the peoples of different language backgrounds.

The Commission recommended that the emphasis in higher education should be on quality, so that the products of our colleges and universities could compare favourably with those of overseas institutions.

[1] *Report of the Commission on National Education*, p. 6 (Government of Pakistan, Karachi, 1960).
[2] Ibid. p. 5.   [3] Ibid. p. 8.

To achieve this, it was imperative that the quality of college and university teachers be improved. This, in turn, would depend ultimately upon our ability to recruit people of high calibre to the teaching profession, upon their dedication to teaching and scholarship, and their willingness and ability continuously to refresh their knowledge and methods through personal study and research.

To improve the qualifications of teachers already in service, and as part of a permanent programme through which college teachers could bring their knowledge up to date and acquaint themselves with new and improved techniques and to stimulate their thinking, the Commission recommended that a series of summer courses be instituted to cover various academic disciplines in each course. These would be attended by university and college teachers and supervised jointly by eminent local and foreign specialists in each discipline. Fortunately, this part of the Commission's recommendations could be implemented right away and a modest beginning was made within months of the acceptance of the Report by the government.

Regarding secondary education, the Commission pointed out that the nation-building needs required a large number of people with a variety of technical skills relating to industry, commerce, and agriculture, and that the new State required men of great integrity, patriotism, and dedication to the ideals of service. The secondary school programme in the past had paid little attention to these matters and, in fact, their tradition of aiming at a literary, or arts, education had been so strong that resistance to any change had frustrated all previous attempts at reform. The main emphasis of the secondary school programme had been on the preparation of the students for joining the universities. To correct this weakness the Commission recommended that secondary education should become a distinct stage with its own purpose, rather than act only as a preparation for higher education.

As for primary education, the Commission was of the view that economic development would require for its rapid achievement a generally literate population who would be able to understand and apply the new discoveries of science and improved technical and agricultural practices, and who could, as in any democratic system, understand local and national issues and could choose wisely from among alternative candidates and courses of action.

The major objective of the educational reforms really was to prepare our people for sharing the burden of developing their country and defending it. It is going to be a slow process, but I would like to believe that we have made a start in this direction. But we have had setbacks. For instance, throughout the whole of 1963, Dacca University operated for only twenty-seven days. We are spending large sums of money to bring the two Provinces to a level of parity. Unfortunately our progress has been hampered by many students wasting their time and allowing politicians to misguide them. These are heart-breaking things. I think, however, that the educational reforms are beginning to take effect and, in another two or three years, we should be getting much better products out of our universities.

As for foreign influence, I believe we should adopt good things wherever they can be found. Unfortunately, it is so much easier to adopt bad things, gaudy and vulgar. I do not have any mistrust of foreign ideas, attitudes, and manners, but I do believe that we should maintain and hold firmly to our own traditions, adopting only such foreign ideas as can be usefully assimilated in our life.

Most of the newly-emerging countries adopted the western system of government because they did not have time to work out a system of their own. As a result, governments have been functioning in a state of tension with their people. The behaviour of the politician, the student community, and the Press, has contributed to this tension. Student demonstrations are a common phenomenon in all new democratic countries like Pakistan, Iran, Turkey, the Philippines, and Japan. In the old days, one would hear a lot about lawlessness among the student community in Cairo. Since the pattern of government there has changed, the students have settled down. In new countries, such as ours, traditions of responsibility are not sufficiently developed; irresponsibility comes easy, since it so often goes unpunished.

But it is also true that governments have not really been providing the facilities which the students require. There were reasons for this. We just did not have the means. There were far too many students and not enough buildings, laboratories, libraries, or even areas for games and recreation.

Some of these shortages can be soon met if vigorous and perhaps unconventional methods are tried, on individual initiative. Organized physical training, for example, in our schools and colleges could take the place of more complicated and expensive games. One instructor on a platform with a loud-speaker can take a very large body of students at one time, and just half an hour a day should build up their bodies and minds, and take the devil out of them.

The language problem has been a major hindrance in the development of a sound and uniform educational system in the country. The Commission advocated teaching through both the national languages, Bengali and Urdu, and referred also to the question of the two scripts but did not go into the difficulties which teaching in two languages and two scripts presents to a developing society seeking to build itself into a unified community professing a common ideology and committed to a common destiny. The language problem has to be viewed essentially as an academic and scientific problem. Unfortunately it has become a highly explosive political issue and the result is that no one wishes to talk about it for fear of being misunderstood. The intellectuals who should have been vitally interested in the matter have remained on the touch-line lacking the moral courage to face up to the problem. Their attitude has been to leave it to the political leaders to come up with some solution and face the odium, so that they may be able to sit back in comfort and criticize whatever solution is offered.

It is quite clear to me that with two national languages we cannot become a one-nation State; we shall continue to remain a multi-nation State. I am not necessarily arguing against this; I am just stating a fact of life which has to be recognized. For it is the case that one language cannot be imposed on the whole country; neither Bengali nor Urdu can become the language of the whole of Pakistan. It is equally true that if the people—both in East and West Pakistan—want to develop cohesion they must have a medium to communicate with each other. And this medium must be a national medium. To evolve such a medium we have to identify common elements in Bengali and Urdu and allow them to grow together through a common script. Admittedly it will be a long process, but with growing understanding and knowledge of each other a national medium is bound to emerge and take shape. I cannot enforce this idea. All I can do is to pose the problem and to emphasize the need for solving it if we are to preserve national identity and unity.

Of all the reforms we initiated, in pursuance of the philosophy of the Revolution, the reconstruction of the system of education was the one closest to my heart. No economic planning, social progress, or spiritual enlightenment could make much headway without a sound and realistic base for education. This immense task requires the pooling of all the talent in the country and I sincerely hope that this will be forthcoming in implementing the intentions underlying the reforms. Only then can we have an educational system which will meet the individual and collective needs of our people.

V

As far back as 1954 I had written that 'there is the problem of our legal system, which is most expensive, ineffective, dilatory, tyrannical and totally unsuited to our genius. This would need complete overhaul and made humane, quick, and cheap. The answer would seem to lie in

having a Jirga-cum-judicial system and revision of evidence and procedural laws with only one right of appeal. The highest judicial court
for dealing with cases other than constitutional would have to be created
in each sub-unit. The federal or the provincial high courts should deal
only with cases of a constitutional nature.'

I remember my father telling me on one occasion that after the
First World War there was a demand from the people who had supported the British that they should be compensated for it. The British
Government asked District authorities to explain to the people how
much Britain had done in the way of introducing reforms to help the
people of India. The Deputy Commissioner of Hazara, a Colonel
James, called a meeting of leading people in Haripur. There was only
one chair for the Deputy Commissioner and the audience had to squat
on a carpet. My father, who had been invited to this meeting, resented
this and stood under a tree. The Deputy Commissioner said that
everything possible was being done by the government but the general
backwardness could not be removed overnight. He specifically referred
to litigation, which seemed a widespread occupation in the area, and
said that everyone came to the courts with false complaints and then
asked for justice. My father said that it was true that people concocted
and fabricated cases and told all kinds of lies, but this was not because
there was anything wrong with the people. The whole system was
fundamentally alien to their temperament and needs. People had discovered, through trial and error, that the legal system introduced by the
British was heavily weighted in favour of those who indulged in lies and
falsehood. The administration did everything to encourage individuals
to make allegations against their own people. It was no use blaming
the people: what was required was a re-orientation of the system.

Penderel Moon, a former member of the Indian Civil Service,
observes in his book *Strangers in India* that the legal system is beyond
the comprehension of a large majority of the people. It is intricate, it is
dilatory, it is expensive. And what is worse, it does not even give you
justice. If you do succeed in getting justice out of this system, you are
just plain lucky. It is a system that has destroyed the morale of the
people because to prove the truth you have to tell lies and in order to
disprove a lie you have to tell more lies. It works well enough in the
place of its birth, but not in our circumstances. The effect has been
that our moral values have been undermined by this system. Penderel
Moon says, and I agree with him, that in an attempt to make it work,
we have corrupted it and the system in turn has completely corrupted us.

I, for one, have little faith in the present legal system. Now I know
that people blame the legal profession for the deficiencies in the

system: I do not. They did not invent this system; it was forced on them. But what is surprising is that I do not see any urge within the legal profession to bring the system into line with the pattern of life in Pakistan. There are many lawyers who are dissatisfied with it, but they show their dissatisfaction in private and not openly because some of their own colleagues in the profession will resist them fiercely. And any form of major change would inevitably come up against vested interests.

A large number of people in Pakistan have joined the legal profession. It is grossly over-manned and has absorbed considerable talent, much of which could be far more usefully employed in other walks of life. To make life a little easier for our poor people in the villages, we have given the Basic Democrats certain comparatively simple judicial functions. Even this has not been taken gracefully by some in the legal profession. I can understand their reasons, but something has to be done to relieve the distress of the people who are being demoralized and oppressed by the legal system. I am not a legal expert, and it is very difficult for me to put down any guidelines, but I would like to see the procedures simplified and the courts giving decisions a little more quickly. I personally feel that our Evidence and other procedural Acts should be fundamentally altered. If Martial Law had continued, I might have done something about it.

There is a peculiar weakness for verbosity among some of the lawyers and the judges; they love to be long-winded. I remember a recent case in one of the high courts which had to do with the divorce or marriage of a woman. There were four or five judges and they vied with one another in writing lengthy judgements, the shortest running to about seventy-two pages. And what was the result? In the end they all recommended that in order to resolve the problem, there should be a conference of leading *ulema* (religious scholars) from all over the Muslim world so that they could establish a uniform pattern to deal with such cases. Now there seems to be nobody who can tell them that their function is to interpret the laws of the land, not to write long theses. There is so much artificiality in the whole thing. It just does not inspire confidence. During the Martial Law period I appointed a Law Reforms Commission to go into the whole matter. They produced a good report, but I feel that it barely touched the fringe of the problem. Fundamentally, this legal system is ruinous.

The Report deals with solutions of a long-term nature, designed to simplify procedures and reduce delays; separation of the judiciary from the executive; appointment of an Islamic Laws Commission; appointment of a committee to revise and consolidate the laws; reduction of court fees; setting up of low-level courts with limited jurisdiction, ranging from summary courts in metropolitan towns to judicial *panchayats* in the villages and the *mohallas* or ward-*adalats* in the urban areas; abolition of frontier crimes regulations; achievement of unformity of laws all over the country; extension of the jurisdiction of West Pakistan high courts to special areas of Baluchistan and replacement of *Qazi* courts in Baluchistan by regular judicial courts; amendment of defamation laws; appointment of a committee to examine the structure of existing court laws, and so on.

Some of the recommendations were implemented, such as the amendment of the Civil Procedure Code in order to reduce the technicalities of the procedural law. The first hearing was made more comprehensive and easy adjournment of hearings made impossible. The appeal from the judgement of a single judge of a high court to a bench of two (Letters Patent Appeal) was eliminated.

However, as I have said, this does not touch the hard core of the problem. I was not so much worried about the material damage being done by the legal system as by the grievous psychological and moral damage. A perfectly good man, an honest man, who would never tell a lie in his own village, goes to a court and is prepared to tell any number of lies. And this is because he has no faith in the system. He does not think it is his system; it is somebody else's system. So he argues to himself that there is nothing wrong if he violates a system which is foreign and has been thrust upon him.

The interminable discussion which goes on and the laxity of the courts in allowing extraneous matters to be brought in suggests a serious lack of discipline. Perhaps the substantive law is all right, but the application of the law in evidence and procedures lends itself to gross misuse and exploitation. The procedures are still cumbersome and slow and, I think, the judiciary and the magistracy find themselves powerless to amend matters and speed things up. Now I sometimes get mercy petitions from persons convicted of murder and sentenced to death: I rarely see a case which is decided in less than two years. That is a big cheque for any legal system to earn in a criminal case. On the other hand, in any civil case, if you have the money and you want to ensure that no decision is arrived at, you can go on indefinitely.

I once asked a judge, whom I have known for a long time, what life was like in the high courts. He said: 'Well, you know, in every case there are two sides—the prosecution and the defence, and in civil cases there are two parties. One just sits there and listens to lies from beginning to end, from both sides, lies and rubbish, and the task is to make sense out of it all and give a decision. This is my life.'

My own feeling is that we should really have this system examined very carefully not by lawyers alone but also by the people who suffer. I now think it was a mistake to appoint pure lawyers and judicial commissioners on the Law Commission. I should really have put in some people who knew something of the sufferings of those involved.

I feel that in our society, when something occurs in a particular area, the people of that area know who has done it and would name the fellow, if they were given a fair chance and protection. I therefore think that the more these things are put in the hands of local bodies the greater justice and satisfaction would be provided. Experience has shown that the handling of minor cases by local bodies has been very encouraging. And what is more, they get people to come to a compromise; they do not just deliver sentences. If they did, they too would become controversial. The conclusion is inescapable that some decentralization of the administration of justice is necessary, except for complicated matters like contractual laws.

I have been thinking deeply over the question of making our laws Islamic. If we succeeded in that, our legal system would become more humane and workable. It is now for the the Legislature to take the initiative in the matter; I would be prepared to endorse any reasonable move in this direction. But while there is a lot of loose talk on the subject, no one, not even the *ulema*, has so far come forward with any concrete ideas. I have set up an Advisory Council on Islamic Ideology and an Islamic Research Institute who should be able to examine our legal problems in the light of religion and advise the government. That should help our legislators to adapt our laws in conformity with the tenets of Islam. But to be workable, these laws must take account of the needs of society today.

It is not an easy task, I know. Any attempt at interpreting the tenets of Islam and adapting the laws to conform to the requirements of the time is a signal for the *ulema* to raise the slogan of 'heresy'. Take the institution of marriage: a Muslim is allowed by Islam to have more than one wife, under certain conditions. This permission has been used to practise indiscriminate polygamy, causing immense misery to innumerable tongue-tied women and innocent children. Thousands of families have been ruined because of the degenerate manner in which men have misused this permission to suit their convenience. A Commission, headed by a former Chief Justice of Pakistan, was set up in 1955 to examine the marriage and family laws and to suggest reforms in those laws. The members of the Commission were all persons of learning. When I came to office in 1958 I found that the Commission had produced a report and made a number of recommendations. Except for one note of dissent the recommendations were supported by all members of the Commission. The previous government avoided the responsibility of implementing the report through their fear of the *ulema*. I had the report examined by distinguished jurists including Justice Mohammad Ibrahim of East Pakistan and Mr. Manzur Qadir, ex-Chief Justice of the High Court of West Pakistan. The recommendations of the Commission did not interfere in any way with any Islamic injunction on the subject; they only provided a procedure for the proper and judicious implementation of the Islamic principles relating to marriage. I decided to implement the procedure recommended by the Commission because I considered it my duty as a Muslim and as Head of the State to do what was necessary to eliminate a grave social malpractice which was affecting the lives of the people. Accordingly, the Muslim Family Laws Ordinance was promulgated in 1961. A section of the *ulema* immediately accused me of interfering with Islam. Some went to the extent of suggesting that I had rewritten certain sections of the Qur'an. Fortunately the social benefits of the new law made an immediate impact on family life: people in general, and the womenfolk in particular, supported the reform and the obscurantists found themselves isolated. I have mentioned this to underline the difficulty of adapting laws to suit contemporary conditions.

VI

The Indus Basin waters dispute between Pakistan and India has a long and chequered history. While Kashmir is basically a political problem, the canal waters was a technical and economic issue which turned into a bitter feud because of India's intransigence. A major contributory factor was the policy of weakness and vacillation followed by successive governments in Pakistan.

Soon after the promulgation of Martial Law, I told a news conference in Karachi that if the Kashmir and canal water disputes were settled peacefully the new régime should be able to work out some mode of coexistence with India. I decided to deal with both the problems in a pragmatic spirit.

The Indus, with its five main tributaries, is one of the great river-systems of the world. Its annual flow is twice that of the Nile and three times that of the Tigris and Euphrates combined, amounting to almost 170 million acre-feet, or enough water to submerge to a depth of one foot the whole area of France or the State of Texas in the United States. The rivers, together with the system of irrigation developed over the past hundred years, support a population of about 40 million in Pakistan and 10 million in India, or almost one-tenth of the combined population of the two countries. The Indus Basin irrigation system is the largest in the world, irrigating about 30 million acres, or a larger area than that irrigated in Egypt and the Sudan by the Nile.

The partition of the sub-continent in 1947 left the headworks of some of our major irrigation systems in Indian territory. All the canals of what are known as the Central Bari Doab and the Sutlej Valley projects depended for their supplies on headworks and rivers under Indian control. The rivers Sutlej, Beas, and Ravi, whose waters flowed into these canals, originated and ran for long distances in Indian territory before they entered Pakistan.

Soon after Partition, India chose to take the drastic action of withholding water supplies to our canals and created a grave crisis for us. Water was released only under certain conditions to which we had no option but to agree, for the alternative was the physical devastation of vast fertile areas. The problem was made more complex because, until then, the Indus Basin irrigation system had been developed entirely from river flow and without reservoir storage. Water supplies were governed not only by seasonal variations, but also by the yearly variations in the flow of the rivers depending on rainfall in the upper reaches of the Himalayas.

India was trying to appropriate for her own use all the waters of the Sutlej, the Beas, and the Ravi; and, perhaps, some waters of the Chenab. As an upper-riparian, she was in a position to deprive us of all this water which flowed through her territory. Tempted by the prospect of quick economic development by utilizing easily available water, India started on huge engineering works which could only result in the complete desolation of vast areas of land in Pakistan.

The sharing of the waters of the Indus system had been a matter of dispute for many years. Before Partition, there were water claims continuously in dispute between the Sind and Punjab provinces of undivided India. Partition drew the border between India and Pakistan right across the Indus system. Pakistan became the downstream riparian, and the headworks of two of the main irrigation canals in Pakistan were left on the Indian side of the border. The sharing of the use of the waters then became an international issue. Somewhere about 1955 or 1956, when I was Commander-in-Chief, there was a great deal of talk in the Press about the Indus Basin dispute. The Indians seemed determined to cut off water supplies to our canals. If that had happened, the country might well have found itself involved in an armed conflict with India. I knew very little about the problem, so I asked for elucidation. The West Pakistan government sent two engineers who explained the case in great detail to me. My main worry was the vulnerability of Pakistan. The sources of the rivers were in India along with the headworks. India had made arrangements to divert the waters and the Indian Army was three times the size of our army. I felt that if negotiations with India broke down, and the Indians did decide to divert the waters, we should be facing a situation of war. Every factor was against us. The only sensible thing to do was to try and get a settlement even though it might be the second-best, because if we did not, we stood to lose everything.

In October 1958, very soon after the Revolution, I undertook a closer study of the facts of the case and acquainted myself with the issues involved. I came to certain definite and firm conclusions. By May 1959 the main issues had crystallized and the World Bank had reached the stage when they could make us a definite offer. Agreement was reached on the general principles on which a water treaty should be based. The World Bank conceded our demand for the construction of a system of replacement works. This was to be a part of the settlement arrangements, with India making a financial contribution. The World Bank team, headed by its President, Eugene Black, offered us the Mangla Dam plus certain headworks and the diversionary and link canals. They also offered a dam at Rohtas near Jhelum. The resources for these gigantic works were in the main to be provided by the friendly countries, especially the United States; some by India and some by Pakistan.

But before I write of the negotiations with Eugene Black, I should like to describe the confrontation I had with our own technical experts and administrators. I sensed that they did not fully realize the gravity of the situation and were asking for the moon when we were in a position of weakness all along the line. They were also trying to dictate policy and were taking up extreme positions. Some thirty or forty of them were assembled in Government House, Lahore, where I addressed them. I said: 'Gentlemen, this problem is of far-reaching consequences to us. Let me tell you that every factor is against Pakistan. I am not saying that we should surrender our rights but, at the same time, I will say this: that if we can get a solution which we can live with, we shall be very foolish not to accept it. Now when I say that, I am in fact saying it to myself because I shall have to take the responsibility for the solution.

'The responsibility does not lie on any one of you, so let me tell you very plainly that the policy is going to be mine. I shall consult you whenever I am in doubt regarding technical details, but if any one of you interferes with the policy, I shall deal with him myself. This prob-

lem, if not tackled properly, may well mean the end of the country.
I mean every word of it. So, don't let any one make any mistake about
it.' I think they understood my meaning.

Eugene Black's offer came to about 600 million dollars in terms of
money. I then consulted my technical advisers, who were firmly of the
view that in addition to a dam on the river Jhelum at Mangla, we
should need a dam at Tarbela to store the surplus flow of the Indus
River. This would not only cater for replacement requirements but also
provide some water for development, especially to feed the canals in
Sind. So a dam at Rohtas was no answer. The difference in cost was of
the order of about 200 million dollars. This was a staggering figure, and
I knew that when Eugene heard it he would hit the roof. And so he did.
But I told him, and I quote the words as I recall using them: 'I have
been around these areas which are going to be affected by the withdrawal of waters by India. People have told me very plainly that if they
have to die through thirst and hunger they would prefer to die in battle
and they expected me to give them that chance. Our *jawans* and the
rest of the people feel the same way. So this country is on the point of
blowing up if you don't lend a helping hand. This is a human problem
of a grave nature and cannot be blinked away.

'What we are being called upon to do is to barter away naturally-
flowing waters into our canals, for storage water, and the history of
storage is that it begins to silt the moment it is completed. Besides, we
are going to be put back by about ten years or so by building these
storages and link-canals. All this effort could have been put to more
constructive effort. So, we are making great sacrifices.

'I know certain countries have been very kind in offering us assistance, but unless we get our additional needs of water, apart from re-
placements, there is going to be chaos in this country. So a dam at
Tarbela is a must.'

Eugene Black thought I had made his task very difficult. He did not
know how he was going to persuade the donor governments to provide
another 200 million dollars. He wanted to have some time to think
over the matter. I urged him, 'Must you have time to think over an
obvious thing like this?' We went over it again and again. Finally, he
agreed to support our demand and said that he would ask the donor
countries for the additional sum—the difference between Rohtas and
Tarbela. In the end we got a promise of over 740 million dollars. I
understand that, earlier, Chaudhri Mohammad Ali was prepared to
settle for 100 to 150 million dollars, and that in the form of loans.

We should be grateful to the friendly countries and to Eugene Black
for what they have done for us. Later they promised to give an additional

350 million dollars for Tarbela or its equivalent, because costs had gone up. For the latter sum all credit is due to George Woods who succeeded Eugene Black as new head of the World Bank.

The Indus Waters Treaty was based on the division of the rivers, according to which, after a transitional period of ten years, extendable at Pakistan's request up to thirteen years, the three eastern rivers—Ravi, Beas, and Sutlej—will be allocated exclusively to India, while the waters of the three western rivers—Indus, Jhelum, and Chenab—will be available exclusively for Pakistan, except for limited uses by India in upstream areas in Indian-occupied Kashmir, eastern Punjab, and Himachal Pradesh. During the transitional period, Pakistan will undertake to construct a system of works, part of which would replace, from the western rivers, such irrigation uses in Pakistan as had hitherto been met from the eastern rivers.

The Indus works programme will be the largest of its kind to be undertaken anywhere in the world and will cost about 1,070 million dollars, of which about 870 million dollars will be spent on the works in Pakistan. These works will include two large storage dams, one on the Jhelum river (with a reservoir capacity of 4·75 million acre-feet) and the other on the upper Indus (with a capacity of 4·2 million acre-feet), five barrages and eight link canals nearly 400 miles in total length, transferring waters from the western rivers to areas formerly irrigated by the eastern rivers; that is, to replace the supplies for areas served by the Central Bari Doab and Sutlej Valley canals. Power stations will be installed at the Jhelum dam with a capacity of more than 800,000 kw. Tube-wells will be installed and drainage undertaken to overcome waterlogging and salinity in irrigated areas totalling 2,500,000 acres. While this system of works is being built, India will continue deliveries from the eastern rivers according to an agreed programme, which will take into account some development needs of Pakistan as well.

During the course of the protracted negotiations, it had become apparent that the cost of financing the system of work in Pakistan and India, to which the two governments had agreed as one of the features of an acceptable settlement, was far beyond the capacity of these two countries. The World Bank, therefore, set up an Indus Basin Development Fund to finance the whole programme. India undertook to contribute to the Fund about 174 million dollars, and the cost of the works in Pakistan will be financed out of the Indus Basin Development Fund.

Details of the agreement show that the division of the total waters of the Indus system under the Treaty would be in the proportion of 80 per cent for Pakistan and 20 per cent for India. The Treaty was signed in Karachi on 19 September 1960 by me, Mr. Nehru, and the World Bank Vice-President, Mr. Iliff.

As I explained to my people at the time of signing the Treaty, the solution that we had finally arrived at was not the ideal one but it was the best we could get under the circumstances. It should be realized that it was the immediate danger to the peace of this sub-continent posed by the dispute that had impelled the World Bank to step in as mediator in 1951. We had no alternative but to make a genuine and determined effort to assist the Bank to find an engineering solution to this grave problem which constituted a threat to peace between the two countries—a solution that we could live with and that would provide financial and technical resources to enable us to construct works which would divert the waters of the western rivers to the canals taking off from the eastern rivers. After years of negotiations of the utmost complexity, heart-breaking delays and frequent stalemates, we had, I felt, been able to obtain a solution which was adequate. So, whereas there was no cause for rejoicing at the signing of the Treaty, there was certainly cause for satisfaction that a possibly very ugly situation had been averted.

When one is dealing with a sensitive problem of this nature, one has to be realistic and judge the situation dispassionately in order to formulate a rational approach. Very often the best is the enemy of the good. We abandoned the chase of the ideal and accepted what was good after a careful and realistic appreciation of the overall situation. Had we not done that, we might have drifted into a conflict at a time when many factors were against us. The basis of this agreement, therefore, as far as we were concerned, was realism and pragmatism. Emotions had no place in it, nor could they be allowed to have any place where the future and safety of millions of people depended on a solution. I have nothing but admiration for President Black and Vice-President Iliff and for the Bank's technical team headed by General Wheeler, who made this dispute an issue of technical skill and human needs and lifted it from the plain of political controversy.

We are also grateful to friendly powers whose contributions to the Indus Basin Development Fund were a vital factor in making the terms of settlement acceptable to us. The cost of the works was far beyond our capacity. That these friendly countries, including the U.S.A., the U.K., Australia, New Zealand, Canada, and West Germany, have so readily come forward with offers of financial assistance, is not only a tribute to their sympathetic understanding of the issue, but also a proof of their interest in the stability and well-being of this sensitive part of the world. The World Bank, by its initiative, offered a distracted world an example of how problems could be solved by generosity and goodwill. I must also say that in the final stages of negotiations Mr. Nehru's personal intervention helped to remove certain differences which had arisen over arrangements during the transitional period.

The experience of the spirit that prevailed during the closing stages of the Treaty negotiations gave me hope that the problem of Kashmir might also get resolved in an amicable and just manner. The very fact that Pakistan had to be content with the waters of three western rivers underlined the importance for us of having physical control over the upper reaches of these rivers to secure their maximum utilization for the growing needs of West Pakistan. In my mind, therefore, the solution of the Kashmir issue acquired a new sense of urgency on the conclusion of this Treaty.

With the signing of the Treaty, a chapter of long and uneasy negotiations and suspense in our national affairs came to an end. We entered a period of sustained hard work to provide the huge storages and immensely long link-canals for alternative sources of water. By 1970 we hope to have completed these works, and when that is done we shall be independent of India in the matter of water supply.

9

Foreign Policy I

Nobody gives you freedom: you have to fight for it. Nobody fights for you: you have to fight for yourself.

Pakistan's foreign policy has a deep moral content. It is inspired by a consciousness of the equality of all nations and the right of all peoples to govern themselves according to their ideology. The principle objectives of Pakistan's foreign policy are security and development. The consideration of security embraces the defence of our country and the preservation of our ideology. The requirements of defence are complicated by the fact that we are divided into two parts, separated by a hostile distance of over a thousand miles, and each part has to be protected within the framework of collective defence. This physical separation underscores the need for welding the peoples of the two parts into a united and indivisible whole. Without complete unity, the security of the country would always remain vulnerable. And since we live in a world of combating philosophies, we have to fight to preserve our ideology which is the basis of our national existence. The consideration of development springs from the knowledge that survival without development is not possible. Survival cannot be an end in itself: it must have some purpose. Our purpose can be no other than the happiness and progress of our people according to their faith. But these considerations can best be promoted in an atmosphere of peace. This gives us a vested interest in peace generally, and peace in this part of the world particularly.

We do not have unlimited resources or unlimited time to make the grade. We must, therefore, utilize the time and resources available to us in a judicious manner, building up our gains and cutting down our losses. We must develop a national outlook and national policies. The current jargon is 'independent' foreign policy. By 'independence' is meant the freedom to criticize and curse everybody else. Now, we cannot afford the luxury of indulging in unbridled criticism of others just to prove our 'independence'. Our foreign policy has to be a national policy which must take into account our vital interests and operate towards the advancement of those interests. We do not have to indulge in histrionics; we have to be quiet and earnest.

The world today is fighting for equality—equality among individuals as among nations, regardless of whether they are big or small. This requires an unequivocal recognition by the world that every nation is entitled to equal rights and opportunities. The degree of a country's sovereignty and self-respect is not determined by the size of its territory or its resources. This sounds simple enough and no one would openly contest the claim, yet there are no means to enforce it. It is a world of the Big—Big Two, Big Three or four or more. It is they who preside over the destinies of the world and determine its direction. The smaller countries, particularly those in the early stages of industrial development, belong to a lower stratum of existence. They have thrown off the yoke of imperialism but most of them have yet to develop an identity and vision of their own, after sweeping away the cobwebs of colonial influences. We too have to establish our identity and fight for a position of equality and honour.

History has placed us in the pathway of the conflicting interests of major powers. Our location gives us a strategic significance both in South-East Asia and in the Middle East. But the cause of our major problems is India's inability to reconcile herself to our existence as a sovereign, independent State. The Indian attitude can be explained only in pathological terms. The Indian leaders have a deep hatred for the Muslims, and since they must disclaim and deny it all the time, they are the victims of continual tensions. From the beginning, India was determined to make things difficult for us. The colossal problem of refugee rehabilitation was created by India to cripple our economy. This was accompanied by denying us our share of the assets of undivided India and the threat of diversion and stoppage of river waters flowing into our territory. Contrary to all agreements and principles, India forcibly occupied a major part of the State of Jammu and Kashmir and concentrated her forces there, thus posing a constant threat to our security.

At the back of it all was India's ambition to absorb Pakistan or turn her into a satellite. The Indian leaders made no secret of their designs. Mr. Acharya Kripalani, who was President of the Indian National Congress in 1947, declared, 'Neither the Congress nor the nation has given up its claim of a united India'.[1] Sardar V. B. Patel, the first Indian Home Minister and the 'strong man' of the Congress Party, announced at about the same time, 'Sooner than later, we shall again be united in

[1] *Amrita Bazar Patrika*, Calcutta, 18 August 1947.

common allegiance to our country.' From the day of Independence, Pakistan was involved in a bitter and prolonged struggle for her very existence and survival. By 1954 Pakistan was compelled to align herself with the West in the interests of her security. She became a member of the Baghdad Pact and the South-East Asia Treaty Organization, both of which were suspect in the communist world.

By the time I became responsible for the affairs of the country in 1958, as President, the political identification of the country with the West was complete. As Commander-in-Chief of the Pakistan Army I was associated with the Baghdad Pact, which after the revolution in Iraq came to be known as CENTO, but my interest was exclusively in terms of the defence of the country. I was anxious to take maximum advantage of this arrangement to build up the defence forces of Pakistan. With the South-East Asia Treaty Organization I had no direct dealings and, in fact, the army was informed only after Pakistan had accepted membership of this Organization. I shall go into the genesis of these arrangements later.

Here I want to state the precise situation in which I found the country at the time of the revolution in October 1958. India had built up massive military strength by acquiring arms from the Soviet Union as well as from some western countries. She had consolidated her hold over the occupied area of Jammu and Kashmir by establishing a reign of terror: most of the Kashmiri leaders were languishing in jail and all civil liberties had been completely suppressed. The United Nations no longer seemed interested in having its own Resolutions, to which both India and Pakistan were pledged in honour, implemented so as to give the people of Jammu and Kashmir a free and fair opportunity to determine their future.

We had few contacts or dealings with the communist world. The Soviet Union regarded us with suspicion and distrust as some kind of a camp-follower of the United States. With the People's Republic of China we were on terms merely of nodding acquaintance. In the Middle East our position had been compromised by some of our leaders who handled the situation, at the time of the Suez crisis, in a clumsy fashion. President Nasser and certain other Arab countries under his influence thought that we were involved in some deep conspiracy to divide the Arab world. With the Afro-Asian community we had no association and Africa was a dark continent as far as we were concerned. This then was the picture in October 1958.

We could not change all this overnight. But clearly the whole pattern of our relations with others required fundamental re-thinking. Some of the essential elements in our geographical situation had not been recognized, nor was there a clear concept of the nature of the political compulsions to which we would be subjected. I think it was the force of events which compelled us to undertake this exercise.

The earlier years had proved conclusively that the threat from India to our security and existence was both real and constant. Indian efforts in the field of foreign policy were all directed towards one aim, the isolation of Pakistan and its disintegration. I had dealt with the problems created by this threat as the Commander-in-Chief, and I knew the weaknesses and deficiencies in our position. We had done all that we could to convince India that we wanted to live in peace with her, but India could not accept the existence of a strong and independent Muslim State next door. We therefore had to examine our situation dispassionately and realistically and organize our relations with other countries, particularly with our neighbours, in a manner consistent with the needs of our security.

Faced with this problem, I was deeply struck by the geopolitical situation of the country. The first question I asked myself was, 'which are the major countries interested in Pakistan?' The exact nature of their interest had then to be identified. The object was to try and evolve a pattern of relationship which would protect the country from any threat of aggression and give us time to develop the country and unite the people.

Take the geographical location first. Here is East Pakistan surrounded on three sides by India and the only approach is from the sea which is not difficult for an enemy to control. West Pakistan is wedged in between three enormous powers with the Soviet Union at the top, the People's Republic of China in the north-east, and India in the south and east. I know of no other small country which has the somewhat dubious distinction of having three such mighty neighbours. Now, this location is a source of weakness in physical terms but it could be converted into a source of strength if we could establish normal and mutually acceptable relations with the countries hemming us in.

With one of them, India, the prospects of establishing normal relations do not appear to be in sight. We must, therefore, accept the situation of implacable Indian hostility and learn to live with it.

Then there is the Soviet Union. By joining SEATO and CENTO we had alienated her and lost her sympathy. Since we had never been a party to any design against her and our membership of the Pacts was dictated solely by the requirements of our security, it should be possible to come to an understanding with the Soviet Union by removing her doubts and misgivings.

And then there was the People's Republic of China fast emerging as a power to be reckoned with. China was making significant progress in all spheres of life, and seemed anxious to have friendly relations with her neighbours. All we had to do was to convince her of our sincerity and friendly intent.

From this it was easy to deduce that if we could not establish normal relations with all our three big neighbours, the best thing was to have an understanding with two of them. They might have their internal differences but we did not need to get involved in that. This was a vital element in our new thinking: to keep clear of the internal disputes and conflicts of other countries; neither to philosophize about their problems nor to act as busybodies. It was on this basis that I set out to normalize our relations with the People's Republic of China and the Soviet Union. It is in this sense that our geographical location and the political compulsions inherent therein have determined the course of our foreign policy in recent years.

Then there was the necessity of developing the country to provide the people with better living conditions, and through this process bring about greater unity among the people of the two wings. Development presupposes resources, and in our social conditions and our scheme of values these resources cannot all be generated or mobilized through regimentation. Therefore we have to look for external assistance to build up the social overheads and provide the initial capital investment. This necessitates our having good relations with the United States and other western powers who are in a position to help us economically. Now any assistance creates certain liabilities; we have to ensure that we do not incur such liabilities as would compromise or damage our national interests.

All this must seem an over-simplification. But from our point of view the approach was rational and pragmatic. The objective was to establish normal relations with the four major powers involved in Asia without antagonizing any one of them. A simple strategy was evolved to achieve this objective. We should endeavour to set up bilateral equations with each one of them, with the clear understanding that the nature and complexion of the equation should be such as to promote our mutual interests without adversely affecting the legitimate interests of third parties. The merit of this approach was that our people, who believe in honest and straightforward dealings, would be able to appreciate and understand it.

I was not unconscious of the pitfalls. No bilateral equation could be established in isolation; other equations would influence its level. In the end each equation would be determined by the limits of tolerance of third parties. So each equation would have to be acceptable to third parties with whom we might be able to establish bilateral relations of mutual benefit. That is where all the complications and difficulties would arise. It would be like walking on a triangular tightrope. It would be vital to determine clearly the limits of tolerance within which bilateral equations might be constructed. To illustrate, the United States would not be too eager to provide us with unlimited economic and military assistance if we were to establish bilateral relations with the major communist powers without any regard to American interests or strategy in Asia. If we cannot in an unlimited way identify ourselves with American interests, we must learn to do with less than unlimited American assistance.

Similarly, we must be able to explain to the United States the extent to which we could go along with them without compromising our own interests. It is not in our interest to alienate the People's Republic of China. Similarly, it is in our interest to develop normal and friendly relations with the Soviet Union. It should be possible to convince the United States that our relations with the People's Republic of China or with the Soviet Union are not directed against American interests in Asia. In return for economic assistance, we offer to the United States our goodwill and growing opportunities for collaboration in the field of trade and industry. But we cannot give in return something that would harm a third country. If their global policy is served by our understanding of their problems and by our not acting against them, well and good. But if the demand goes beyond that and requires us to do something that is against the interests of another power, then we will have to decline because that would be going against the interests of Pakistan. I realized that in our new approach such a choice might be forced on us at times. In that event people in positions of responsibility would have to weigh the alternatives: either to succumb to the pressure of a major power or to forgo whatever assistance might be involved, political, military, or economic. The decision would ultimately rest with the people of Pakistan.

There is reason to believe that such a situation may not be forced on us if we conduct ourselves with moderation and sobriety. Because of the emergence of China, the earlier polarization between the Soviet Union and the United States is gradually disappearing. And for many years to come all three of them will be involved in a relentless struggle to create areas of influence for themselves in different countries. None of them can afford to isolate and antagonize any of the developing countries completely. In any case, whether the choice is forced on us or not, the only way in which we can survive is to tell the major powers that we cannot afford to get involved in their squabbles. All we want is to be left alone to work for the security of our country and the unity and development of our people. We are not in the market for becoming partisans in their struggle for power.

Now this approach can be easily confused with the kind of 'neutralism' that India tried to practise during the early fifties, and that came a cropper in the end. There is a fundamental difference. India's neutralism was at best a posture of sitting on the fence and seeing how best it could take advantage of both sides; at worst it was a kind of sanctimonious hypocrisy and a subterfuge. For a time India could get away with it because of its size and strategic position in Asia. India's 'neutralism' was an attempt to act 'big' and to create a cover for the expansion of her influence. We entertain no such illusions. Our approach is essentially intended to conserve our resources and to cut our commitments.

India had set herself up as a beacon light, ranging far and wide, a true guide to errant humanity. She could sustain this pose so long as there was tension between the United States and the Soviet Union. She could act as a bridge between them. As the major powers were engaged in a struggle of their own, and China had yet to discover the Indian mind, it was possible for the Indian leaders to preach philosophy and promote India's designs against her smaller neighbours. I think they overreached themselves and, as time passed, the contradictions between their profession and their practice became more and more difficult to rationalize and explain away.

Our approach to world powers and to our neighbours is dictated by a sense of our limitations. We have neither the desire nor the capacity to get mixed up in their wranglings. We are not in a position either to influence their decisions or to solve their problems. The basis of our foreign policy thus is that we stay within our own means, political as well as economic. All we expect is that we should be left alone to deal with our internal affairs, to bring about greater unity among our people, to promote their welfare and to preserve our identity, political and ideological. It is within this framework of understanding that we seek assistance from other countries. And we have no intention of making any demands on them which would be likely to strain either their willingness or their capacity to help. Our objective is to move into a position where we have to make fewer and fewer demands on them. Neutralism aims at establishing strong bargaining positions. Our concept of developing bilateral relations aims at establishing equations within our resources and limitations and within the resources and limitations of others; we have no intention of bargaining with others.

We expect them to help us to the extent they can and, in return, we will help them to the extent we can.

It has been suggested that this would mean Pakistan having the minimum of relations with the major powers, and with her neighbours in particular. From there it is argued that if Pakistan were to get into a situation of real trouble she would find no one willing to come to her rescue. Now I accept that. But we must never forget that we shall have to defend Pakistan ourselves. No other country can be expected to do that on our behalf. That is the basis on which our defence effort and other endeavours should be planned. The major powers have their own problems and their policies may change with events and we may be ultimately left entirely alone. That is where our faith in God Almighty must reassure us. It is His law that if an aggressor rears his head in one place someone equally strong emerges in another place to frustrate him in his tyrannical designs. Conflicts between nations cannot remain isolated. Should a conflict take place between India and Pakistan other powers will inevitably get drawn into it. But we must develop the capacity and the will to stay the course regardless of what the others may or may not do.

II

Having stated the general principles I shall now try to trace the actual development of the various equations and discuss the problems we had to face in establishing them.

I shall deal first with the Indo-Pakistan equation. The background of Indo-Pakistan relations since Independence is well known. The last twenty years have been years of frustration for Pakistan in all her attempts to find some level of existence as good neighbours with India. I think political leaders in Pakistan before the Revolution tried very hard to come to some understanding with India. The argument from the Indian side has been on the following lines: 'Let us forget our disputes; let us have a "no-war pact"; let us have more trade, more freedom of movement between the two countries and more cultural exchanges. This will soften feelings on the two sides and once an atmosphere of goodwill and understanding develops, all problems will resolve themselves.' To the Indians this sounds highly plausible and they often claim, with an air of injured innocence, that their sincere and genuine overtures have met with no response from Pakistan.

What is Pakistan's position? It is to ask how goodwill and understanding can develop when basic differences and disputes remain unresolved. If India is willing to enter into a 'no-war pact' with Pakistan why should she be engaged in building up a tremendous war-machine? The Indians reply that their war potential is intended to contain Chinese aggression. How is it then that the type of machine which they are evolving can operate essentially in the plains? How can Pakistan ignore the fact that India is in a position to unleash vast forces against Pakistan at a few hours notice? In matters of defence, countries do not formulate their policies on the basis of the intentions of others; it is their capability which must be taken into account. If a big country like India has the capability to attack Pakistan, the intentions can always change, pact or no pact. A 'no-war pact' can make sense only if it is accompanied by an agreement about the maintenance of forces at a specified level.

We have also to consider how the need for a 'no-war pact' has arisen. It has arisen because of the existence of disputes which can lead to an armed conflict between the two countries. Now, if nothing is done to resolve these conflicts on a just and honourable basis, how does the danger of conflict disappear merely because of the existence of a 'no-war pact'. To make sense, a 'no-war pact' must at least provide reasonable machinery to deal with the disputes and to bring about an honourable solution of those disputes. Such machinery should have the confidence and support of both sides and must indicate how, in the event of disagreement between the two sides, the issue would be resolved in a peaceful manner. Without the reduction of force and without the provision of any machinery for the solution of problems, a 'no-war pact' would only mean the expression of pious intentions at a given time. In isolation, such a pact would certainly help India to strengthen her claim in the world that she has peaceful intentions; it would certainly not help Pakistan who can foresee those intentions changing any minute.

Finally, the assumption that disputes get resolved with the passage of time is open to serious question. Fundamental disputes affecting the life and freedom of people cannot be swept under the rug; nor do they get buried under the dust of time. They have a habit of erupting because human beings cannot be kept eternally in bondage.

This is the point which India, and indeed the world, has to realize when dealing with the problem of the people of Jammu and Kashmir who are engaged in a life-and-death struggle to establish their right of self-determination. And when India says let goodwill grow and the problems will solve themselves, it gives no assurance that, in the meantime, the problems will remain frozen. In fact, all the available evidence shows that the Indians are busy solving the problems on their own terms. A large part of the State of Jammu and Kashmir is under their forcible occupation; they are busy consolidating their occupation; they are changing the complexion of the population of the State. Their thesis 'let goodwill grow' means 'let's have it our way'.

There is then the record of previous agreements between India and Pakistan on a number of issues. One has only to go through that record to see in what manner and to what extent India honoured those agreements. I have mentioned how Pakistan was denied her share of assets, finances, stores, and ammunition at the time of Independence. Each one of these items was governed by an agreement to which both the countries were pledged. There is the United Nations Commission for India and Pakistan Resolution dealing with the Jammu and Kashmir dispute, to which both India and Pakistan are parties. Yet every time an attempt is made to implement the Resolution, India finds one pretext or another to frustrate it. First she said that conditions in Jammu and Kashmir must be allowed to become normal before the people could be given an opportunity to exercise their right of self-determination. And when conditions returned to normal, she said that now that the situation had settled down matters should not be disturbed by ascertaining the wishes of the people. This has been the constant pattern of Indian policy: 'Let things become normal and we will deal with the problem'; and 'now that things are normal why raise the problem'.

I had two meetings with Pandit Jawaharlal Nehru: one at Palam airport, New Delhi, on 1 September 1960, and the other when he came to Pakistan to sign the Indus Waters Treaty between 19 and 23 September 1960. The Palam meeting lasted about two hours. We issued a joint statement at the end in which we stressed the need to conduct relations on a rational and planned basis. We also agreed that outstanding issues and problems should be settled in accordance with justice and fair play, in a spirit of friendliness, co-operation, and good-neighbourliness. Later, while speaking to the Press, I suggested that there was 'need for reappraisal, for forgetting and forgiving, and for a more realistic, rational, and sensible relationship with each other'.

I did not get the impression that Pandit Nehru was extraordinarily pleased to see me, but he was quite moved by some of the suggestions I made to him. He struck me as a tired man, though he still had a reserve of fight and political acumen. I missed the idealism or starry-eyed thinking which is often attributed to him. I told him I considered that relations between India and Pakistan had been dictated by drift rather than by any rational design. The reason, I thought, was that neither side had drawn up any plan for neighbourliness. People on both sides thought that all social and economic ills were due to the British and once they left everything in the garden would be lovely. Events proved that they were not entirely right, though a good deal of our misfortunes were due to British occupation. Much distress and hatred was generated and people in both countries began to believe that they should have nothing further to do with each other. I felt it was not too late to formulate a plan to put our relationship on a rational and sensible basis.

Pandit Nehru talked of the no-war declaration. I explained to him that before we entered into any such declaration there should be an agreement on the setting up of machinery for the solution of outstanding problems, and then that for a no-war declaration to be effective it would be necessary for us to disarm in relation to each other. In military thinking the crucial factor was 'capability'. If a country had decisive military capability it could always change its intentions and act aggressively. I reminded him of the concentration of the Indian Army against us in 1950 and again in 1951 when there was hardly any military cause for doing so.

I then raised with him the Kashmir problem. I put it to him that it was the people of Kashmir who should have the decisive say in the matter. It was vital that a solution satisfactory from the point of view of the people of Jammu and Kashmir be found. Mr. Nehru did not disagree with my ideas but emphasized the need for the creation of a background of understanding between the two countries and for eliminating, as a start, border incidents and firing.

We took up the threads during the second meeting in Murree, on 21 September 1960. I again broached the subject of Kashmir. I told him that this was the most propitious moment for settling this dispute, to bring peace to India and Pakistan. He was an accepted leader in India and perhaps people in Pakistan would be prepared to listen to me, too. Such a coincidence might not occur again for a long time, so it would be a great pity if we were to lose this opportunity. Any thought that time would make Pakistan forget the need for an honourable and fair solution to the problem of Jammu and Kashmir was highly unrealistic. The whole country was united on this issue and no government in Pakistan could possibly forget the problem.

I showed him a map of Kashmir and West Pakistan and how all our major rail and road communications and canal headworks were completely outflanked. The security of Pakistan required a fair solution of the problem. There was also the economic reason now that West Pakistan was dependent on the use of waters of only three rivers. Pakistan had to conserve every single ounce of water in these rivers and that could be done only in the hilly areas of Kashmir. Similarly the further power requirements of Pakistan could only be met by hydro-electric generation in those areas. For India and Pakistan to live as good neighbours this problem would have to be solved one day. If it could be solved peacefully and honourably and in accordance with the commitments of the two governments, both sides would derive enormous advantages. India should then be able to reduce its army by half and we too should be able to cut down our military expenditure proportionately.

On this occasion Pandit Nehru started replying haltingly but with deliberation. He said that the Kashmir problem had become very complicated with the passage of time. Hard positions had been taken up and it was not easy to go back on them. Two 'elections' had been held in Kashmir and a third was in the offing. India had spent an enormous amount of money, apart from military expenditure, on development work in Kashmir. There was also the question of a large Muslim minority in India which was being integrated. Any hasty action on Kashmir, he thought, would upset this process. India was trying to divert people's energy into constructive channels and if the *status quo* was disturbed in Kashmir, people's energy would be diverted into negative channels.

I told him that he knew very well the kind of 'elections' that had been held in the State in the absence of any civil liberties. There was no denying the fact that the people of Jammu and Kashmir were most unhappy about the continued occupation of their State by the Indian army. As regards the Muslim minority in India, they could not be held as hostages and their future did not have to be linked with the problem of Jammu and Kashmir. There was little prospect of the Indian Muslims being integrated into Indian society so long as there was no settlement between India and Pakistan over Kashmir. As regards diverting people's energy into constructive channels, it could only be done if a society had an ideology. We had a considerable argument over this.

Nehru finally asked what, accepting the fact that there was need for peace between the two countries and also that the room for manoeuvre for settlement of the Kashmir dispute was limited, I thought should be our first step. I told him that this would depend on the objective we had before us. Once the objective was determined, an organization could be established to work out the method. Mr. Nehru said that he foresaw serious political opposition in his country. He mentioned that Indian public opinion had reacted violently to Chinese 'occupation' of 'Indian territory'. I could not see the relevance since Kashmir had never been Indian territory and was the subject of an international dispute on which the two countries were pledged to a solution, in accordance with a United Nations resolution.[1]

I did not get the impression that Nehru was interested in any long-

[1] See also Appendix I, p. 242.

term and lasting solution. He was, perhaps, not averse to the dialogue going on for the time being, but he was not visualizing a future of understanding between the two countries. Had he been interested in such a future, I think he would have given more serious thought, for example, to the proposal for joint defence which I made in May 1959. For some odd reason he thought it was an attack on India's integrity and self-respect. There was nothing sinister in the proposal, nor was I the first one to have made it. The Quaid-e-Azam thought that it was of vital importance to Pakistan and India, as independent sovereign States, to collaborate in a friendly way jointly to defend their frontiers both on land and sea against any aggression. Dr. Eric Streiff, Special Correspondent of the *Neue Zürcher Zeitung*, Zürich (reported in *Dawn*, Karachi, 12 March 1948), had asked the Quaid-e-Azam: 'In international affairs, will Pakistan and India work jointly and also join hands for the defence of their borders—both land and sea—and co-operate against any outside aggression?' The Quaid-e-Azam replied:

Personally I have no doubt in my mind that our own paramount interests demand that the Dominion of Pakistan and the Dominion of India should co-ordinate for the purpose of playing their part in international affairs and the developments that may take place, and also it is of vital importance to Pakistan and India, as independent sovereign States, to collaborate in a friendly way jointly to defend their frontiers both on land and sea against any aggression.

But this depends entirely on whether Pakistan and India can resolve their own differences and grave domestic issues in the first instance. In other words, if we can put our house in order internally, then we may be able to play a very great part externally in all international affairs.[1]

In April 1953 Mohammad Ali Bogra, who was then Prime Minister of Pakistan, declared that, once outstanding disputes between the two countries had been settled and a suitable climate created, 'joint defence of India and Pakistan could be advantageously considered by the two countries'. He added that through joint defence, both countries 'would be able to save a lot of defence expenditure which we could usefully employ for the national good and for raising the standard of living of the masses'.[2]

On 24 April 1959 I said that in the case of external aggression both India and Pakistan should come together to defend the sub-continent. The Indian leaders thought that I was suggesting some kind of a defence pact and their reaction was one of fright and distrust. A few days later in Quetta I clarified my proposal, explaining that it did not mean any

---

[1] As reported in *Dawn*, Karachi, 12 March 1948.
[2] *Times of India*, Bombay, 26 April 1953.

special type of pact about which India need be so perturbed. What I had in mind was a general understanding for peace between the two countries. I emphasized that the prerequisite for such an understanding was the solution of big problems like Kashmir and the canal waters. Once these were resolved, the armies of the two countries could disengage and move to their respective vulnerable frontiers. This would give us the substance of joint defence; that is, freedom from fear of each other and freedom to protect our respective frontiers.

Mr. Nehru deliberately chose to misunderstand the proposal and declared in the Lok Sabha on 4 May 1959, 'We do not propose to have a military alliance with any country, come what may.' He elaborated this by saying, 'I am all for settling our troubles with Pakistan and living normal, friendly and neighbourly lives—but we do not want to have a common defence policy which is almost some kind of a military alliance—I do not understand against whom people talk about common defence policies. Are we to become members of the Baghdad Pact or SEATO or somebody else?'[1] Later, in January 1960, Mr. Nehru, while speaking at the annual Congress Party meeting in Bangalore, asked 'What does the military pact mean? Does it mean that armies must march across India?' He then added with some heat, 'Whatever the consequences, India would never allow foreign armies on her soil even for her defence.'[2]

What Mr. Nehru missed completely was that I was neither suggesting any change in the foreign policies of the two countries nor any formal defence arrangement. His vision of Pakistan armies marching over Indian soil on the pretext of defending India's borders was essentially intended to divert public opinion from the real issue, which was to come to a settlement on outstanding disputes and to live on peaceful terms. I kept coming back to this proposal and clarifying it more and more to enable the people of India to recognize its merits. I first tried to assure the Indian leaders that the proposal did not violate the 'nonalignment policy' professed by India. The crux of the proposal, I stated in unequivocal terms, was that, once differences between the two nations were resolved, the Indian and Pakistani forces then facing each other could be released to defend their respective territories.

The Indian Prime Minister, however, refused to see any merit in resolving disputes with Pakistan or living at peace with her. The two countries had been locked in confrontation ever since Independence and their armies were facing each other in Kashmir and on the international borders between India and Pakistan. My proposal was

---

[1] *Dawn*, Karachi, 5 May 1959.
[2] *Morning News*, Karachi, 16 January 1960.

intended to bring home the fact that these armies were in the wrong place: once the disputes were resolved, they could go to their right positions and the people of India and Pakistan would be rid of the fear of each other. There was also in the proposal the inherent possibility that some understanding could be arrived at to ensure that if either country was engaged in war with some third power she would not have the apprehension of being stabbed in the back by the other.

It was not the Indian Prime Minister alone who chose to misunderstand the proposal. There were people in Pakistan, too, who thought it might lead to some kind of a confederation between India and Pakistan. How they came to such a conclusion was beyond me. Only those who had neither knowledge nor appreciation of history could think on these lines. India and Pakistan could never work as a confederation even if such an arrangement were to be brought about by force. And the reason is simple: Indian nationalism is based on Hinduism and Pakistan's nationalism is based on Islam. The two philosophies are fundamentally different from each other. These two nationalisms cannot combine, but it should be possible for them to live side by side in peace and understanding. This is our foreign policy objective towards India. Those who talk of confederation ignore the past history and the temperament of the people, their whole ideology and philosophy. When Sheikh Abdullah and Mirza Afzal Beg came to Pakistan in 1964, they too had brought the absurd proposal of confederation between India, Pakistan, and Kashmir. I told them plainly we should have nothing to do with it. It was curious that whereas we were seeking the salvation of Kashmiris, they had been forced to mention an idea which, if pursued, would lead to our enslavement. It was clear that this was what Mr. Nehru had told them to say to us: I did not blame them because they were obviously acting under the compulsion of circumstances but they left me in no doubt that their future was linked with Pakistan.

I think Pandit Nehru and his people could not believe that I had put forward the proposal in all sincerity; they might have thought I was trying to get a solution of Kashmir on the cheap. What they did not realize was that I was thinking in terms of establishing a long-term basis for peace between the two countries. Of course I wanted the future of the people of Jammu and Kashmir to be decided according to their wishes, but I also wanted a change in India's aggressive attitude and hostility towards Pakistan. I was working for co-existence, for relaxation, and for understanding.

That was not to be. History had offered India and Pakistan a great opportunity. It was missed because the Indian leaders felt they must go on arming themselves regardless of the ruinous burden they were imposing on their people. They decided that they must have not one army but in fact two armies, one for their wars with China and the other to intimidate Pakistan and other smaller neighbours of India. The equation between the two countries, instead of stabilizing at a certain level, was thus destined to have a disturbed and violent future.

III

The equation between the United States of America and Pakistan has been one of close friendship and alliance. This equation was firmly established by the time I became President. I was certainly associated with those elements in it which had a direct bearing on the defence services, but the essential content was determined by the political leaders. My own thinking, at that time, was that it was natural for the United States to be deeply interested in the welfare and safety of smaller powers in Asia. My reasoning was that the Soviet Union and the People's Republic of China, and even India, in spite of her serious internal weaknesses, would like to create and extend their spheres of influence, and it was unlikely that they would be able to agree on the kind and extent of influence that each one of them should exercise. They would, however, be agreed on one thing, and that was not to let the United States, an off-shore power, have any permanent foothold in Asia.

Now, wedged in between these three big countries are a number of small nations starting from Turkey, Iran, Afghanistan, Pakistan, and extending to Nepal, Burma, Malaysia, Indonesia, the Philippines, and Korea. These are strips of geography caught between masses of land and their main concern, quite naturally, is their own security. It was not unreasonable to assume that these smaller nations would be looking for such friends as might help them in protecting themselves. Assuming that the United States, too, wanted to have an area of influence in Asia, it was logical for her to present herself as a natural friend to countries like Pakistan. For some time the United States' policy conformed to this line of thinking, but with the emergence of the People's Republic of China as an Asian power and, more particularly, after the conflict between India and China over the question of border demarcation, the United States' thinking and policies in Asia underwent a complete and fundamental change.

The United States' thinkers and planners developed an anxiety to build up certain countries in Asia as bulwarks against China. They selected Japan and India for this purpose. Building up India meant providing her with vast quantities of military hardware which naturally created a sense of apprehension among her smaller neighbours. Since Pakistan was regarded by India as her enemy number one, Pakistan was the first to be affected by the change in American policy. To Understand the exact significance of this change it is necessary to go over the history of Pakistan–United States relations.

Pakistan became an ally of the West in May 1954, when the Mutual Defence Assistance Agreement with the United States was signed. Later that year Pakistan became a member of SEATO along with the United States, Britain, France, Thailand, the Philippines, Australia, and New Zealand. A year later Pakistan joined the Baghdad Pact, another mutual defence organization, with Britain, Turkey, Iran, and Iraq. The United States did not join this organization but remained closely associated with it from its inception. In 1958, when Iraq left this Pact, it was re-named CENTO (Central Treaty Organization). It continued to comprise Turkey, Iran, and Pakistan, as its regional members. Early in 1959 Pakistan signed (as did Turkey and Iran) a bilateral Agreement of Co-operation with the United States, which was designed further to reinforce the defensive purposes of CENTO. Thus Pakistan was associated with the United States through not one, but four mutual security arrangements. In this sense, she was sometimes regarded as 'America's most allied ally in Asia'. She was the only Asian country to join both SEATO and CENTO.

Pakistan came in for bitter criticism from India when she joined these alliances. India charged that by so doing, 'Pakistan had brought the cold war to the sub-continent'. The real purpose of the Indian out-cry became clear, however, as time advanced, and more particularly when in 1959 Pakistan signed the bilateral Agreement of Co-operation with the United States of America. According to this Agreement, the United States was required, under certain circumstances, to assist Pakistan if she became the victim of aggression. India demanded and, according to Mr. Nehru, received a specific assurance from Washington that this Agreement 'could not be used against India'.[1] Shorn of sophistry, this demand amounted to seeking an assurance that if India should commit aggression against Pakistan, the United States would not come to the assistance of Pakistan under this Agreement. There could not be a more illuminating commentary on India's historic attitude towards Pakistan.

This attitude also explains why India has, throughout, opposed the grant of military aid to Pakistan. Not that she feared Pakistan: after all, India is five times her size and Indian armed forces are four times the size of Pakistani forces. In actual fact the military aid to Pakistan

[1] Nehru speaking in the Indian Parliament, 14 March 1959.

13a Sheikh Mohammad Abdullah, the 'Lion of Kashmir', at a meeting with the author in Rawalpindi soon after his arrival from New Delhi, 24 May 1964

13b At formal talks with His Highness King Zahir Shah of Afghanistan in Kabul, 1 July 1964

14*a* With Mr. Jomo Kenyatta, Prime Minister of Kenya, in London,
6 July 1964

14*b* With President Jamal Cursel of Turkey (centre) and His
Imperial Majesty the Shahinshah of Iran (left) at the summit meeting
in Istanbul, 21 July 1964

was designed to provide merely a deterrent force. There was no question, therefore, of Pakistan posing any kind of threat to India.

I have spoken of India's hostility to Pakistan's alliance with the United States. She had resorted earlier to direct pressure to try to prevent Pakistan from joining it. In August 1953, after bilateral negotiations lasting some months, Nehru and Mohammad Ali Bogra, Pakistan's Prime Minister at that time, issued a joint communiqué on Kashmir. In it, they agreed that: 'It was their firm opinion that this [Kashmir dispute] should be settled in accordance with the wishes of the people of that State. The most feasible way of ascertaining the wishes of the people was by fair and impartial plebiscite.'[1] Further, it was decided that the Plebiscite Administrator should be appointed by the end of April 1954. He would then make such proposals as he thought proper for preparations to be made for the holding of a fair and impartial plebiscite in the entire State.

Shortly after this, Nehru got wind of the fact that Pakistan was likely to enter into alliance with the United States and receive military aid from that country. In a protracted and strongly-worded letter he indicated that if Pakistan went ahead with the project, the Indo-Pakistan agreement on Kashmir would lapse.[2] Mohammad Ali replied that he did not see why any military assistance that Pakistan might receive from the United States for purely defensive purposes should make it less imperative for them to improve India–Pakistan relations by settling the Kashmir dispute. In particular, he did not see why, if Pakistan joined an alliance with the United States, this should disqualify the people of Kashmir from exercising their right, which the United Nations, India, and Pakistan had acknowledged, to a free vote to decide whether their State should accede to India or Pakistan.

In December 1953, although Pakistan had not by then either entered into any pact with the United States or received any military assistance, Mr. Nehru indicated that he could not go forward with the agreements set out in the joint communiqué on Kashmir because 'the whole context in which these agreements were made will change if military aid comes [to Pakistan] from America'.[3] Obviously Pakistan

---

[1] Joint Communiqué by the Prime Ministers of India and Pakistan, 20 August 1953.

[2] 'We, in India, have endeavoured to follow a foreign policy which we feel is not only in the interests of world peace but is particularly indicated for the countries of Asia. That policy is an independent one and of non-alignment with any power bloc. It is clear that the policy which Pakistan intends to pursue is different. It means that Pakistan is tied up in a military sense with the U.S.A. and is aligned to that particular group of powers. This produces a qualitative change in the existing situation and, therefore, it affects Indo-Pakistan relations, and, more especially, the Kashmir problem.' (Nehru's letter of 21 December 1953 to the Pakistan Prime Minister.)

[3] Statement in the Indian Parliament, 23 December 1953.

could not allow Mr. Nehru to dictate her foreign policy. In May 1954 Pakistan went ahead with the signing of the Mutual Defence Assistance Agreement with the United States. From that point on, the fact that the Indian Prime Minister would repudiate the joint communiqué on Kashmir became a foregone conclusion. Pakistan's efforts to save it eventually collapsed when the two Prime Ministers met for the last time in May 1955.

In that same year the alliance with the United States came under still heavier pressure. The Soviet Union reacted when, in 1955, Pakistan joined the Baghdad Pact (now CENTO). Up to that time, the Soviet Union had maintained a neutral stand on the Kashmir dispute; its representatives had abstained from voting whenever the issue came up in the Security Council. But now the Soviet Union charged that, by joining the Baghdad Pact, Pakistan had become a member of 'an aggressive western alliance', and it responded by radically altering its stand on Kashmir. Thenceforth, the Soviet Union began to subscribe to India's claim that no plebiscite was possible or necessary in Kashmir and that Kashmir was an 'integral part' of India.

In contrast, over the last decade, the policies of the United States have undergone a change which has operated progressively to the disadvantage of her ally, Pakistan, vis-à-vis neutral India. When we first joined the alliance with the United States, neutralism—'non-alignment' as India prefers to call it—was suspect in American eyes. It was in fact regarded as 'immoral'; it was another name for 'playing both sides of the street'. Over the years, it has come to assume a mantle of respectability in American eyes. Indeed, in the late fifties it gradually began to be actively supported, in some cases in competition against the Soviet Union. In particular, influential American circles began to advocate 'massive aid' to India.

At the same time, there grew a feeling among the allies of the United States—not in Pakistan only—that, in a variety of ways, they were increasingly being taken for granted. Gradually, as a result of this change in American thinking, neutral India became by far the largest recipient of U.S. economic aid, while she continued freely to castigate the United States in the United Nations and outside, whenever opportunity offered. Pakistan watched this transformation in American foreign policy with increasing perplexity and dismay. Our concern arose from the fact that the Indian military build-up was aimed largely against Pakistan. The pronouncements of Indian leaders and the continuing massing of India's army on Pakistan's borders clearly suggested that.

Until 1962, however, the policy of the United States continued to distinguish between a 'non-aligned' India and the American ally, Pakistan. Although under a Mutual Defence Assistance Agreement signed in 1951 (reaffirmed in 1958), India also was receiving military aid from the United States—without accepting any of the obligations that devolve on an ally—American policy continued generally to maintain, in the matter of direct military aid, a substantial difference between an ally and a neutral. However, this distinction between Pakistan and 'non-aligned' India disappeared after the border disputes between India and China which flared up into an armed clash in 1962.

Despite the fact that over the decade the distinction in American eyes between an ally and a neutral had become increasingly blurred, Pakistan continued steadily to stand by the alliance. Our view has been that, so long as we were in this alliance, we must continue honourably to discharge, as far as we could, whatever obligations devolved on us as a member.

In 1963, however, Pakistan received a new cause for disillusionment with American foreign policy. Following the India–China border clash, the United States proceeded to rush arms to India on a scale which to us seemed totally unjustified by the requirements of the situation. Since then, arms aid has been flowing into India continuously on a very substantial scale, not only from the United States but also in equal measure from Britain and, to a smaller extent, from some other members of the Commonwealth.

People in the United States sometimes ask: is not the military assistance given to India by the U.S.A. meant exclusively for fighting Communist China? Has not India pledged that she will not use these arms against Pakistan? Have not the United States and Great Britain also given assurances that if India employed these weapons in an aggression against Pakistan, they would act to thwart the aggression? Are not these assurances, they ask, sufficient to protect Pakistan against the possible misuse of western arms against her?

Before I proceed to answer these questions, let me briefly recapitulate the facts leading up to the western policy of arming India.

On 12 October 1962 Mr. Nehru announced that he had instructed the Indian army to 'throw the Chinese' out of the disputed areas. This announcement was described by the New York *Herald Tribune* (15 October) as 'tantamount to a formal declaration of war', while the British newspaper, the *Guardian*, called it an 'ultimatum'. That the Indians fired the first shot was suggested by a subsequent report in the *New York Times* of 19 April 1963, which mentioned that 'General Maxwell D. Taylor, Chairman of the Joint Chiefs of Staff, indicated in secret Congressional testimony made public here today that India might have started the border fight with Communist China'. On 20 October 1962 fighting flared up between China and India at a number of points along their disputed border in Ladakh (Kashmir) and in the North-East Frontier Agency (NEFA) area lying east of the state of Bhutan.

What happened subsequently is, however, fairly generally known. During two brief bouts of fighting—the first in October and the second in November—the Indian army met with serious reverses. By 20 November the Indians had surrendered another 2,000 square miles of disputed territory in Ladakh, thus putting the Chinese in control of almost the entire 15,000 square miles of territory which they claimed in that part of Kashmir. In the NEFA area, the military rout of the Indian forces assumed even more serious proportions. By 20 November, not only the entire disputed NEFA territory but even Assam seemed exposed to the rapidly-advancing Chinese forces. Then suddenly, on 21 November, the Chinese declared a cease-fire and offered unilaterally to withdraw to points behind the McMahon Line from the entire territory they had overrun. This undertaking they subsequently fully carried out, offering at the same time to negotiate their border differences with India peacefully. Since then there has been no significant military incident on any part of the entire disputed border.

At Nassau, on 29 December 1962, long after the cease-fire on the India–China border, the United States and Britain decided to continue to supply India, on an emergency basis, with up to 120 million dollars' worth of military aid. The programme included a variety of military equipment, but its central feature was the arming of six Indian divisions for mountain warfare. Arising also from the Nassau decision, a United States–British–Canadian Air Mission visited India to examine what would be India's air needs should China attack again. And another U.S. Mission went out to India to study the question of how to expand India's arms-production capacity. Subsequently, on 30 June 1963, at Birch Grove, the United States and Britain decided on a further substantial programme of military aid to India, over and above that agreed at Nassau. Apart from additional arms, this programme provided for extensive radar communications, air transport and training facilities, as well as for American and British assistance to expand greatly India's own armament production.

India has also been assured that there is no need for her to enter an alliance with the West in order to continue to qualify for military assistance against China. Indeed, she has been given to understand that it is in the western interest that she should continue to remain 'non-aligned' and receive military aid from the Soviet Union as well. Taking advantage of this favourable western response, India decided to raise her standing army from 11 to 22 divisions as rapidly as possible, and to expand substantially her air force and navy—all ostensibly for use against China.

Let us first examine briefly whether the arming of India on this extensive scale is necessary or justified. The American-British military aid programme to India was originally put in motion at a time when the West feared that the India–China conflict might escalate into a major war. From the very outset it has been our view that the fighting was only in the nature of a border conflict. On 5 November 1962, after the first India–China clash, I made a statement to that effect, and expressed concern over the western decision to rush military aid to India on a scale based apparently on an assumption that India was faced with a major war with China. There was no valid basis for this assumption. It made no sense militarily, I said, that China should have decided to launch an invasion of India over the Himalayas at the height of winter. Under the circumstances, it seemed logical to conclude that the Chinese objectives were limited. Later, when I visited China, the highest authority in the country told me that the Sino-Indian conflict on the Tibetan border was the direct outcome of Indian military provocations. A stage had been reached when their Premier and the Chief of Staff could bear it no longer. They therefore decided to hit back. Subsequent events have proved that the Chinese had not planned to embark on a major attack on India. Since then, the Chinese have demonstrated their willingness to settle the dispute peacefully. The Indians, on their part, are anxious to avoid any further fighting with China and have been working steadily for a peaceful settlement. Yet India continues to demand—and receive—an increasing amount of military assistance.

India currently presents three faces to the world: one to the West, simulating a resolve to fight China in order to secure the maximum of western arms assistance; a second to the Soviet Union, stressing her resolve, nevertheless, to remain 'non-aligned'; and a third to China, seeking a peaceful settlement of the dispute by secret peace overtures through neutral emissaries.

It is my belief that the Sino-Indian dispute can and will be resolved peacefully. Therefore, the continuance of military aid to India is unjustified. Even in the unlikely event of a recrudescence of border fighting between China and India, the Indians could not, considering the mountain terrain, deploy more than three to four divisions against the Chinese. One may justifiably ask, then, why is India doubling the size of her standing army to 22 divisions? Even allowing for the necessary reserves, who are the remaining divisions aimed against? The fact of the matter is that, taking advantage of the favourable western response to her demands for arms, India is planning to raise two armies, one with which to face China and the other to use against Pakistan and her other smaller neighbours in pursuance of her expansionist objectives. Any army meant for China would by the nature of things be so positioned as to be able to wheel round swiftly to attack East Pakistan. Thus both the armies pose a grave threat to Pakistan.

Having built up this enormous war machine, India's leadership would need to justify the great hardships it had imposed on the Indian people in the process. It might also want to regain face, which it lost in the fighting with China. It was possible, therefore, that India might decide to do so—as soon as a suitable opportunity offered itself—by throwing her massive armour against Pakistan and possibly striking in the first instance against that part of Kashmir which is under Pakistan's control but which India claims to be 'Indian territory'.[1]

I have tried to recapitulate the events which put under strain the Pakistan–United States equation. It was clear to me even at the time of the Kennedy–Nixon Presidential contest that the United States was out to appease India and to get her in its orbit of political influence by all possible means. If Pakistan did not feel happy about it, it was just too bad and there was nothing that the United States could do.

At the invitation of President Kennedy, I had visited the United States in July 1961. President Kennedy said, in his welcome address, that Pakistan was 'a friend of immediacy and constancy'.[2] He also observed that 'Americans in private and in their public life appreciate the value of friendship and the constancy of friends'. I was heartened by this because the value of friendship rests on reciprocity.

I addressed a Joint Session of the Congress of the United States on 12 July 1961. I explained at some length the basis of the partition of the sub-continent. Our demand for a homeland of our own was based on the realization that we would have no place worth the name in a society which was governed by a rigid caste system. The demand was not based on bigotry or intolerance. It was, in fact, an escape from the bigotry and intolerance to which we had been subjected for decades in the Indian society. We were not wanting to create a priest-ridden society but a liberal and enlightened one in which we should be able to live according to our own ideology and faith. In our society there would

---

[1] The substance of pp. 129–36 is based on an article I wrote on the Pakistan-American alliance, subsequently published in *Foreign Affairs* (Jan. 1964), an American quarterly review. Later events proved how well-founded my fears were.

[2] 11 July 1961, at Andrews Air Force Base.

be no place for colour prejudice or race prejudice. 'We people are, shall we say, colour-blind and race-blind.' I reminded the Congress of their responsibilities and world obligations. There was applause when I said, 'the only people who will stand by you are the people of Pakistan', but, before the applause died down, I added, 'provided— provided you are also prepared to stand by them. So, I would like you to remember that, whatever may be the dictates of your commitments, you will not take any steps that might aggravate our problems or in any fashion jeopardize our security. And as long as you remember that, I have no doubt in my mind that our friendship will grow in strength.'

Throughout my visit, I emphasized the need for bringing about a just and honourable settlement of the Kashmir dispute, without which there could be no peace in the sub-continent. I urged the United States to use their growing influence in India to persuade the Indian leaders to realize the value of living at peace with Pakistan. I was asked by a Pressman how far President Kennedy could go in persuading Mr. Nehru to resolve the Kashmir dispute. My answer was: 'We will see how far he can go. He should be able to go a long way.'[1]

A few days earlier I had a luncheon meeting with the National Press Club in Washington. One of the questions put to me there was: 'How would Pakistan react if arms aid was given to India?' I said, 'We have made our position clear to the United States and indeed to the whole world. We want to live at peace with India. We are stuck on Kashmir. The problem of Kashmir involves the feelings and wishes of the people of Kashmir. It is also a manifestation of India's hostility towards Pakistan. Apart from that there are considerations of economy and security. India does not seem prepared to have peace with Pakistan. India's armed forces are three times our strength, out of which no more than 15 per cent can really face China, the rest are poised against Pakistan. In a situation of this kind, if any arms aid is given to India, Pakistan would feel insecure, and there would be a tremendous ground swell of public opinion in Pakistan against such a move. And it will put a tremendous strain on our friendship with the United States.'

In my meetings with President Kennedy I tried to impress upon him that the situation in the sub-continent could not become stable so long as India and Pakistan remained on inimical terms over Kashmir. I suggested to him that the U.S. Administration was in a decisive position to exert a healthy influence on India in this matter, and that their policy objectives could not be achieved unless there was peace in the Indian sub-continent.

[1] Meet-the-Press, Sunday 16 July 1961.

I also asked President Kennedy about the shift in American policy towards non-aligned countries and how it would affect Pacts like CENTO and SEATO. I told him that regional members would find it difficult to justify their membership of these Pacts in view of the change in American attitude. President Kennedy assured me that he was acutely conscious of the need for collective security. He felt that he had not been correctly understood on the question of aid to 'neutrals'. He was not thinking in terms of abandoning friends and embracing 'neutrals': all he had in mind was that 'neutrals' should not be treated as enemies. He particularly wanted to know how SEATO and CENTO could be strengthened and how the United States could be of assistance in helping to settle the disputes between India and Pakistan.

I also asked him about the U.S. Administration's intentions to enlarge the scope of the Mutual Security Act to include neutral countries. Would that mean giving arms aid to India? I left him in no doubt that such a move would have serious repercussions on public opinion in Pakistan. Already people, not only in Pakistan but from Korea to Turkey, had started wondering whether the United States could distinguish between 'friends' and those who were 'not friends'. I was assured that nothing would be done which might create difficulties for us and that we would be consulted *before* any military aid was given to neutral countries under the amended Act.

I described to President Kennedy the background of the Kashmir dispute at some length. While India and Pakistan faced each other with loaded guns, essential development remained insufficiently cared for. If this dispute could be resolved it would be a great service not only to this region but to the whole world. I told him of my meeting with Nehru in London in May 1960. Nehru had not been particularly responsive when I raised the question of Kashmir with him. I had told Mr. Nehru then that there was a general belief that his attitude towards Kashmir was governed by certain emotional considerations. He had replied that if that were so, the valley could be turned into a kind of Switzerland for him to visit as often as he chose. He also added that his mother came from Lahore, yet he had no emotional involvement with the place.

It was obvious, I told President Kennedy, that Nehru was exploiting the fact that he was in forcible occupation of a large part of Jammu and Kashmir and that to him that was the end of the matter. The point I was trying to get across was that arms assistance to India would only encourage her to remain in occupation of areas which did not belong to her and the prospects of any just settlement of the dispute would be eliminated.

President Kennedy agreed with me that there was urgent need for a solution of the Kashmir problem. But he seemed to think that he was not in a position to play an active and direct role in the matter. He struck me as a preoccupied and lonely man. He had not been long in office and seemed under considerable strain, perhaps because of the Bay of Pigs fiasco. He seemed unsure of his grasp of things and I could see that he was surrounded by too many theoreticians, who are useful people to have but can sometimes divert one from the right and practical course of action. You need to have hard-headed, realistic, and experienced men around you, particularly in times of crisis. President Kennedy mentioned to me that he would like to have a half-hour talk alone with me. He took me by the arm and led me to a seat under a tree on the lawns of the White House. When we sat down he spoke of the Berlin situation and asked me what I would do in similar circumstances. Obviously he did not expect me to give him a solution; all he wanted was to talk about a matter which was causing him considerable worry. I came away with the impression that he was under great stress and could not really open his heart to anyone.

I returned from the United States satisfied in the sense that I had put across my point of view to President Kennedy without any reservation. I could only hope that the United States would realize the dangers inherent in allowing the Kashmir dispute to remain unresolved and would not embark on large-scale supply of arms to India in a hurry.

The United States at that time was beginning to show some concern about the agreement for oil exploration which we were negotiating with the Soviet Union, and the prospects of demarcation of the boundary between Pakistan and China. My position on both these issues was that in view of the changing situation it was important for us to normalize our relations with the Soviet Union and the People's Republic of China. We could not afford to carry unnecessary political burdens.

I have mentioned above certain events during the Sino-Indian conflict in 1962. I think it is necessary to trace the development in greater detail in order to show how the United States reacted to the situation and how we came to a gradual and painful realization that as between India and Pakistan, the United States had chosen India.

The Chinese authorities in Tibet issued an order in July 1959, declaring both Indian and Tibetan currencies illegal. Indian nationals were advised not to enter Tibet in the interest of their own safety. In August 1959 a Chinese force occupied the border post of Longju on the Assam–Tibet border; they also occupied another post in Ladakh. This was followed by an exchange of protest notes between India and China.

In November 1959 Nehru declared: 'I want to disabuse any suspicion that might lurk in some people's minds that we will not be able to defend our integrity if the Chinese invade us. We have confidence in our strength and determination to meet this challenge, and we will meet it with our full strength.' Mr. Chou En-lai suggested to Mr. Nehru that both sides should withdraw their troops 20 kilometres along the entire length of the 2,500-mile border, thus creating a 25-mile demilitarized zone pending 'a friendly settlement of the boundary question'. Mr. Nehru rejected the proposal. The Chinese government, however, issued orders to its frontier units to stop sending out patrols, in order to avoid incidents.

In April 1960 there was a meeting between Mr. Nehru and Mr. Chou En-lai in New Delhi but the talks did not resolve the differences. There followed a series of meetings at the official level. In March 1961 some Chinese nationals were ordered to leave India. Throughout 1961 the relationship between China and India remained under considerable strain. Nehru was beginning to adopt a belligerent attitude. Both sides complained of violations of their airspace and territory. Mr. Krishna Menon, who was Defence Minister, stated in the Lok Sabha on 11 April 1961 that the Indian government had 'taken all necessary steps' to defend the Himalayan borders and that the idea that communist invaders could 'just walk in at any time', was no longer true.

In July 1962 there were two other border incidents. In September 1962 the Chinese proposed, once again, that 'the armed forces of both sides should withdraw 20 kilometres along the entire border in order to ease tension'; the proposal was again rejected by India. Towards the middle of September 1962 there were further border clashes at the eastern end of the Himalayan frontier. The NEFA border remained quiet until 10 October when a serious clash took place at the extreme western end of the McMahon Line. On 13 October the Chinese again called upon Nehru to 'pull back from the brink of the precipice', as, according to them, China was 'absolutely unwilling to cross swords with India'. A week later there was serious fighting in Ladakh. The Chinese did not advance in Ladakh beyond the line claimed by them. In the NEFA the Chinese overwhelmed two outposts. Their attack then developed into a general offensive at both ends of the McMahon Line. In three days the Chinese forces covered some 90 miles, capturing Se La Pass and Bomdila. The Chinese government announced a uni-lateral cease-fire on 21 November 1962, and started withdrawing their forces to positions 20 kilometres behind the line of actual control which existed between India and China on 7 November 1959.

President Kennedy wrote me a letter on 28 October 1962. He expressed alarm at the situation which had arisen as a result of the Sino-Indian conflict and informed me that the United States intended to give the Indians what help they could for India's immediate needs, and to ensure that whatever help they gave to India would be used only against the Chinese. He argued that Pakistan was in a position to make an important move which, according to him, only Pakistan could make, and that was to signal to the Indians, in a quiet but effective way, that the concern, which President Kennedy himself thought totally un-justified but which had led the Indians to maintain the greater part of their militiary power on their borders with Pakistan, should be put aside in that crisis. He suggested that perhaps an effective way would be a private message from me to Nehru telling him that he could count on Pakistan's taking no action on the frontiers to alarm India. President Kennedy emphasized that no possible outside aid could increase the ability of the Indians to withstand the Chinese offensive as much as a shift in their own dispositions. He said he knew the history of Kashmir and was not making the suggestion lightly. He did so in the hope and belief that the painful moments which India was then experiencing would teach them how much more important the threat from the North, as he put it, was to the whole of the sub-continent than any regional quarrels within it. He assured me that action taken by me in the larger interests of the sub-continent would do more in the long run to bring about a sensible resolution of Pakistan-India differences than anything else he could think of.

I give below in full the reply which I sent to President Kennedy on 5 November 1962:

Dear Mr. President:

I am grateful to you for your kind message of October 28, 1962, which was delivered by your Ambassador.

For the last fifteen years, India has posed a major military threat to Pakistan. She has built up her forces, may I say, mainly with American and British equipment three to four times our strength and has openly declared that Pakistan is her enemy number one.

Eighty per cent or more of her Armed Forces have already been ear-marked against us and the bulk of them remain concentrated on our borders on ten days' state of readiness. We have been exposed to these aggressive designs all these years simply because the Indian Prime Minister himself is not prepared to honour his pledge in regard to so many agreements and especially in regard to the solution of Kashmir in which Pakistan is vitally interested for profound economic and security reasons. Therefore, by and large, we have spent these fifteen years in a state of mobilization which has been forced upon us by India. On top of all this, the recent conflict between India and China has led to developments of grave concern to us.

However, our own information, although meagre, leads us to believe that the Chinese intention seems to be to occupy the territory which they believe belongs to them and over which there has been a dispute between her and India. Even Mr. Nehru thought it fit in his wisdom to declare in the Indian Parliament in 1954 with reference to the Chinese position in Tibet that 'I am not aware of any time during the last few hundred years when Chinese sovereignty, or if you like suzerainty, was challenged by any outside country. All during this period, whether China was weak or strong, or whatever the Government of China, China always maintained its claim to sovereignty over Tibet. . . . The British Empire in the days of Lord Curzon had expanded into and made several types of arrangements in Tibet. Now it is impossible or improper for us to continue any such arrangements. . . . These maps and treaties are all prepared by the British Imperialists. These treaties and maps are intended to show that we must act as they did.'

Militarily, however, we do not believe that China can bring to bear against India her major forces through the difficult terrain of the Himalayas to achieve decisive results, and even if she has any such intention the way to do it would be to outflank India through Burma. In our opinion that would be a simpler way of doing it and in cost it would be cheaper. If the Chinese intentions were more than limited and they were to expand into the territories of Assam, we would have as much cause for concern as India, as our East Pakistan would be directly affected. We are making this appreciation about the actual situation in no light-hearted mood.

Why has such a situation developed on this sub-continent and around India? We believe that this is the direct outcome of distorted and fallacious thinking on the part of Mr. Nehru and his associates and a consequence of a baseless foreign policy that he has been following. This foreign policy has been based on the following factors:

(a) bending over backwards to appease communism;
(b) hoist the white flag of neutralism to appease communism and get other wavering nations to join India in order to be able to create a world nuisance-value for themselves;
(c) intimidate and threaten Pakistan in order to politically isolate it and economically weaken it; and
(d) abuse the West, and especially the U.S.A. in season and out of season.

The events have proved that all that is happening to Mr. Nehru is the direct consequence of this warped thinking. We have been warning and pointing to this all along.

Mr. President, what you now ask of us is to give an assurance to Mr. Nehru of a kind that will enable him to deploy his troops, at present concentrated against us, elsewhere. I am surprised that such a request is being made to us. After all, what we have been doing is nothing but to contain the threat that was continuously posed by India to us. Is it in conformity with human nature that we should cease to take such steps as are necessary for our self-preservation? Or, will our own people ever accept such a position?

According to our information, India has withdrawn an infantry division and a half away from us but there are definite indications that they are moving forward their reserve armoured formations of one division and one brigade to battle locations against Pakistan. Similarly, they now have a corps headquarters to control troops deployed against East Pakistan. The bulk of their Navy, barring a couple of small vessels, have been concentrated in Bombay harbour, ostensibly for refit but in reality to pose a threat to us. Under no stretch of imagination, Mr. President, can these moves be described as indications of peaceful intentions towards us by India. So, how can we, in a situation like this, be expected to show our friendship to them?

No, Mr. President, the answer to this problem lies elsewhere. It lies in creating a situation whereby we are free from the Indian threat, and the Indians are free from any apprehensions about us. This can only be done if there is a settlement of the question of Kashmir. This matter is sometimes stated as very difficult to resolve. I do not agree with that. I believe that if there is a change of heart on the part of India, it should not be difficult to find an equitable and an honourable settlement.

Our object is to have peace, and especially with our neighbours. I am very grateful for the assurance you have given that the arms you are now supplying to India will not be used against us. This is very generous of you, but knowing the sort of people you are dealing with, whose history is a continuous tale of broken pledges, I would not ask a friend like you to place yourself in an embarrassing situation. India's conduct over the question of Junagadh, Mangrol, Hyderabad, Kashmir and Goa should be well-known to you. Our belief is that the arms now being obtained by India from you for use against China will undoubtedly be used against us at the very first opportunity. However, in the light of the promise that you were good enough to make, namely, that we shall be consulted before you gave any military assistance to India, we did expect to be consulted and also informed as to the types and the quantities of weapons and equipment which are now in the process of being supplied to them. It is regrettable that none of this has been done.

I would also like to draw your attention to the fact that although India today poses as an aggrieved and oppressed party, in reality she has been constantly threatening and intimidating, in varying degrees, small neighbouring countries around her. Let me assure you that in the eyes of many people in Asia, Indian intentions are suspect and the Indian image as a peace-loving nation has been destroyed.

You have referred, Mr. President, to press comments in Pakistan. While we have endeavoured to restrain expression of extremist views in our newspapers, it is not possible to interfere with the freedom of the press which reflects the real sentiment of the people. It must be realized that public opinion is gravely exercised by the new developments as the result of arms aid to India, more so, as India continues to pose a serious threat to our security. I am afraid it is going to be extremely difficult for my Government to discount public opinion.

With kind regards,

Yours sincerely,
Signed:
Mohammad Ayub Khan.

The *New York Times* carried a despatch in its issue of 31 October 1962 on President Kennedy's letter to me. The despatch indicated that the letter was sent to me at the same time as President Kennedy sent a letter to Mr. Nehru, 'assuring him of United States' support and sympathy in his country's battle against China'. The despatch further said that, 'United States officials are said to be aware of Pakistan's misgivings about any increase in India's military potential, but it is the hope in Washington that Marshal Ayub's Government will understand the motives of American military aid. It is also hoped here that the Pakistanis will not make any new move now in their long-standing dispute with India over Kashmir.'

On the same day the *Washington Post* editorial suggested that,

rude as the Indian awakening has been, it is not yet clear that the great Asian power is fully alert to its peril. While it casts about for military re-sources to meet the Chinese onslaught, it still has not felt sufficiently en-dangered to draw upon military strength immediately at hand. While its military forces engaging the Chinese fall back because they are outnumbered and ill-equipped, the bulk of the powerful Indian Army faces the Pakistan frontier, immobilized, tied down, sterile. . . . There is no help that the Western world can give the sub-continent that would be as useful as the help that India and Pakistan could give themselves by settling the quarrel [over Kashmir]. . . .

There was a section of the U.S. Press that warned the U.S. Administration of the danger of blindly giving arms aid to India. The *Philadelphia Enquirer* wrote editorially on 30 October 1962:

Nevertheless, there is good reason not to rush in blindly, handing out largess we can't afford or weapons which might shortly be turned about and aimed at the Free World. This country has already given India billions of dollars' worth of economic aid, while that country, starting in 1947 with Junagadh and Kashmir, engaged in a long list of military adventures against weaker peoples, conquest of Goa being only the latest. In none of these cases did India call upon the United Nations or permit the peoples involved to voice their personal desires through plebiscite. Pakistan, one victim of Indian policy, is now understandably alarmed at the idea of massive gifts of arms to its neighbour. . . . Prime Minister Nehru's reputed desire to 'pay for the weapons' should be encouraged in so far as it is not an excuse to con-tinue on a path of aggression in the name of non-alignment or so-called neutrality.

Our Ambassador to the United States had a meeting with a State Department official on 2 October 1962. He inquired about the kind of arms aid the Indians had asked for from the United States. He was told that the Indians had not yet specified their requirements for arms but that Mr. Nehru had seen Ambassador Galbraith in New Delhi that very morning and had asked him for United States arms aid against China. Ambassador Galbraith, on the authority of the United States government, had informed Mr. Nehru that the United States would give arms aid to India, and that it was for Mr. Nehru to indicate his requirements. The United States had already agreed to stand aside in the matter of priority for two Caribou transport aircraft the Indians wanted to acquire from the Canadians.

Our Ambassador recalled the assurance given by President Kennedy to me that Pakistan would be consulted *before* any decision was taken on the question of giving arms to India. Obviously, the United States government had ignored two very important points, that their decision to give arms aid to India was arrived at *without prior consultation* with Pakistan; and it was communicated to India *before* it was communicated to Pakistan. The Ambassador expressed the hope that Pakistan would be consulted before decisions were taken regarding the terms and volume of aid and the type of equipment to be supplied to India. He was told that military aid might be provided to India either under lend-lease, against payment in local currency, or against deferred payment.

It was conveyed to our Ambassador that the United States was anxious to act without any loss of time. They regarded the Chinese move as the biggest since Korea. In Korea the U.S. decision had been taken with great rapidity and the same speed was necessary to meet the present situation. The Indians had taken five years to wake up to the Chinese reality and their illusions had now been shattered. The United States was anxious to give full support to India, subject, of course, to receiving suitable assurances that the arms would be used only against China.

In another meeting in the State Department, the following day, our Ambassador was informed that a specific request for arms aid had been received from Mr. Nehru. The request consisted of two lists: one contained items for delivery over a period of 120 days, and the other contained items which were required immediately and would be air-lifted. The equipment was to be given to the Indians for rupees which would be deposited in a fund and used as in the case of the PL-480 programme. A provision was also being worked out for a waiver for the initial shipment. The requirements indicated by the Indians were intended to meet the specific combat situation plus related reserves. The United States aim was to provide immediately material to stiffen Indian combat capability. Our Ambassador was advised that the U.S. arms would not be used by India against Pakistan and that he should 'take the United States' word for it'. He was also told that Pakistan need have no anxiety regarding a situation of imbalance developing in the sub-continent as a result of the supply of arms to India. He was advised that Pakistan should forget the past and make a gesture of goodwill and co-operation towards India. Such a gesture would make a tremendous impact on India and her attitude would, undoubtedly, soften towards Pakistan. And who knew that this might not lead to a satisfactory solution of the Kashmir problem. That, in brief, was the American point of view.

It was obvious that the United States had decided to give long-term arms assistance to India, apart from providing emergency relief. It was also clear that while the United States wanted to see an amicable settlement of the Kashmir dispute between India and Pakistan, they were not prepared to use their full influence directly lest India should feel that she was being subjected to pressure. The U.S. attitude, in fact, was that India should have all sympathy and support and that Pakistan would be well advised not to raise any difficulties.

Mr. Nehru wrote me a letter on 27 October 1962 in which he gave me his version of the dispute that had arisen between India and China on the question of border demarcation. I sent him the following reply on 5 November:

It is a matter of great regret to us that this dispute should have led to intensified military activities and induction of new war potential, thus endangering the peace and stability of the region in which Pakistan is vitally concerned.

I agree with you when you say that no effort should be spared to eliminate deceit and force from international relations. In this respect I am constrained to point out that various outstanding disputes between India and Pakistan can also be resolved amicably should the Government of India decide to apply these principles with sincerity and conviction.

We in Pakistan are pledged to a policy of peace and friendly relations with all neighbouring countries, especially India. We have accepted this course for we believe this is the only method through which we can pursue the gigantic tasks of economic and industrial development which must be carried forward in the interest of the prosperity and well-being of the people.

Mr. Harold Macmillan sent me a message through his High Commissioner on 25 October 1962. A few days later I received a similar message from the Australian Prime Minister, Mr. R. G. Menzies. To both of them I replied in very much the same terms as I had replied to Mr. Kennedy's letter, repeating especially my reasoned belief that the Chinese were not undertaking a full-scale military invasion of India. I was hoping that the western countries would take our point of view into account before embarking on large-scale supplies of arms to India, but it seemed that in their anxiety to rush to help her with arms and ammunition they were neither willing to accommodate us nor to take

15a With the Indonesian President, Dr. Soekarno, at the President's
Guest House, Rawalpindi, 19 September 1964

15b With Chairman Liu Shao-chi and Chairman Mao Tse-tung
at the N.P.C. Hall, Peking, 4 March 1965

16a   With His Imperial
Majesty the Shahinshah of
Iran at Mehrabad Airport,
1 July 1964

16b   Welcoming Mr.
Chou En-lai, Premier of
the State Council of the
People's Republic of
China, on his arrival at
Chaklala Airport, Rawal-
pindi, 2 June 1965

the long-term view of the serious imbalance which their action would create in the sub-continent.

There was a definite attempt, I think, to panic India into believing that there was going to be an attack by China with 25 to 30 divisions through Burma and over Tibet. Mr. Nehru, who had started talking about 'a long fight' with China, convinced himself that a Chinese invasion was inevitable. It suited him to talk about such a possibility.

How much interference there was from Delhi in the conduct of the battles I cannot say, but such interference is always fatal. A commander in the field must be carefully chosen, then given his task and left alone to carry it out in the manner he considers best. General Kaul, the Indian Army Commander on the north-eastern front, was a supply and transport officer and had no experience of serious fighting. An Indian Brigade was put right out on the forward slopes of the Se La Pass, in full view of the Chinese. No experienced commander would have done such a thing. The Chinese made a frontal demonstration against this Brigade and then went round it. Kaul panicked and ordered the rear Brigade to move forward in support. When this happened the Chinese made a second encircling movement and got into the trenches that the rear Brigade had left. When the rear Brigade found they could not break through the cordon of Chinese surrounding the forward Brigade, they turned about in an attempt to return to their original dispositions. They found to their utter astonishment their trenches occupied by the Chinese. They broke to avoid destruction, and, in the meantime, the Chinese made another encircling movement, and entered the plains of Assam, where the civil population fled in panic. By this time the Indian Army itself was on the run and had ceased to be a fighting force. Given better leadership, correct dispositions, and reserves held for counter-attacks on the flanks, the results might not have been so disastrous.

The Chinese fought most skilfully under brilliant leadership. Of course, they are much tougher people than the Indians and are used to soldiering in that climate. The mere fact of living in Tibet at a height of about 18,000 feet is a great advantage. But the fact remains that despite this talk of 25 to 30 Chinese divisions, which was nothing but a figment of Indo-U.S. imagination, the Chinese had no more than 6 to 7 light divisions in the entire area and in the limited area of NEFA they brought to bear against the Indian Army not more than one or one and a half divisions in any given sector. Yet, fighting with remarkable skill, they made rings round the Indians.

But let me not denigrate the Indian soldier, for some of them are as good as any in the world. They were badly served. Had they been better led they would have given a more satisfactory account of themselves.

IV

The Indians believed that they would soon be facing a full-fledged invasion by China. In this view they were encouraged by the United States. The result was the arms rush, of formidable magnitude. The United States thought that all that need be done for Pakistan, in consideration of past understanding and alliance, was to give some kind of an assurance that their arms would not be used against Pakistan and to prepare the ground for direct talks between India and Pakistan to resolve the Kashmir dispute.

The public assurance came in the form of a State Department release, on 17 November 1962:

> The Department of State released today the text of Exchange of Notes concerning the provision of defence assistance by the Government of the United States of America to the Government of India. In the Exchange of Notes it is stated that the assistance will be furnished for the purpose of defence against outright Chinese Communist aggression now facing India.
>
> In 1954 when the United States decided to extend military aid to Pakistan, the Government of India was assured that if our aid to any country, including Pakistan, was misused and directed against another in aggression, the United States would undertake immediately, in accordance with constitutional authority, appropriate action both within and without the United Nations to thwart such aggression.
>
> The Government of the United States of America has similarly assured the Government of Pakistan that, if our assistance to India should be misused and directed against another in aggression, the United States would undertake immediately, in accordance with constitutional authority, appropriate action both within and without the United Nations to thwart such aggression.
>
> Needless to say in giving these assurances the United States is confident that neither of the countries which it is aiding harbors aggressive designs.

President Kennedy himself issued a statement on 2 November 1962, saying, 'In providing military assistance to India, we are mindful of our alliance with Pakistan. All of our aid is for the purpose to defeat Chinese communist subversion. Our help to India in no way diminishes or qualifies our commitment to Pakistan and we have made it clear to both governments as well.'

In arranging direct talks between India and Pakistan, Mr. Duncan Sandys, then Secretary of State for Commonwealth Relations in the U.K. Government, and Mr. Averell Harriman, U.S. Assistant Secretary of State for Far Eastern Affairs, played a significant role. The following joint statement was issued by the Government of India and the

Government of Pakistan over the signatures of Nehru and myself on 29 November 1962:

The President of Pakistan and the Prime Minister of India have agreed that a renewed effort should be made to resolve the outstanding differences between their two countries on Kashmir and other related matters so as to enable India and Pakistan to live side by side in peace and friendship.

In consequence, they have decided to start discussions at an early date with the object of reaching an honourable and equitable settlement.

These will be conducted initially at the ministerial level. At the appropriate stage direct talks will be held between Mr. Nehru and President Ayub.

Signed:	Signed:
M. A. Khan.	J. L. Nehru.
F.M.	29.11.62
29.11.62.	7.10 p.m.

Hardly had the joint statement been signed when Nehru made some observations in the Lok Sabha which strengthened my doubts about his intention to enter into any meaningful and constructive talks about the Kashmir dispute. Mr. Duncan Sandys was shown the text of Nehru's observations on 30 November, when he arrived in Karachi from New Delhi on his way back to London. He was so surprised that he decided to fly back to Delhi to clear the matter up. From the airport he drove straight to the Prime Minister's house and caught Nehru as he was going to bed.

Nehru first tried to show that he did not seem to understand what all the fuss was about. He said that he had made his statement as he always did without a prepared text. His remarks had been made in answer to a question of which he had had little notice, about a rumour on the B.B.C. which suggested that the idea of partitioning Kashmir was already under discussion. He added that it was wrong to read too much into particular phrases. He did not like the idea of making any statement which could be interpreted as a retraction. However, at Mr. Duncan Sandys's suggestion, he agreed that some statement might be worked out which, while not involving any eating of words, would put a more favourable construction on what he had said and would help to allay some other doubts which his statement in the Lok Sabha had aroused. The result was the following statement by Nehru on 1 December 1962:

There has never been any question of pre-conditions or of any restrictions on the scope of the talks which the two governments are initiating. As I indicated yesterday in the Lok Sabha, the problem of Kashmir is complicated and difficult. But I am sure that with goodwill on both sides it should be possible to work out an honourable and equitable solution of this as of other problems.

In the meantime, Nehru had sent another urgent request for military assistance to the United States. Twelve C-130 military transport planes were sent to India by the United States on 20 November 1962. Further assistance in the form of mountain-warfare equipment followed. The planes were to be used for transporting supplies within the Indian territories, and would perform 'priority tasks' in connection with the formation of fresh defensive positions by the Indians in the NEFA area.

The military situation looked dismal from the Indian point of view at that time. The Chinese were moving rapidly at both ends of the valley in the NEFA area; major parts of the Indian forces in the NEFA area—one to one and a half divisions—had been rendered ineffective. It appeared that the Chinese might take Tezpur, Jorhat, and Digboi. A high-level team comprising officials from the Pentagon and the State Department and a representative of the White House came to India in the third week of November to assist the U.S. Embassy there in 'assessing Indian needs' and to advise 'on relevant policy considerations'. The American assessment at that time was that if the Chinese moved into India beyond the disputed territory, the conflict would no longer remain 'only India's business': it would become 'something more than that'.

It was in this situation that Nehru had signed the joint statement under which India and Pakistan were to make renewed efforts to resolve the Kashmir dispute. Within weeks of the unilateral declaration of a cease-fire by China, the Indian attitude changed completely and the talks, which had never held much promise, got bogged down in procedural wrangles and academic inanities.

President Kennedy and Prime Minister Macmillan intimated to me the extent of the arms they were supplying to India. I wrote to President Kennedy on 2 January 1963:

> Only a speedy and just Kashmir settlement can give us any assurance that the contemplated increase of India's military power is not likely to be deployed against Pakistan in future.

> I agree completely with your judgement that no single step could contribute as much to the security of the sub-continent as the resolution of the Kashmir problem. Despite the discouraging and provocative utterances of Mr. Nehru on the subject, we are pursuing our sincere efforts to negotiate with India a solution which would meet three requirements: respect of the wishes of the people of Jammu and Kashmir; protection of the vital interests of Pakistan; and due regard for such claims of India as can be considered legitimate.

> It is only with reference to these three basic criteria that a correct judgement can be made as to the one-sidedness or otherwise of the intransigence which India is very likely to show in the negotiations.

To Prime Minister Harold Macmillan I wrote on the same day:

My dear Prime Minister,

I thank you for your message of December 24th. Sir Morrice James has also explained to me the extent of the military assistance which you and President Kennedy have decided, at your Nassau meeting, to extend to India.

The extent of the military assistance which Britain and the United States have decided to extend to India for the present without making it contingent on a Kashmir settlement, gives us cause for great concern. The Nassau decision based on the assessment of your military experts, may seem, in the context of your global strategy, to be the minimum aid necessary to enable India to defend itself from an attack through NEFA and Ladakh. We on the other hand find it hard to believe that any invasion of the sub-continent is likely to occur from these directions and consequently the quantum of military support to India, quantitative as well as qualitative, which you will be extending is fraught with serious consequences to the maintenance of the present ratio of military strength in the sub-continent and hence to the security of Pakistan.

I have always held the view that the most effective way of safeguarding the security of the sub-continent is through a disengagement of the armed forces of the two countries. A Kashmir settlement will assure to both the substance of disengagement. Without a settlement, sizeable military aid to India is more likely to be deployed against Pakistan than for the defence of the north-east or the western sectors of India's frontier with China.

We have kept the British High Commissioner informed of the talks that took place a few days ago at the level of ministers in Rawalpindi. This meeting was purely exploratory. The real test of India's intentions regarding Kashmir will come in the next ministerial meeting in New Delhi about the middle of January.

Pakistan's attitude will not be rigid. I have instructed my delegation to be guided by three basic principles in its approach towards possible solutions that may be discussed:

(i) whether the solution is likely to be acceptable to the people of Jammu and Kashmir;
(ii) whether it safeguards the vital interests of Pakistan; and
(iii) whether it meets the legitimate claims of India.

I have no illusions that any formula which satisfies these three requirements will not be beset with difficulties; but if India sincerely desires an end to the dispute, and given goodwill on both sides, there is no reason why the two countries should not be able, with the assistance of Britain and the United States, to reach an equitable and honourable settlement within the next month or two.

Public opinion in Pakistan is such that while I am willing to exercise due patience, I will find it extremely difficult to convince the people of the virtue of this quality if one round of discussion after another does not open the way to a solution.

I remain convinced that the key to a just and peaceful settlement lies with you and President Kennedy. If the flow of your arms supply is so regulated as to influence India to be in a more amenable frame of mind, positive results are bound to follow from negotiations now under way.

With best wishes for your health, happiness and prosperity in the New Year.

Yours sincerely,
Signed:
Mohammad Ayub Khan.

I recall that during this period the Chinese Ambassador called on me one morning. This was after China had declared the cease-fire. He had been instructed to convey to me that inspired statements were being made in certain quarters to create doubts in the minds of Pakistanis about the Chinese attitude towards the Kashmir settlement. He assured me that the Chinese Government would be very glad if an honourable settlement were to be reached between India and Pakistan.

I do not have to go over the details of the negotiations which followed between India and Pakistan. It was the same old story. The Indians were playing for time. They had been able to secure a great deal of arms aid from the West and a joint statement promising talks on Kashmir did not seem too big a price to them. We had known all along that without direct U.S. interest India would not budge an inch, but the United States thought that in existing circumstances a direct U.S. role in the talks would not be productive. The great opportunity which history had offered for a settlement of the Jammu and Kashmir dispute was thus lost. Once the United States and other western countries had decided that they would not link arms aid to India with a settlement of the Kashmir dispute, the Indians were under no compulsion to enter into any serious discussion with Pakistan.

I had a meeting with General Maxwell Taylor in December 1963. He mentioned the American desire to station a nuclear task force in the Indian Ocean. I said that the U.S.A. was free to do what it liked on the high seas, but I could not understand what military or political advantage they would get from such a move. They were in a position to achieve their objectives from their existing locations. Where was the need to add another element of tension in the Indian Ocean littoral? Politically, the move would be most unpopular and countries in Africa and Asia would strongly resent it. So far as Pakistan was concerned, such a force would only add to her problems and encourage India to act in an even more irresponsible manner.

There was at that time, as I have mentioned, a bilateral arrangement between the U.S.A. and Pakistan under which the U.S.A. was to come to Pakistan's assistance should the latter be subjected to attack from any quarter. On several occasions proposals were made by the U.S.A. to fly out a task force to Pakistan. We wanted to know whether such a force would carry out a contingency plan with us in which our combined forces would have a definite role to play. The Americans would not agree to this; all they wanted was to demonstrate to us their ability to fly out to Pakistan from far-off bases. In this we were not interested. Since they did not agree to participate in the kind of exercise we had suggested, we felt that no useful purpose would be served by having a U.S. task force come to Pakistan for any exercise. By this time it was becoming clear to us that, in the event of India attacking us, it was most unlikely that the U.S.A. would honour its commitment and come to our assistance.

10

Foreign Policy II

I have mentioned earlier that Pakistan was the only Asian country which joined both SEATO and CENTO. I have a feeling that the reasons why we joined these Pacts are not always fully understood, even in Pakistan. The crux of the problem from the very beginning was the Indian attitude of hostility towards us: we had to look for allies to secure our position. Then there was the strong desire which has always existed in Pakistan that we should forge closer relations with our neighbours in the Middle East and particularly with other Muslim countries, not only because of the existence of common bonds of faith but because we have an identity of attitudes and values and we share the same historical experience and face similar problems.

The Baghdad Pact was sponsored by the United States. Originally the United States was willing to come into the Pact as a full member. The strong reaction of President Nasser, however, made her change her mind and she decided to participate only as an observer. The American interest in the Pact was well known; they wanted to establish a counterpoise to communism in the Middle East. It was this fear of communism that had impelled the Christian world to help the Muslim world, for the first time in history. The Muslim world occupied an area which was vital strategically and economically and that was the reason why the United States and other western countries thought it worth their while to befriend the Muslims. The Muslim world itself was at that time emerging from the domination of western powers. It needed material assistance and also time and the technical know-how to develop its human and material resources. There was no reason why we should not have taken advantage of the opportunity. For us, our own needs for development were paramount and that was the reason we joined the Pacts.

There is no doubt that if a larger number of countries in the Middle East had come into the Baghdad Pact it would have provided an excellent opportunity and a unique platform for the Muslim countries to get to know one another and to co-ordinate their policies and plans. The Muslims had no forum and the Baghdad Pact offered a promise of becoming a powerful forum where the Muslim peoples could explore areas of co-operation.

It was a great misfortune that the Arab countries did not take kindly to the idea. One can understand the reasons why they were suspicious of the Pact right from the beginning: they had suffered at the hands of imperialists and the misadventure of Suez by the British and the French, supported by the Israelis, did not help to soften the Arab attitude towards the alliance. They were not prepared to trust any form of association in which the British had any interest. I visited Cairo in November 1960. There was a rally of the National Union. I said during my address that Pakistan's representatives may have acted in a 'clumsy' manner at the time of the Suez crisis but every sensible man in Pakistan had been deeply distressed by the invasion and their sympathies were all with Egypt. As Commander-in-Chief of the Pakistan Army I had approached the government at that time and warned them about the possibility of Egypt being attacked by Britain in conjunction with others. My anxiety was that the Egyptian authorities should be alerted and something done to avert the disaster. While Pakistan has always supported Arab causes, and the U.N. records are available to prove this, Pakistanis have reason to feel aggrieved that they do not always get support from the Muslim world in their own struggle.

Another reason for Pakistan joining the Baghdad Pact was the appreciation that the Middle East was a vulnerable area, containing vast natural resources which could become a source of conflict between the Soviet Union and the western world. Once such a conflict started, it would spread to our borders and seriously endanger our security. It was natural that we should have been deeply interested in associating with any arrangement for the defence and security of this area. We also hoped that through this Pact we would get a certain measure of protection against Indian designs in the Middle East. Our neighbours would get to know our problems and understand more closely the threat from India to which we were exposed. Through this process we should be able to get their sympathy and support.

To sum up, our objective in joining the Baghdad Pact was to secure our position and to contribute to the general consolidation and stability of the entire region, particularly of the Muslim world. We wanted to promote peace and stability, but some of the Arab countries felt that we were there to serve the interests of western powers. Now, I do not deny that the objectives which the western powers wanted the Baghdad Pact to serve were quite different from the objectives we had in mind. But we never made any secret of our intentions or our interests.

I do not know whether we could have convinced the Arab countries of our *bona fides* if we had tried harder, but it is a matter of great pity that what could have been a powerful Muslim forum was undermined by the Arab attitude, however understandable that attitude might have been. Our objectives in the Pact did not run counter to Arab objectives and, in fact, this get-together under the auspices of the Baghdad Pact might have proved much more effective than the Arab League. As it was, we were misunderstood and even accused of indulging in divisive activities in the Arab world. It was alleged that we had enticed Iraq into the western sphere of influence. Now there was nothing that we could have gained by dividing the Arab world. How would it help our national interests? It pains us to see the Arab world divided. The Baghdad Pact was not the cause of this division; had it been so, the breach would have been repaired after Iraq left the Baghdad Pact. Our action was designed not to divide the Arab world but to bring all Muslims, including the Arabs, together on a common platform.

Another major loss we suffered in joining the Pact was that we were deprived of the opportunity to understand the Soviet Union earlier. The Russians were our neighbours and, as later events proved, we would have been able to understand each other better if some contact had been established between us. Because of the absence of any contact, many misunderstandings cropped up and the leaders of the Soviet Union decided to give full support to India. This more than nullified whatever economic and military advantages we gained from the Pact.

But it is not all a negative story. A major benefit of the Pact was the association and friendship which we were able to develop with the governments and peoples of Iran and of Turkey. It was on the basis of this association and friendship that we were finally able to evolve the scheme of Regional Co-operation for Development. People in Iran and Turkey came to believe in our sincerity as we learnt to appreciate theirs.

Another indirect and paradoxical advantage of the Baghdad Pact was that we came to realize the disadvantages and dangers inherent in any political or military alliances of a regional character. I worked out the concept of RCD on two assumptions: the first was that, irrespective of size, each member should have an equal say in any regional alliance. Any arrangement in which there is a dominant partner would run into difficulties. The second assumption was that we should exclude politics and military affairs as far as possible. I believe that if an alliance is restricted, at least in the initial stages, to collaboration in the economic and cultural fields and in the field of development, it can establish a firm base of understanding on which it may be possible to raise a lasting structure.

When I put the RCD idea to His Imperial Majesty the Shahinshah of Iran and to President Gürsel and Prime Minister Inönü of Turkey, they received it most graciously. I am not suggesting that they found the idea so convincing that they agreed to adopt it the moment they heard of it. Their own circumstances had led them to believe that a regional understanding was a necessity. Small countries living in isolation have no place in the world today; they have got to collaborate with one another to command respect and to offer a strong and viable front. We were not unconscious of our internal limitations. Turkey, for example, is placed in a strategic position. It is an associate of the European Common Market and has to rely heavily on NATO. But even within our limitations we discovered that there was a large enough area for co-operation. But for the Baghdad Pact we would not have had the necessary experience of each other which helped us to evolve the RCD pattern of association.

The other Pact that we joined was the South-East Asia Treaty Organization. I do not quite know the reasons that prompted the Government of Pakistan to join this Organization: one must really ask Chaudhry Zafrullah Khan, who was then Foreign Minister. We soldiers were not consulted; I think we learnt of it in the General Head-quarters after the Foreign Minister had already signed the Pact. Even at that time I thought that Pakistan had no reason to join SEATO at all. Perhaps the main consideration was to oblige the United States, who had been giving us considerable economic help. Beyond that I really did not see any purpose in our being a member. If anyone thought that membership of this Organization would in any way strengthen the position of the eastern part of Pakistan, then he was obviously overlooking the fact that the real danger to East Pakistan was from India which surrounded it on all sides.

Both the SEATO and CENTO Pacts have lost much of the value they had, though they still retain some kind of a formal significance. One of the reasons why these Pacts have lost relevance is that we now have bilateral arrangements with most countries, including the United States; though the value of these arrangements, too, is doubtful. The only real value these Pacts still have is that some of the member countries might feel it their duty to express their sympathy for another member in times of difficulty; but as far as their military value is concerned, I think they are more an irritant than a help. I doubt if it would do anybody very much harm if both these Pacts were done away with. For the present, no member country wants to take the blame for breaking the arrangement. The United States, for all their dislike of the Pacts, would not snuff them out because they would not want to give the impression that they were withdrawing their interest from this area. Such an impression would create a vacuum which other bigger powers would like to fill.

The Pacts do offer some kind of a façade and give the United States a measure of political influence. While these considerations might weigh with the United States, I think there is increasing consciousness of the fact that these regional arrangements are no longer realistic in present-day conditions. The change in the American attitude towards the Soviet Union has certainly reduced CENTO to an anachronism.

II

I have recounted how the years between 1960 and 1964 caused us grave concern with regard to our relations with the United States. I had the feeling that the United States was allowing its policies to be determined by events and that the changes it was introducing were affecting the confidence of people in the moral content of U.S. policies and programmes. People in Pakistan were becoming disillusioned; a relationship which had been built up after a great deal of hard work during the fifties was ceasing to command respect. We could not ignore the growing military strength of India and we could not rely on the United States coming to our assistance if India were to embark on aggression against us. We had no means of preventing the United States from following a policy that we knew could only weaken its position in Asia in the long run. The U.S. government's whole thinking was dominated by the fear of China and they were desperately clinging to the prospect of India providing an answer to what they regarded as the Chinese threat.

We reasoned with the United States as I have tried to show in the previous chapter, but we got no response. We could not even convince them that so long as relations between India and Pakistan remained what they were, there could be no stability or peace on the subcontinent. I think the British were more conscious of the need for bringing about an agreement between India and Pakistan, but they had very little leverage in terms of economic and military influence. It was the United States alone that had the requisite influence but it declined to exercise it. I have a feeling that the armed forces in the United States were more sympathetic to our point of view, but they were not in a position to influence the planners in the State Department. We remained extremely careful throughout this period of stress and strain not to do anything which would give unnecessary offence or provocation to the United States. But we could not afford to ignore our national interests and we therefore had to take certain steps to normalize our relations with our neighbours. It is possible that this peeved the State Department who could not reconcile themselves to the idea that Pakistan should be acting in the field of foreign affairs without their permission. Some among them may have thought that the United States had given substantial aid to Pakistan and, even though the circumstances might have changed, Pakistan had no right to protect herself and ensure her security in whatever manner she thought fit and proper.

This is the only way in which I can explain the attempts that were made by the United States to put the squeeze on Pakistan. What they did not realize was that no government in Pakistan worth the name could have ignored the very real danger posed by India and allowed the security of the country to rest on flimsy assurances and paper guarantees. Also, I think the United States did not quite realize the extent to which the people of Pakistan would be prepared to accept economic distress and hardship for the sake of the honour and integrity of their country. People in developing countries seek assistance, but on the basis of mutual respect; they want to have friends not masters. We knew of the U.S. relationship with China but the U.S., too, must recognize our political and geographical compulsions.

It was only after our compulsions were understood and recognized by the United States that our relationship was re-established on the basis of a new understanding. In normalizing our relations with the People's Republic of China and the Soviet Union we were not going into the communist orbit with all its concomitants of military alliances. The process of normalization followed clearly defined limits.

III

The Americans thought that as a result of the conflict between India and China something important and fundamental had happened in Asia. The shock of the conflict and the Indian defeat had altered India's orientation. Before this conflict, India had no military policy except in relation to Pakistan, but now India had suddenly come to believe that she had a long-range enemy in China. The shift in Indian orientation was, for the United States, one of major importance. In the short run it put America in a position of leverage on the question of arms aid to India and all its military build-up. India had been forced to review her political philosophy in the realm of international affairs. Events had shown that she must establish closer economic and military ties with the United States in the interest of her own security. From the U.S. point of view, India had been awakened from slumber by China. The United States could not afford to lose this opportunity to bring about a better balance in Asia.

The Americans interpreted the Chinese move as something pregnant with ominous possibilities. They thought that in order to consolidate their hold on Tibet, the Chinese were looking towards the Himalayan kingdoms of Nepal, Bhutan, and Sikkim, as well as towards the NEFA region.

Also, there were indications that the Soviets and the Chinese had had profound differences. Evidence of this was provided by the closing of Soviet consulates in China, the reduction in Soviet economic aid to the Chinese, and the Soviet demand for payments on schedule. A dialectical argument of considerable seriousness was also going on between the Soviet Union and the People's Republic of China. All evidence pointed to a deep division in the communist camp. The Chinese had been expected to produce the atom bomb in 1962, but this was delayed owing to a variety of factors, including the failure of the Chinese agricultural programme. From all this the United States experts inferred that the Chinese were in sore need of victories and successes to counter-balance these failures. They would, therefore, want to make something important out of their conflict with India. The Chinese wanted to establish a good position along the Himalayan border region. This area was 'softer' than the off-shore islands of South-East Asia. Working on this hypothesis, the American planners came to the conclusion that the Chinese would attack India again over the Himalayas and the eastern Assam border, based on Tibet and Burma respectively.

To me the whole thing looked a military absurdity. Conquest of even a portion of India in Ladakh and Assam would only expose the Chinese to U.S. intervention and nuclear war, putting a tremendous burden on their transportation, resources, and economy. I could not believe that the Chinese would embark on such a futile and fruitless venture. What would they get in return? If 120,000 Chinese soldiers sitting in Tibet, with the Himalayan barriers between them, could scare India into increasing her armed forces to about 1·2 million and her military budget by 300 per cent regardless of the fearful privations to which the people of the country were being exposed, China's purpose was fully served. India would crumble under the weight of her own problems. It was only a matter of time; all that was required was to leave her to her fate.

It suited the Indians to tell the world that they were beaten because they were heavily outnumbered. They conjured up visions of the Chinese descending on them in 'human waves'. The fact of the matter is that the Chinese had only six or seven light divisions in Tibet and not more than a division or two in each sector; and they were not within supporting distance of each other. The suggestion that the Indian Army failed to stem the Chinese advance because they were armed with bolt-action rifles is nonsense: this type of rifle is still very effective. In any case, even automatic rifles would have made little difference since the Chinese did not throw themselves on the Indian firepower. From the military point of view, the Indians failed because of poor leadership and inadequate training. The basic reason for their collapse was that their military thinking had not advanced with the times and they fought the war on the 1939 pattern. The Indians lacked skill and experience and their method of fighting was inferior to that of the Chinese. They occupied defensive positions thickly, thus presenting better targets to their opponents; and their defended localities were not within supporting distance of each other. Also they held narrow fronts and had no counter-attack elements in their dispositions, and they failed to carry out reconnaisance on their flanks.

In the event, the Chinese moves came as a complete surprise to the Indians, culminating in the total collapse of their defensive positions.

IV

When the Chinese came into Tibet and the Dalai Lama sought refuge in India, relations between India and China began to get strained. I thought at the time that McMahon might have drawn a line on a map, but unless the line was demarcated on the ground there was bound to be friction as soon as either side took up the question of patrolling the border.

A similar situation could arise on our own undemarcated borders in the Sinkiang and Baltistan areas. We had been receiving reports from time to time that Chinese patrols were coming up to Shamshal. There had been no shooting incident, but the Chinese had driven away some cattle in certain areas. I thought it might be a good idea to approach the Chinese and suggest to them that the border be demarcated. After all, neither side had anything to gain by leaving the border undefined. I inquired whether any attempt had been made in the past to demarcate this border and I was shown the relevant maps and papers. Some attempts had been made by the British. I asked our experts to mark what from our point of view constituted the actual line of control on the map, and this was done. We also found that we could legitimately claim control up to a point opposite the Shamshal Pass. The people of Shamshal village could, according to custom, take their cattle for grazing in a fertile valley on the other side of the Pass where the Chinese had established a couple of posts. They also used to get salt, a rare and valuable commodity, from the soil in that area. I mentioned this matter at a Cabinet meeting, but the feeling was that the Chinese were unlikely to respond to any suggestion for the demarcation of the border. I felt that there would be no harm in preparing a memorandum and getting in touch with the Chinese authorities. This happened towards the end of 1959.

There was no response from the Chinese government for a long time. Meanwhile, the question of the admission of China to the United Nations had assumed considerable importance. We had, of course, all along been of the view that China had a right to be in the United Nations. I had made Pakistan's position clear during my visit to the United States in 1961. I had publicly stated that it was only fair to allow the People's Republic of China to occupy her legitimate position in the United Nations. And for this I was criticized in the American Press which felt that as a guest in their country I should not go openly against the American position on the question.

On my return from the United States in December 1961, the Chinese Ambassador came to see me. He asked for our support for the proposition that the Chinese entry into the United Nations should be decided on the basis of a simple majority rather than a two-thirds majority. I asked him about our suggestion of demarcating the undefined border between China and Pakistan. He said that that was a very complicated matter. I told him that if border demarcation was a very complicated matter, China's admission to the United Nations was even more complicated. I suggested to him that we should look at the two problems on merit regardless of whether they were simple or complicated. We should be prepared to do what was right and sensible. We were supporting China's case for admission to the United Nations not to please China but because we genuinely felt that China had a right to be in the United Nations. I expressed surprise that the proposal to demarcate the border between China and Pakistan had evoked no response. I think the Chinese Ambassador was impressed by what I told him.

Our Foreign Minister, Mr. Manzur Qadir, later took up the matter with the Chinese Ambassador and asked him pointedly whether they

17 Meeting ex-service men on Dushak Day in Rawalpindi, 14 October 1961

18   Seeing the building plans for Islamabad, 15 September 1963

were refusing to discuss the demarcation of the border because of the disputed nature of the Kashmir territory. The Foreign Minister got the impression that that was the real reason, and that China at that time did not want to get involved in another argument with India. We were able to explain to the Chinese government that all we were asking for was the identification of the line between two stated points. The area to the north of the line would constitute Chinese territory; the status of the area to the south of the line did not have to be determined. China would be responsible for the defence of the area north of the line and the defence of the area south of the line would be Pakistan's responsibility. Soon after this the Chinese told us that they were prepared to discuss the problem of demarcation of the border with us. The two sides nominated their teams of experts to examine the problem.

It was at about this time that Mr. Nehru visited Pakistan to sign the Indus Basin Treaty. He asked me whether we had approached the Chinese to demarcate the border and I informed him of the position. He wanted me to show him the map on which we were basing our claim and wanted to know exactly the area to which our claim extended. I told him quite frankly that we had no intention of claiming any area which we did not honestly believe to be covered by the actual line of control as determined by our experts. We might ask for certain areas beyond the line of control to provide facilities for the local population.

Mr. Nehru asked me to let him have a copy of the map and I agreed to this in principle. As soon as he went back to India, he started criticizing us for having approached the Chinese to demarcate the border. He mentioned the map I had shown him and said that we did not even know where the border was and that we were acting in a childish manner. That was Mr. Nehru's style: he quite forgot the spirit in which we had discussed the matter and used the whole thing as a debating point. Simultaneously, he sent an official request for the map. Our people said that, considering the attitude he had adopted, we should decline to give him the map. My reaction was that Mr. Nehru was responsible for his own conduct and I was responsible for mine. Since I had promised to give him a copy of the map we should do so, irrespective of what he was saying or doing. And the map was sent to him.

Formal discussion with the Chinese started soon after. The Chinese were very difficult in the beginning, but once they realized that we were there not to outwit them but to seek an honourable solution their attitude changed. They produced a map on the basis of which they claimed certain areas on our side of the actual line of control, the

valley of Khanjarab and some areas near K-2. Eventually they agreed
to the actual line of control as shown on our map and it was adopted
as the demarcation line with certain marginal adjustments. The watershed of the Indus Basin rivers was shown on our side and the watershed
of the rivers of Yakang and certain adjoining areas on their side. There
was some argument about K-2 and it was agreed that the line of control
should be put right on top of K-2, thus letting the mountain peak belong
to both sides as had been done for Mount Everest with Nepal. Once we
had agreed on the demarcation line, aerial surveys were undertaken
and the whole matter was settled amicably and without any difficulty.

We raised the question of the grazing ground which covered several
hundred square miles on the other side of the Shamshal Pass. We proved
to the Chinese representative that this area had been traditionally under
the use of the people of Shamshal and that if they were denied access to
the area it would cause them great hardship. The Chinese said they
would check with the people of Sinkiang but agreed, in principle, that the
matter be resolved on merit. They finally agreed to let us have the area.

This agreement on border demarcation was the first step in the
evolution of relations between Pakistan and China. Its sole purpose was
to eliminate a possible cause of conflict in the future. But as a result of
this agreement, the Chinese began to have trust in us and we also felt
that if one was frank and straightforward one could do honest business
with them.

This agreement was followed by the establishment of air communications between China and Pakistan. Pakistan International Airlines
had purchased Boeings, which are expensive aircraft. We could only
pay for these by earning a fair amount of foreign exchange. It was in
this context that the question of exploring the possibility of opening
foreign routes was taken up. I think that PIA suggested to the Chinese
at their own level that they should be allowed to fly to Japan through
China instead of Hong Kong. I believe PIA was experiencing some
difficulty in flying through Hong Kong. At that time a number of other
airlines, including KLM and BOAC, too, had approached the Chinese
for flying rights.

The Chinese accepted the PIA proposition, presumably because
they thought it better to establish dealings with a neighbour rather than
with a European power with whom they did not even have diplomatic
relations. Even France did not have diplomatic relations with China at
that time, and with the British relations were only at the Counsellor
level. I believe the Chinese told the British that the question of flying
rights could be discussed only after an exchange of Ambassadors.

So far as we were concerned, the whole thing was essentially dealt with as a commercial transaction. After the transaction had been concluded, all kinds of political interpretations were put on it. It was said that Pakistan had opened a window for the Chinese to look into the rest of the world. Now that was obviously overdrawing the picture. Surely, if we had not entered into the arrangement, KLM or BOAC would have bagged the contract. And there was no lack of windows for the Chinese through which to catch a glimpse of the world. After this there was increased travel between China and Pakistan, though even before, the Chinese Prime Minister had visited Pakistan when Suhrawardy was Prime Minister, and Suhrawardy had also visited China.

I think that western misgivings about our dealings with China were due mainly to the fact that we started taking a more active part in Afro-Asian affairs. Afro-Asian conferences have always been suspect in western eyes, and it was thought that we were collaborating closely with the Chinese in building up the Afro-Asian forum, the 'Third World'. I must say that the Chinese never tried to influence us, nor did they ever approach us for support on any particular proposal in Afro-Asian gatherings.

Our interest in the Afro-Asian world was principally economic and in the exchange of ideas and experiences. The object was to establish some pattern whereby the developing world could live and trade with the developed world. We had been put at a great disadvantage as primary producers and it seemed necessary for us to establish a reasonable economic relationship among Afro-Asian countries to carry on trade on a mutually advantageous basis. Some of us were entering into the manufacturing stage and we found avenues for exports blocked or severely restricted in the European and American markets.

These were the kind of things that we intended to talk about in Afro-Asian conferences and we had made this clear not only to the Chinese but also to other members of the conferences. But the western powers thought the conferences had only one aim and that was to attack western colonialism and neo-colonialism. Far from joining in a tirade against the West, we wanted to operate as a steadying factor and a moderating influence. Indeed, at the first meeting of Foreign Ministers which took place in Djakarta in 1964, in connection with the organization of the Algiers Conference, a resolution was sponsored by several members condemning American action in Vietnam. It was as a result of our intervention that the resolution was dropped. Our argument was that no good would come of such a resolution and it would only act as an irritant. We pleaded that the Conference concentrate on constructive and positive matters.

It is possible that some of the western countries thought that by coming into contact with the People's Republic of China we would get converted to communism. I told some of my American friends that nothing could be more absurd. After all, they had been our close friends for a long time, but neither had they converted us to Christianity nor had we converted them to Islam. Communism is not something which is imported; it springs from the socio-economic conditions within a country. Wherever conditions deteriorate to an extent that people lose all hope, they rise to demolish the existing oppressive order. A communist dignitary once expressed surprise that though Karl Marx was a German, Germany never took to communism. I told him that even at the worst of times, after the two wars, there had been no complete breakdown of the socio-economic structure in Germany, so there was no need to resort to desperate measures. In Russia on the other hand, and later in China, this phenomenon did occur. Society was completely shattered and the only way it could find its salvation was through adopting communism. Communism is not an exportable commodity; it is a panacea for an acutely diseased society. How far it will be efficacious after the disease has been overcome remains to be seen. Pakistanis have an ideology of their own—an ideology of hope—and it was inconceivable that they should abandon this ideology and accept some alien philosophy of life. This argument did not impress the Americans, perhaps because in their life religion does not play the same decisive role as it does in ours. The Americans think of communism more as a contagion than as the result of economic distress and social disintegration.

I think the limits within which Pakistan's relations with China can develop are fully understood and respected on both sides. There are two factors that can influence the development of this relationship. One is the Chinese feeling that the United States, in collaboration with the Soviet Union, are trying to draw a ring round China so as to contain and isolate her. Now, if Pakistan were to join in any such arrangement either with the Soviet Union or with the United States of America, then the relationship would collapse. So we have to convince the Chinese that we are not in the market for any such deal and that, therefore, they need have no fear or doubt about us.

The other factor is the possibility, sometimes talked about, that India and China may come to an understanding. There is no doubt that the Indians have been sending emissaries and using the good offices of third countries to explore the possibilities of a *rapprochement* with China. Personally, I do not foresee the restoration of the 'Bhai Bhai'[1] situation

---

[1] Meaning 'Brothers', this was used as a popular slogan when India and China were on friendly terms.

between India and China in the near future for several reasons. For one thing, the Chinese are not going to trust the Indians again in a hurry. That is the impression I get from my meetings with the Chinese leaders. And the Indians are not going to come to terms with the Chinese because they are doing very well with the United States and they see no reason why they should lose such a profitable source of income. With India's dependence on the United States becoming more and more pronounced, the Chinese would find it impossible to accept that India was not aligned with the United States against them or that in the case of an armed conflict India would hesitate to provide all facilities to the Americans for use against the Chinese.

It is sometimes suggested that India and China will always remain apart because they are competing for the leadership of Asia. I do not think the Indians are in the race. India will never offer any real challenge to China because of the texture of her society and her way of life. Far from playing a leading role in the affairs of the world, she will always be dependent on some major power even for her survival. The Indians realize the limitations of their social, economic, and political structure. What can happen is a breakdown of the structure due to growing frustration within the Indian society. In that event, the question will be which mode of communism will dominate India. Will it be Chinese-oriented or Soviet-oriented? I think if communism were to come to India, it would be the Soviet type and it would then have to adapt itself to the rigid caste structure of Indian society. That would only estrange relations between India and China still further.

V

The Chinese are deeply engaged in unifying their people and their territories. What is worrying them is the future of Taiwan (Formosa). Connected with this is the American presence and American bases around them. It seems unlikely that the Taiwan problem will be resolved for a long time. There are people in the United States who think that it would be in the interest of the United States to come to a settlement with China on Taiwan. But the Americans are heavily involved in military as well as political terms with Chiang Kai-shek, who commands an army about 600,000 strong. Meanwhile, a war is going on in Vietnam which can at any time escalate into a major confrontation between China and the United States. The Chinese regard this as a real possibility and are making preparations to defend themselves.

Although the Chinese are worried about Taiwan and the possibility of a general war, yet I think they are primarily concentrating on

developing socialism in their country so as to build their society and
fully utilize their resources. My personal feeling is that while they are
extremely self-confident and determined, they are unlikely to do anything rash which might provoke a war. The long-term objective of the
People's Republic of China is to secure for themselves an equal status
with the Soviet Union and the United States. That is going to take
time. The world must get used to the idea of continued tension and
conflict between China, the United States, and the Soviet Union.

The understanding between the Soviet Union and the United
States came about when the Soviet Union developed the capability of
hitting the United States directly from their land mass. It was then that
the two countries started thinking in terms of establishing some measure
of coexistence to prevent the possibility of mutual destruction through
some terrible mistake, if not through design. The understanding between China and the United States and the Soviet Union will also come,
but only after China has developed a similar capability. That might
take another fifteen years or so. In the meantime, any one of these
powers would be happy to see the other two locked in a limited conflict
which would have the effect of weakening them. There is very little that
any of the smaller powers can do in this situation. All these ideas of
dispatching peace missions are unlikely to produce any positive results.
Major powers do not change their policies until there is some compulsion for them to do so.

It might help to ease some of the tension if the People's Republic of
China were to be admitted into the United Nations. I think direct
dealings and dialogue between the West and China might help to
remove unnecessary fears and misunderstandings. The United States
has a feeling that once China comes into the United Nations most of
the developing countries of Asia and Africa will line up behind her. My
belief is that no emerging country would like to be wholly identified with
any of the big powers. They know that identification of this kind would
cost them their freedom of action and might also expose them to internal
instability.

VI

It was not until April 1965 that Pakistan was able to establish direct
contact with the U.S.S.R. For eighteen years we knew little about each
other at the human level. Inevitably, both sides acted under precon-
ceived notions and suffered from a sense of distance. Liaquat Ali Khan
had accepted an invitation to visit the Soviet Union at one time, but
unfortunately that visit never materialized.

I mentioned earlier that our membership of the Baghdad Pact introduced an element of strain in our relations with the U.S.S.R. The Indians were not averse to exploiting the situation and presented us to the Soviet Union as some kind of theocratic State opposed to all liberal movements. In Pakistan, too, there was a certain inhibition about the U.S.S.R. and a section of the people believed that contact with Russia would encourage the growth of communism in the country.

But the main cause, to my mind, was that even though our civilization and culture had close connections with Central Asia, two hundred years of British occupation had wiped out these connections. By the time the British left, the contact had been lost. When we achieved independence, our natural tendency was to look to the West rather than towards our immediate neighbours, and the western countries were not too anxious for us to have any dealings with the Soviet Union. My visit to the Soviet Union in 1965 was essentially intended to recover the lost links. The fact of neighbourhood was a physical and geographical one, and I wanted to re-establish the validity and compulsion of this fact.

I had my first meeting with the present Soviet leaders on 3 April 1965. We had a formal conference in Mr. Kosygin's office on a bitterly cold and gloomy afternoon. Mr. Kosygin had Mr. Polyansky, Mr. Gromyko, and some other members of the government with him. The atmosphere inside the room was no less cold in spite of central heating. The Soviet delegation looked stolid and sullen. After the usual exchange of courtesies, I waited for the Soviet Prime Minister to make the first move. But Mr. Kosygin thought that as guests in their country it was for us to make the opening statement; that, he said, was their custom. 'A very convenient custom, Mr. Prime Minister', I said. 'You would not like us to have inconvenient customs, Mr. President', Mr. Kosygin rejoined.

I realized that the Soviet reputation for opening gambits in chess was not ill-founded! The best thing, I thought, was to go straight to the point, so I outlined our assessment of the world situation. I described the relations the Soviet Union had established with India and the manner in which these relations were affecting us. I touched on Soviet relations with the United States and China and explained how we viewed them in our context. The question was to consider how relations between Pakistan and the U.S.S.R. could be improved and an area of understanding established.

Mr. Kosygin started speaking, I thought, with considerable caution and restraint. He mentioned the progress which the Soviet Union had made in different fields and summed up by suggesting that Soviet policy was to establish the broadest possible co-operation with the East as well as the West. I intervened to say that, placed in the middle as the Soviet

Union was, she could establish such co-operation with great advantage. He did not miss the point and said smilingly, 'You live in the East but even you find it advantageous to co-operate with both sides.'

The ice was beginning to thaw. Mr. Kosygin sensed it too and said, 'We should soon be able to get along without an interpreter.' He warmed up and started dealing with specific points which I had raised. He seemed anxious about the situation in Vietnam. It had been reported at that time that the United States had used gas in Vietnam. Mr. Kosygin found it impossible to accept the explanation given by President Johnson that this had been done by the military commanders without his approval. 'Surely the U.S. President has control over his army!' He accused the United States of having launched unprovoked aggression in Vietnam, in violation of the Geneva Agreement. His reading was that the U.S. would get more and more entangled in Vietnam and would not know how to disengage itself. He mentioned the assistance which the Soviet Union was giving to North Vietnam. As he saw it the immediate question was how to end the war. It was for those who had engineered the war to answer this question: so far as the Soviet Union was concerned she would stand by North Vietnam.

Mr. Kosygin then said that perhaps the United States was trying to take advantage of Sino-Soviet differences. But the U.S. should know that these differences would not stand in the way of the Soviet Union coming to the help of the Vietnamese. The differences between the Soviet Union and the People's Republic of China were 'not organic'; they were a temporary phenomenon and the Vietnam situation would not accentuate them, it would only help to resolve them. The Soviet Union and the People's Republic of China belonged to 'a common theory'. A great tradition of friendship among the people of the Soviet Union and the people of China existed and the Soviet people had great respect and admiration for the Chinese people.

Mr. Kosygin then turned to the Indo-Pakistan differences. As he was explaining the rationale of Soviet military aid to India, I said that by a peculiar coincidence the policies of the U.S.S.R. and the United States seemed to have coincided in India. This did not please Mr. Kosygin. He said with some emotion, 'Only some enemy of ours could have told you that.' I maintained that we did not have to be told by anybody; we had come to this conclusion ourselves. After all, the security of the sub-continent was not served by the massive supply of arms to India whether the arms came from the western countries or from the Soviet Union. The motives and reasoning might be different but the effect was the same, and the safety of the smaller countries in the region had been jeopardized by the arms build-up in India. The U.S. assumption was that India needed these arms because she was going to be attacked by China. That made no military sense to us at all.

I went on to say that the Soviet Union was providing arms for India because she did not want to leave the field to the United States. All this was helping India to pursue her aggressive and expansionist policies. I mentioned how India had recently driven out half a million Muslims into Pakistan and how she was blatantly violating the cease-fire line in Kashmir. We were unable to resolve our differences with India because the increased military strength she had acquired was encouraging her to perpetuate her forcible occupation of a large part of the State of Jammu and Kashmir and to flout the United Nations resolutions with impunity. Whenever we brought the matter to the world forum, India had the assurance that she would be bailed out by the Soviet veto.

Mr. Kosygin heard me with great patience and consideration. He thought that the differences between India and Pakistan were not due to the arms which were being supplied to India by the West or by the Soviet Union. The differences were really a legacy of imperialism and the imperialists were still interested in maintaining tension between India and Pakistan. He then raised the question of Pakistan's membership of SEATO and CENTO, in which, as Mr. Kosygin put it, 'the U.S. rules the roost'. He talked specifically of the U-2 incident which had generated much mistrust.

The Soviet Union had legitimate cause to complain about the Pacts; but they had to appreciate our position. India's avowed policy was to isolate us and we had to seek friends somewhere. We had not joined the Pacts to encourage aggression in any direction; our sole concern was our security. In the U-2 incident we were clearly at fault, but the whole thing had been as much of a shock to us as it was to the Soviet Union. I then explained that our presence in the Pacts was serving as a moderating influence and, in any case, the Pacts were not hurting the U.S.S.R. Mr. Kosygin said, 'They may not be hurting us, but they give us no pleasure either.' He then reverted to Indo-Pakistan problems and advocated direct negotiations.

I think this first meeting, which lasted for nearly three hours, helped us to understand each other. There was a great deal of plain talk from both sides and one could see from the worried and tense faces of the diplomats in the two delegations that the talks had not followed protocol.

We met next day at a *dacha*, about twenty-five miles from Moscow. It was an old country house located in the heart of a pine and birch forest, by the bank of Moscow river, which was frozen. We had some recreation shooting at clay pigeons.

We started our discussions at about 11.30 a.m. and went on till half past one. Mr. Brezhnev joined the Soviet delegation for this meeting. By and large we covered the same ground as in the first meeting but the atmosphere was distinctly different; already, there was much warmth and understanding. I reverted to the question of the Indian arms build-up. If it was inconceivable that China should attack India then what was she arming herself for? Could she have any objective other than expansionism? The Indian theoreticians were claiming boundaries from the Oxus to Mekong. We could not attribute everything to the im-perialists. India was not content with her present sphere of influence and she knew that Pakistan had the will and the capacity to frustrate her expansionist designs. She wanted to browbeat us into subservience. All we wanted was to live as equal and honourable neighbours, but to that India would never agree. It was Brahmin chauvinism and arrogance that had forced us to seek a homeland of our own where we could order our life according to our own thinking and faith. They wanted us to remain as serfs, which was precisely the condition in which the Muslim minority in India lived today. There was the fundamental opposition between the ideologies of India and Pakistan. The whole Indian society was based on class distinction in which even the shadow of a low-caste man was enough to pollute a member of the high caste.

Mr. Kosygin thought that Indo-Pakistan relations had become extremely complicated. He explained that the Soviet Union was against arming any nation and that it would not like to see a situation of military confrontation develop in any part of the world, much less in our own region. He conceded the ideological differences between India and Pakistan but thought that the answer lay in evolving some mode of practical coexistence. The Soviet Union supplied arms to various countries to fight imperialism. I wanted to know which particular brand of imperialism or colonialism India was fighting against. Mr. Brezhnev intervened at this stage to suggest that India was non-aligned and was not a member of any defence pacts. I expressed my surprise to hear that India was regarded as 'non-aligned' in spite of her providing bases for propaganda, joining in joint exercises, seeking a nuclear umbrella, and receiving massive military aid. If all that added up to non-alignment, what was alignment?

We came back to a discussion of the Pacts, and I restated our position at some length. I think by then the Soviet leaders had begun to see our point of view with more sympathy. We discussed various possibilities of co-operation between the Soviet Union and Pakistan on a bilateral basis. Mr. Kosygin observed that we had been able to do considerable positive work in less than twenty-four hours and that we had achieved more in one day than others had done in eighteen years. 'All we knew about you was', Mr. Kosygin said, 'that you were a member of certain pacts—even though paper pacts—and we were doubtful and cautious about you.'

I think there was general recognition on both sides that the meeting might prove a turning point in our relations and that there were tremendous possibilities of co-operation. I found the Soviet leaders extremely knowledgeable. They were courteous, polite, and hospitable but firm on their basic assumptions. I venture to think that they recognized our sincerity and came to have a better appreciation of our position.

During my visit to the Soviet Union I was also able to get a better understanding of the nature of the Sino-Soviet differences. I was interested in this problem because it has a direct bearing on our security. It was in October 1962 that India provoked the conflict with China and it was at about the same time that the Sino-Soviet differences came out in the open. Both these events led to a closer association between India and the western countries on the one side and India and the Soviet Union on the other. Both the United States and the Soviet Union started competing with each other in supplying arms to India, as we have seen: one to prepare her to face China and the other to maintain the balance in Asia. The effect was that whatever compulsion there was for India to come to terms with Pakistan disappeared.

The general nature of the Sino-Soviet differences is well known and so are the arguments and the accusations used by the two sides. But they do not fully explain the bitterness which persists, particularly in the Chinese mind. The Chinese have a feeling that they were treated unfairly. It is possible that there is a belief in China—how justified it is I do not know—that the Soviet Union would not like to see China emerge as a major power. The Chinese also think that the Soviet attempt to establish coexistence with the United States contains an element of hostility towards China. In other words, though the arguments are mostly exchanged on an ideological plane and are couched in philosophical jargon, the reasons for mistrust are basically nationalistic. China's major objective is to attain a position of equality with the United States and the U.S.S.R., and they fear that coexistence between the Soviet Union and the West would delay the achievement of that objective.

The leaders of the Soviet Union argue that with the development of nuclear power, the dangers of conflict between the communist world and the capitalist world have assumed dangerous proportions. Should such a conflict occur, not only would the two sides, but the whole world, be annihilated. They feel that it is vital for the two sides to prevent the tragic possibilities of a nuclear war.

The Soviet Union is entering what one might call a state of satisfaction, economically and socially. It is progressing rapidly and the standard of living of the people is improving. The Russians have found vast resources which will take decades to develop fully. Quite naturally, they do not want to risk what they have achieved and to deny their people a future of happiness by provoking a war. One might find all this difficult to reconcile with Khrushchev's decision to place rockets and nuclear warheads in Cuba. That was the time when the two major world powers looked over the precipice of world disaster and, properly chastened, pulled back just in time. I think it was a terrible mistake, unlikely to be repeated. To my mind it marked the real end of the decades-old cold war when the prospects of confrontation ended and coexistence as a hard fact of life in the nuclear age was forced upon the United States and the U.S.S.R.

I think Sino-Soviet differences will continue even though, as Mr. Kosygin said, they are not of an organic character. But if either the Soviet Union or the People's Republic of China is exposed to attack by a third country, the differences will disappear and the two communist powers will offer united resistance. Whatever may be the views of the leaders in the two countries, the people of one country will not sit back and watch the people of the other country fighting a major war all on their own.

VII

Our relations with Afghanistan have not followed the friendly and fraternal lines which should have been expected of two neighbouring Muslim States. When India and Pakistan came into existence as two independent sovereign states there were two misconceptions in the minds of many Afghans. The first, arising from constant Indian propaganda, was that Pakistan could not survive as a separate State. The Afghan rulers believed this to be true and decided to stake a claim to our territory before Pakistan disintegrated. They consequently laid claim to part of our northern areas where the Pathans or Pushtoons live. In this way the idea of an artificial State of 'Pakhtoonistan' inside our borders was made an issue by the Afghan rulers. Now clearly this was unacceptable to us for no sovereign State can allow another country to interfere in its internal affairs.

In this claim the Afghans were backed by India whose interest lay in ensuring that in the event of a war with us over Kashmir, the

Afghans should open a second front against Pakistan on the North-West Frontier. They also reasoned that if they had this understanding with Afghanistan, we would not be able to use the Pathan tribesmen against them. The Indians thought that they would thus be able to hem us in and embarrass us by a pincer movement.

The second misconception lay in the attitude of the Afghan rulers themselves. If their first premise proved wrong and Pakistan did survive, they realized that it would have a democratic government. This would naturally undermine the position of the rulers in Afghanistan. So they made these claims to our lands and also carried out raids over the Durand Line which divides the two countries; and they hired agents and dissident tribesmen to create incidents in these areas. All this helped them to divert the attention of their people from internal difficulties.

We have throughout followed a policy of patience with Afghanistan. We have given them all possible facilities for the passage of goods on our railways and we have not established exchange control on our trade with them. We have done all this because we have the friendliest feelings towards the people of Afghanistan. They have a land-locked country with no outlet to the sea and we have given them commercial and other facilities at a considerable cost to ourselves.

On several occasions we have discussed our mutual problems at different levels. Our experience has been that the Afghan claims become stronger and more strident when there is a weak government in Pakistan. When Pakistan has a strong and stable government Afghanistan's claims become vague and less insistent. Of course, the Afghans have taken good care never to define their stand on 'Pakhtoonistan'. In the past they produced maps showing areas right down to the Indus, in fact right down to Karachi, as part of 'Pakhtoonistan'. But whenever we have seriously asked them to let us know what worries them they have explained that they have no territorial claims; all they are interested in is the welfare of the people of 'Pakhtoonistan' and that they should have an opportunity to express their will. When we remind them that the Pahktoons have already expressed their will in a free and fair referendum held at the time of Partition, and that every major tribe was then consulted, they have no answer but they remain dissatisfied.

I had a long meeting with Prince Naim in January 1959. I explained to him that Pakistan had come into existence as a result of the struggle of the Muslims of the sub-continent to free themselves from British and Hindu domination. British India had been divided on the basis of religious majority areas and not on a racial basis. On achieving independence, we naturally looked to the Muslim world, especially the Muslim countries in the Middle East, for understanding, friendship, and support. We were disappointed that Afghanistan adopted an attitude of open hostility from the very day of our independence.

Ironically enough, Afghanistan was the only country that opposed our admission to the United Nations. Since then we had been subjected to a campaign of vilification and slander in the Afghan press and radio. On one occasion our Embassy in Kabul was sacked by a mob and our people hounded out of Afghanistan. It was difficult for us to comprehend the Afghan attitude. They had defined 'Pakhtoonistan' in a variety of ways—as a separate independent State, as an autonomous area, as a unit within Pakistan to be called 'Pakhtoonistan', and sometimes only as a demand for a reference to be made to the Pathans to indicate whether they were happy with Pakistan. I told Prince Naim that we could well understand why the proposal they had in mind was being kept deliberately obscure. The Afghan rulers obviously wanted to create a right of interference in the internal affairs of Pakistan before starting on other ventures. What was not realized was that this kind of talk was patently unwarranted and amounted to aggression across an international frontier, the Durand Line, which had been, time and again, solemnly confirmed by the Afghan authorities. The original agreement arrived at in 1893 was confirmed in 1905, reaffirmed in the Anglo-Afghan Treaty in 1919, and finally endorsed when the present ruling family in Afghanistan came to power.

The Afghan attitude could only be interpreted as an indirect attempt at expansionism. The preposterous claims which the Afghan rulers were making could only lead to trouble. All this concern for the Pathans in Pakistan was based on the claim that at one time in history Afghanistan held sway over some parts of what is now West Pakistan. But there were also times, of much longer duration, when Delhi's sovereignty extended up to Kabul and beyond. If old conquests were to be our guide then Pakistan should have more interest in the future of Pathans living in Afghanistan. The world had moved away from old historical positions and life in modern times was not governed by legends of past glories. Pakistan's patience should not be taken for weakness or lack of resolution. I appealed to Prince Naim to abandon the policy of hostility toward Pakistan. 'It would be to our mutual advantage to live as friendly neighbours', I told him.

I think we will have to live with this situation. In the meantime, we must continue to be patient and tolerant; it takes time to create good-will and understanding and it never pays to act in a hurry in such matters. The King of Afghanistan in recent years has accorded a certain measure of participation in the running of the country to people outside the royal circle. If, as I believe, this process of giving more responsibility to ordinary citizens continues, the artificial differences between Afghanistan and Pakistan will disappear and the Afghans will realize the obvious benefits of co-operation with us. Like other countries, Afghanistan too will have to go through a formative period while they are conducting their first experiments with democracy. People there, as elsewhere, have to understand the spirit of working a democratic system. As the common man begins to have more say in the running of the country, I think there will be greater recognition of present realities and less nostalgia for past glories.

I have great admiration for the ruling family and for the King personally, who is a man of wisdom and has shown willingness to share power with the people. We share the same faith with our brethren in Afghanistan and this alone should prove decisive in eliminating present difficulties and providing a basis for good neighbourly relations. In this lies the prosperity of the tribes who live on either side of the Durand Line. The tribes on the Pakistan side have been given opportunities to develop their area and considerable progress has been made towards improvement in agriculture and the setting up of small industries. Our attitude in this matter has been to let the tribesmen decide for themselves what particular development scheme they would like to adopt. All this has helped to integrate the people of this area with the rest of the country. They have an equal share in the country's prosperity and are fully identified with the destiny of Pakistan.

VIII

I have referred to the basic power-groups round the world—the West led by the U.S.A., the Communist Bloc under the dual leadership of the U.S.S.R. and China, and the presence of Hindu India on our borders, a continent by itself. But beyond this lies another world of teeming, though not so articulate, millions, comprising scores of newly-independent countries in Africa, the Middle East, and Asia.

Before the Second World War, one heard of the Socialist Sixth of the World, meaning Russia. With the emergence of China it was borne in upon the world consciousness that every fourth man in the world was Chinese. Yet the balance of power was still in favour of the U.S.A., with its nuclear armoury, till it was challenged by the Soviet technological and scientific break-through.

Simultaneously, there was an awakening in the new nations from Casablanca to Djakarta, from Cairo to Nairobi and beyond. The Third

World of Asia and Africa was responding to the shouts of 'Uhuru', 'Allah-o-Akbar', and 'Merdeka'. What is this Third World, peopled by over seven hundred millions of black and brown races and nations-in-the-making? In this world of have-nots there are no really dominant members to overawe the rest. Numerically the most populous is Pakistan with 110 million people, but it is closely followed by Indonesia with 107 million, Thailand with 28 million, Turkey, the United Arab Republic, and the Philippines with 27 million each.

What is this Third World? It is not a geographic concept, nor a social reality. It is not even a political idea capable of definition or of being translated into a formal arrangement. It is essentially a reflection of the collective consciousness of the people of a large number of countries in different sub-continents at various stages of independence and development. It is a claim staked by the developing world for recognition; it is an urge for acceptance.

Until a decade ago, the world belonged to the two largest industrially developed nations, namely, the U.S.A. and the U.S.S.R., and the only problem seemed to be for these powers to come to an understanding regarding their respective spheres of influence and control. The world at that time really meant the American World and the Soviet World. But these two worlds suffered from serious internal contradictions and were locked in a prolonged cold war for world domination. Meanwhile, downtrodden and subject peoples in different parts of the world were waging a powerful struggle for emancipation, and the internal strife between the two major powers helped them to establish their claim to freedom. One by one they burst forth from centuries of darkness to reach for the sun.

These countries emerged with a vision of the Third World. What gave them some kind of homogeneity was their common experience: they had all been exploited and oppressed. The pain and the misery of exploitation was common to them and so were the hopes and aspirations for a happier and more dignified life, because they all felt that they should have a legitimate share in the good things of life. But the new vision was disturbed and scarred. The problems they had inherited were not all resolved with the running up of flags of independence. In fact, the problems were just unfurling themselves and their solution required more than the fluttering of the spirit. They discovered that their erstwhile masters had left them in a state of isolation, that all traditional ties of cultural contact and communication had snapped. All the old trade routes and channels of exchange of knowledge had disappeared.

The Asian countries were just recovering from the horrors of the Second World War and there was enough bitterness among them to

19*a* Visiting Fenchuganj fertilizer factory in Sylhet, 4 February
1962

19*b* Going round the Karnaphuli Multipurpose Project, 31 March
1962

20*a* Opening the Srakha
Gravity Dam, constructed
by army engineers, near
Quetta, 14 December
1962

20*b* Inaugurating the
installations of the
National Oil Refinery,
Karachi, 21 February
1963

keep them involved in their internal conflicts for centuries. The African countries were in an even more dismal state. The European powers had put the map of Africa on a table and divided it up into a number of countries by drawing straight lines across the map and deciding which country should be governed by which European power. It was like dividing up the spoils of conquest. All they were concerned with was to draw straight lines so that the boundary pillars between different countries would be connected by the shortest possible distance. They were not concerned whether these lines cut across traditions, affinities, cultures, or ethnic and linguistic unities. And the people of Africa had no say in this callous exercise in geometry; they all became victims of straight lines. When these countries gained independence, many of them found that they had neither an administrative structure nor a body of civil servants. Most of them did not have a trained or disciplined army. There was no real education and little had been done to prepare them for the responsibilities which they would be called upon to discharge as citizens of an independent country.

In the Middle East a number of small countries had been carved out by the western powers to suit their own interests after the break-up of the Ottoman Empire. These countries had developed strong national interests, often in mutual conflict. Different patterns of administration had been imposed on different countries. The object of the major powers was to ensure that this area should remain soft and that no country should be strong enough to challenge their interests. They had taken care to create so many inner conflicts that there would be little prospect of these countries forming any association to build up a strong bargaining position.

When the Arab League was established there was hope that some kind of unity might be forged by the Arab nations. This hope remained unfulfilled. Similarly, the emergence of President Nasser and his régime led one to expect that he might be able to bring all the Arab countries on to one platform. Even if they did not join the other non-Arab Muslim countries, unity among the Arabs themselves would have been a great blessing for them and a source of strength to the region as a whole. Unfortunately, differences between the Middle Eastern countries were so deep-seated that they could not be brushed aside. The situation was further complicated by the fact that certain attempts were made, however indirect and disguised, to interfere in each other's internal affairs.

Apart from these problems of physical barriers, absence of contacts, and national conflicts, the Third World had the problem of discovering and evolving its own philosophy and fashioning its own instruments to deal with its problems. Whatever intellectual heritage had been bequeathed them by the colonial powers had no relevance to their cultural needs. They were all set in pursuit of alien ideas and alien objectives. Not that the knowledge they had acquired under foreign rule was futile; far from it. In most cases this knowledge had helped them in their struggle for freedom, but it was the methods and disciplines of that knowledge which were often unsuited to their conditions. These methods and disciplines had been evolved to deal with specific problems which had little in common with the problems and conditions prevailing in the newly-emerging countries.

The major powers left behind them such a heavy atmosphere of intellectual dominance and superiority that any attempt by the people of the newly-emerging countries either to identify their problems according to their own lights or to deal with them according to their own methods was generally regarded by the intelligentsia as something retrograde and reactionary. The only civilized system of government was the system of the West; any deviation from that system was suspect. The democratic structure which had been raised in the West was regarded as the only system capable of sustaining independence and growth. Democracy had taken the place of religion in the life of people in the western countries and they were guarding their pattern of democracy as fanatically as religious zealots nurse and protect their rituals and forms. They were more concerned with the form of democracy than the substance and principles, the assumption being that the principles could find expression only in one particular form—their own.

All these problems and limitations have obstructed the growth of the Third World, and, I am afraid, that growth may remain a dream, or at best a grand strategic aim, for a long time to come.

The most precise expression which the Third World was given was in the Afro-Asian movement. We in Pakistan identified ourselves completely with the Afro-Asian movement and, I think, made a definite contribution in preparing for the Second Afro-Asian Conference. Unfortunately, the Conference could not be held for reasons over which those entrusted with preparatory work had no control. It was a great disappointment and I felt at the time that a dream had been shattered, and that it would take a long time before the pieces could be put together again.

One of the reasons for the failure of the Conference was—and to my mind this might have been decisive—that too much politics, with all the inevitable controversies and tensions, had crept into the movement. The real problem before the developing countries was to work out a system of dealing with the major powers. Instead they spent all their energy in dealing with their own internal differences and disputes.

Even though the Second Afro-Asian Conference could not be held, it taught us some useful lessons. Any get-together of the smaller nations in the Afro-Asian world will be resisted not only by the big powers but even by those who have big-power illusions. Take the case of India: she came out of the First Afro-Asian Conference in 1955, which she had helped to organize, disillusioned and disappointed because Mr. Nehru had not been able to establish himself as the leader of Asia. Ten years later, she approached the Second Afro-Asian Conference with a great deal of hostility because other nations of the area would not accept her leadership and were rather suspicious of her intentions. India started subverting Afro-Asian solidarity, and turned the proposed Conference into an arena of Sino-Soviet tussle.

In 1955 Nehru had successfully blocked Russia's entry into the First Conference by saying that the Soviet Union could not be invited because it was a part of Europe. Now India, ten years later, turned a complete somersault by arguing that Soviet participation in the Second Conference would be a source of great strength to the Afro-Asian world. This point of view was put forward to divide the Afro-Asian countries so that they could not take a unified stand against encroachments from advanced countries. India also tried to impose on the Conference her own definition of self-determination by asserting that self-determination was the right of any country that was dominated by another to liberate itself; but that there could be no self-determination for different areas and regions within a sovereign and independent country, for this would lead to fragmentation and disruption and no country's integrity would be safe. Obviously, this would preclude all discussions on Kashmir. But India's main aim was to divide the Afro-Asian world. She also tried to bring about a clash between the supporters of Indonesia and the supporters of Malaysia by demanding that Malaysia be invited to attend the Conference.

I visualize this Third World as a universe of the developing countries containing a number of constellations, each constellation held together by an internal balance of force. Each constellation should be organized around common ideas, common experiences, and common problems. This is the only way in which the developing world can confront the developed world.

Common sense dictates that Pakistan should belong to a major constellation extending from Casablanca to Djakarta. There should be some association and understanding among countries of this region: not a political or military association but an economic and cultural association. We have common needs and there are a number of things we could do for mutual benefit; we would all gain by combining. A bloc of countries like this would be a very powerful combination and would have an effective voice in the world. Today, the small nations of the world are taken for granted. If we were to speak with one voice, the world would sit up and take notice. What, for example, is the origin of the Turks, Iranians, Afghans, and many Pakistanis? We all have the same origin, the steppes of Central Asia. How is it then that we have forgotten our common ancestry to an extent that we do not even realize that our safety lies in being able to put up a united front against the outside world of major powers and hostile 'isms'?

This particular constellation of ours, if we could bring it into being— and the seeds are there in RCD—would be a shining example for others, particularly the Arab constellation, of which the centre would be the United Arab Republic. In this, I believe, President Nasser could play a key role. I think he is the most important man in the region today and I fervently hope and pray that he will help history to move in the right direction. So long as countries of this area, which have so much affinity and common points in the past and the present, do not develop depth and bulk they will remain vulnerable and the entire zone will continue to be a cockpit of international intrigues and strife.

The concept of one monolithic universe of under-developed countries would not be a very practical one in the present context. But once the basic idea is accepted, any number of combinations can be tried to reinforce the main aim of increasing unity with a common platform to face the world outside. For example, there is great scope for fruitful regional collaboration, say, between three or four countries in the Maghreb, like Libya, Tunisia, Morocco, and Algeria. For one thing, they share a common faith and a similar past. They would be a viable group with about 30 million people spread over two million square miles of territory. It seems to me that it would be a very sound thing if these countries were to get together and have some common arrangements whereby they could collaborate with one another. Similarly, I think that the destinies of Egypt and the Sudan lie together because both depend on the same source of water and communication, and they are in fact contiguous. By the same token, the whole of the Arabian peninsula, also, has a common destiny.

I personally favour such regional associations and then inter-regional groupings so as to be able to get a better deal through collective bargaining. Otherwise we shall be dealt with individually by the big powers, and suffer immeasurably in the process; we would always remain an area of weakness. For whoever finds an opportunity to swallow this part of the world, will not hesitate to do so; in our present state, we shall not have the strength to stop them. The only deterrent at the moment is the rivalry among the big powers. We will remain 'sub-nations' if we do not join together to offer united resistance to power pressures.

The countries in this region from Casablanca to Djakarta are also suspect in the eyes of the major powers because most of them profess the faith of Islam. Whatever may be the internal differences among these countries about Islam, and regardless of the approach to Islam which each one of these countries has adopted, it is a fact of life that the Communist world, the Christian world, and Hindu India treat them as Muslim countries.

India particularly has a deep pathological hatred for Muslims and her hostility to Pakistan stems from her refusal to see a Muslim power developing next door. By the same token, India will never tolerate a Muslim grouping near or far from her borders.

The big-power rivalries, the diffusion of the focus of world power by the emergence of China, and the end of the U.S.-U.S.S.R. tussle for world supremacy, all are hard realities, but they need'not be a source of weakness for small nations acting in concert. With a little far-sightedness it should be possible to create such constellations of power, interlinked with one other, sustaining the whole universe of developing nations and capable of withstanding the ravages of alien meteorites.

IX

Ever since the Soviet Union and the United States have come closer to accepting the gospel of coexistence, the need for their wooing of smaller countries for support has receded. Aid was used as an instrument of the cold war, but in view of the new situation, it may become more and more difficult for the smaller countries to get large-scale assistance. In fact, I doubt very much whether it will remain 'aid' at all; it will pro-bably assume the form of purely commercial transactions. The in-dustrialized countries have discovered that territorial imperialism is no longer fashionable nor easy to maintain. They have tremendous accumu-lated economic power which they find it more advantageous to use.

Now, the developing countries need economic support for their growth. They have also to pay for capital goods which they must import to process their raw materials. They can only pay back what they receive in the form of assistance and loans if they earn enough foreign exchange by selling processed goods in foreign markets. They have limited access to these markets because the developed countries prefer to buy only raw materials from them and have their own arrangements for manu-facture. Prices of raw materials being subject to wide seasonal variations, the terms of trade have always tended to operate against the developing countries. Then there are a variety of quantitative restrictions and tariff barriers which they have to cross before their goods find entry into western markets. So long as the developing countries are not able to buy and sell commodities and goods under free market conditions, the terms of trade will continue to move against them.

All this has put us, in Pakistan as in other countries, at a great disadvantage. Our need to earn foreign exchange arises both from the necessity of satisfying our commercial and industrial needs through imports and from the necessity of paying back the debts which we, like most under-developed countries, have had to incur. Some of these debts are very heavy, carrying interest as high as 6 per cent. I visualize that a time may come when developing countries may have to ask for a complete moratorium on repayment of their loans. If the developed countries are not prepared to trade with us, and are not prepared to buy our finished goods, what are we to do? How are we going to repay and service our existing debts, let alone meet our own requirements of foreign goods? A great clash of interests is bound to take place on a world-wide scale and I think the capitalist countries of the West may eventually find themselves isolated if they do not open their markets to us and bring about such structural changes in their industry as would leave room for small countries to manufacture and sell semi-processed and less sophisticated goods.

A recent U.N. survey indicates that if developed countries were to purchase 10 billion dollars' worth of manufactures by 1980 from under-developed countries, this would substantially benefit the latter, although the transaction would represent just one per cent of the additional demand for manufactures in the world. But will they? It doesn't look like it. All America, for instance, expects and allows Pakistan to export to her is 25 million yards of cloth a year—a ridiculously small quantity. Cloth is one of Pakistan's major export hopes, but this principle also applies to other goods.

Then Britain, which some years ago had no balance of payments problem, imposed an import quota on cotton cloth and yarn from Pakistan. When I took up the question in 1962 with Mr. Duncan Sandys, Commonwealth Relations Secretary, his reply was that the textile industry in Manchester had been very badly hit and that the government had to consider the Manchester votes. When I raised the same question with Prime Minister Macmillan, his reply was, 'This voting business is something that we cannot ignore.'

So much for the ethics and goodwill of the developed nations. When we ask why they don't leave the field of simple manufactures to us and embark on more sophisticated production, they say, 'It is easier said than done. Who will buy these things from us?' This is one reason for their reluctance to free trade, this fear of losing the markets in the easier, profitable goods; the other is that sophisticated manufactures require higher capital investment. The industrialized countries no doubt have their problems, too, but they have exploited these areas for centuries and they should now be prepared at least to do legitimate trade with them. At the first hint of new entrants, they hurriedly put up protective walls of quotas, preferences, and tariffs.

I am afraid the developing nations, particularly those that are switching to light manufactures, will have to do some quick thinking and take urgent collective measures. Salvation in the economic, as in the political, field appears to lie in linking-up, and fast. Countries that produce similar goods should get together. Take tea, for example, or jute or rice or any of the major commodities: if countries producing them were to have an arrangement whereby the world had to trade with a common organization, the producing countries could get better terms. And if a rational arrangement were to be devised, then the profits could be shared according to the volume of production in each country. We, the producers, might well be left with large stocks. What if we are? Let those stocks remain and let no one country profit at the expense of another or undercut another. And why must our trade be tied to Europe or America? Wherever we can, we ought to trade with each other and make common arrangements for trading in commodities that we are producing. I am well aware of the argument that inter-regional trade in Africa was between one and five per cent of these countries' total trade because the African economies produced similar and competitive rather than complementary goods and commodities. The answer is for us all, now and in the long term, to act in conjunction and consider the possibility of changing and co-ordinating our respective patterns of production. This is one very important reason why I so strongly supported the Second Conference of the Afro-Asian countries.

From whatever angle one looks at it, the salvation of the Third World depends on the formation of homogeneous groups to protect common interests and to work for the solution of common problems.

11

The Constitution and Ideology

I

To follow my approach to the constitutional problems of Pakistan it is
necessary to go back a little in time. I was staying on 4 October 1954 at
a hotel in London where I had broken my journey for a couple of days
on my way to the United States. It was a warmish night and I could not
sleep, but it was not the weather alone that kept me awake. The news
from home was disturbing, the portents ominous. I was feeling uneasy
because I had heard that Governor-General Ghulam Mohammad
might do something reckless. He and Prime Minister Mohammad Ali
Bogra were feuding with each other. I had a premonition that Ghulam
Mohammad might draw me into politics which I wanted, above all
things, to avoid.

I was pacing up and down the room when I said to myself: 'Let me
put down my ideas in a military fashion: what is wrong with the
country and what can be done to put things right.' I approached the
question much in the manner of drawing up a military appreciation:
what is the problem, what are the factors involved, and what is the
solution, if there is a solution? So I sat down at the desk in my room
and started writing. In the beginning my mind was confused but soon
everything stood out clearly. In a few hours I had produced a document
which contained my thinking and set out my approach to the problems
facing the country. I came to the conclusion that the affairs of the
country, though in a desperate state, were not beyond redemption.
This is how the document read:

A short appreciation of present and future problems of Pakistan

THE AIM

1. The ultimate aim of Pakistan must be to become a sound, solid and
cohesive nation to be able to play its destined role in world history. This can
be achieved only if as a start a constitution is evolved that will suit the genius
of the people and be based on the circumstances confronting them, so that
they are set on the path of unity, team work and creative progress.

2. Before such a constitution can be devised, it is obvious that certain preliminary steps will have to be taken that will provide the setting for unhindered evolution of such a constitution. Taking of such preliminary steps therefore becomes the IMMEDIATE aim of Pakistan.

FACTORS

General

3 (a) The people of Pakistan consist of a variety of races each with its own historical background and culture. East Bengalis, who constitute the bulk of the population, probably belong to the very original Indian races. It would be no exaggeration to say that up to the creation of Pakistan, they had not known any real freedom or sovereignty. They have been in turn ruled either by the caste Hindus, Moghuls, Pathans, or the British. In addition, they have been and still are under considerable Hindu cultural and linguistic influence. As such they have all the inhibitions of down-trodden races and have not yet found it possible to adjust psychologically to the requirements of the new-born freedom. Their popular complexes, exclusiveness, suspicion and a sort of defensive aggressiveness probably emerge from this historical background. Prudence, therefore, demands that these factors should be recognized and catered for and they be helped so as to feel equal partners and prove an asset. That can be done only if they are given a considerable measure of partnership.

(b) The population in West Pakistan, on the other hand, is probably the greatest mixture of races found anywhere in the world. Lying on the gateways to the Indian sub-continent, it was inevitable that each successive conquering race should have left its traces here. Consequently, this forced mixture of races has brought about fusion of ideas, outlook and culture, despite the linguistic variety that obtained. Strategically and economically, too, this area is destined to stand or fall as a whole. Lying as it does in the basin of the Indus river and its tributaries, its future economic development must be considered as a whole to achieve the maximum results. All this indicates, therefore, that West Pakistan, in order to develop properly and prove a bulwark of defence from the North or South, must be welded into one unit and all artificial provincial boundaries removed, regardless of any prejudices to the contrary, which are more the creation of politicians than real. When doing this, however, regard must be had for the prejudices and fears of people and their future balanced development. This unit should, therefore, be so subdivided that each sub-unit embraces a racial group or groups with common economy, communications and potentiality for development, and administration decentralized in them to the maximum possible.

(c) The creation of one unit in West Pakistan, however, is possible only if the biggest constituent is prepared to show large-heartedness and make a sacrifice for the common good. Punjab is the biggest and the most important province in West Pakistan with more than half its population. If she insisted on proportionate representation the others would at once shy off. Besides, no coalition can work with one dominant partner. Therefore, for its preservation and the glory of Pakistan, Punjab should be asked to accept 40 per cent representation in the legislature of this unit; others having representation in proportion to their population. But before such a unit can be brought into being, the existing provincial and state legislatures and cabinets will have to be done away with so as not to interfere with and impede reorganization.

Deductions from the above

(1) Call East Bengal one unit and give it as much partnership as possible.

(2) Reorganize West Pakistan into one unit and give it similar partnership as above.

(3) Abolish present provincial ministries and legislatures to speed up reorganization.

(4) Subdivide each unit into convenient sub-units, each embracing a racial group or groups with common economy, communications and prospective development. Administration to be decentralized in these sub-units as much as possible.

(5) In order to remove any fear of domination, Punjab to be asked to accept 40 per cent representation in West Pakistan unit legislature.

(6) Both East and West units to have their own legislatures.

4. Given the above, the fear of any one unit dividing and dominating others would disappear; harmonious and unfettered development in each unit would be possible; fear of provincialism will be reduced to the minimum; saving in manpower in eliminating so many top-heavy provincial administrations would be effected; expense of administration would be reduced to the minimum, and the danger of politicians interfering with the local administrators curtailed. In other words, very valuable gains would have been made by such a reorganization.

THE ADMINISTRATIVE STRUCTURE OF EACH PROVINCIAL UNIT

5. Having created two provincial units in Pakistan, the next question is to determine the structure of administration in each unit. Before answering such a question, it would be appropriate to reiterate the fact that our eventual aim must be to develop democracy in Pakistan, but of a type that suits the genius of the people. Our people are mostly uneducated and our politicians not so scrupulous. The people are capable of doing great things, but they can also be easily misled. Unfettered democracy can, therefore, prove dangerous, especially nowadays when Communism from within and without is so quick to make use of its weaknesses. We, therefore, have to have a controlled form of democracy with checks and counter-checks. This indicates that legislature finds the cabinet, whose actions are controllable by a Governor, who, in turn, is controlled by the Head of State (President); in certain circumstances,

Governor having the power to remove Ministers or Ministries. He should also be in a position to protect the rights of the services and have them carry out their obligations.

6. Connected with the elections of legislatures is the question of franchise. It is too late now to resile from universal suffrage however great its shortcomings may be. The answer would be to provide checks here too so as to prevent its becoming irresponsible. We must not forget that democracy is a means to an end and not an end by itself and that there is no set pattern of democracy that can be applied to every country without modifications. It would be advisable, therefore, to enable people to elect a college of people in each sub-unit, who, in turn, elect members for the provincial and central legislatures. Such an election system would be more easily manageable and would make for a good deal of responsibility.

7. As to the size and type of provincial and central legislatures, opinions may differ, but the need for strict economy in men and money would indicate that one legislature for each province of about 150 members each would do. Similarly, the central legislature, of which mention will be made later, should not be of a strength more than that.

8. Whilst talking about administration, there is the problem of our legal system, which is most expensive, ineffective, dilatory, tyrannical and totally unsuited to our genius. This would need complete overhaul and made humane, quick and cheap. The answer would seem to lie in having a Jirga-cum-judicial system and revision of evidence and procedural laws with only one right of appeal. The highest judicial court for dealing with cases other than constitutional would have to be created in each sub-unit. The federal or the provincial high courts should deal only with cases of a constitutional nature.

Deductions from the above

(1) In each province there should be one legislature of about 150 members each, headed by a Cabinet. There should be a Governor in each province appointed by President with powers of control over the Cabinet and the services.

(2) Electoral system should consist of election of electoral colleges in each sub-unit by universal suffrage: these colleges to elect members for the provincial legislature, the central legislature, and also elect the President, of which mention will be made later.

(3) The legal system should be simplified and decentralized to sub-units: introduction of Jirga-cum-judicial system to be examined.

(4) Government Servants' Conduct Rules should be revised so as to make summary dealings in cases of rewards and punishment possible.

THE STRUCTURE OF THE CENTRE

9. Having created two units of the country, their federation on an equal basis without fear of domination of one over the other becomes a practical proposition. This federation should consist of one legislative house of about 150 strong, equally divided amongst the two units, headed by a Cabinet.

This Cabinet should have executive powers as voted by the legislature, subject to some effective control by the President, who should be elected. The President should be made the final custodian of power on the country's behalf and should be able to put things right both in the provinces and the centre should they go wrong. Laws should be operative only if certified by the President except in cases where they are passed by three-fourths majority. No change in constitution should be made unless agreed to by the President. In case of serious disagreement between the President and the legislature, provision should be made for fresh elections of either one or both. Acceptance of the Mohammad Ali formula for election of President and passing of laws would perhaps be necessary.

10. For reasons given before, the provinces should have as much autonomy as possible and that means that in addition to the subjects already in their hands, communications, except inter-provincial, industries, commerce, health, etc., should be handed over to the provinces, leaving defence, foreign affairs and currency in the hands of the centre.

11. The quick development of our resources and raising the standard of living of our people is one of the main problems which Pakistan has to solve. This can be done effectively only if we overhaul our educational system to prepare our manpower for the task and to have well-controlled and well-financed organizations to undertake major development projects. That indicates organization of development board rather on the PIDC-fashion for education, cottage industries, land and power and hosts of other things in each province. This arrangement will help relieve local administrations of a lot of headaches and will ensure quick development.

12. But nothing much will be gained unless we carry out land reforms in a scientific fashion. Possession of vast areas of land by a few is no longer defensible nor is acquisition of land without compensation. The Egyptian example is a very good one; they allowed the owner a certain limit of holding, buying the rest for distribution amongst peasants, who will pay the cost in seventy yearly instalments.

13. It was mentioned earlier that the President should be made the repository of power. He can discharge this duty only if the services are made directly responsible to him. To do that, a system of Joint Staff headed by a Supreme Commander will have to be introduced. The Supreme Commander should be appointed by the President. In addition to other duties, he should be made Defence Member and an ex-officio member of the Cabinet. This will not only knit the services together and lead to economy in pooling things common to all the services, but would put a stop to any attempt by politicians to interfere in the internal affairs of the services to promote their personal interests.

14. The experience of the last seven years has shown how dangerous the use of ambiguous clichés can be. Everybody said we should have Islamic Democracy without ever defining what it was and how it differed from the normally-understood democracy. Perhaps it is not possible to define it. Would it, therefore, not be correct to say that any variety of democracy when worked in the spirit of the Qur'an can be called an Islamic Democracy? We shall perhaps do better and avoid many pitfalls if we accept this concept.

OUTLINE PLAN

15. As a preliminary, abolish provincial ministries and legislatures in West Pakistan and create one province of it under a Governor with the requisite staff.

16. Create sub-units in East Bengal and West Pakistan equivalent to a commissioner's division, each division containing racial group or groups with common language, common economy and communications and common development potential. Decentralize administration so that the head of the division becomes the king-pin of administration.

17. Overhaul the legal system so as to make it cheaper and quicker, placing the highest appellate court in a division, except for cases involving points of constitutional law, for which a federal court or a high court in each province should suffice. A Jirga-cum-judicial system should be evolved and procedural law simplified.

18. Create Development Boards in each province covering education, water and power, land reforms and development, cottage industries, etc.

19. Create a Joint Staff for the three services headed by a Supreme Commander who, in addition to other duties, should be Defence Member and be ex-officio member of the central Cabinet coming finally under the President.

20. The central government to consist of one Legislature of about 150 members equally divided between the two provinces, a Cabinet and the President. The President to have over-riding powers to assume control should things go wrong in the provinces or the centre. To avoid undue domination of one province over the other, apply the Mohammad Ali formula to the election of President and passage of bills.

21. The provincial government in East Bengal to consist of a legislature of about 150 members headed by a Cabinet with a Governor appointed by the President: the Governor to have some measure of control over the Cabinet and the services. Same arrangement should apply in the province of West Pakistan, except that the representation of the present Punjab to have 40 per cent and the rest of the seats divided amongst others in accordance with their population.

22. Provinces to have maximum autonomy possible, the centre dealing only with defence, foreign affairs, currency and such communications as are inter-provincial.

23. Government Servants Conduct Rules should be revised so as to make summary awards or punishments possible.

24. The suffrage should be adult franchise, who should be called upon to elect an electoral college in each division, who will then elect the President and members of the central and provincial legislatures.

25. Finally, hope and pray that this Constitution is worked in the spirit of the Qur'an. If so, our solidarity, strength and future is assured.

II

Shortly after the incident when I declined Governor-General Ghulam Mohammad's offer to take over the administration of the country, he said to me, 'Well one thing you must do, you must come into the Cabinet.' I did so, and my first act was to tell the Governor-General and my Cabinet colleagues that we had to do something constructive. They asked me, 'What is it that you would have us do?' I put forward the 1954 document. 'This is my programme. This is what we have got to do. The first thing is to unify West Pakistan.'

I do not claim that 'One Unit' was entirely my idea; other people, too, were talking about it. But my contribution was that when I joined the Cabinet I wanted to work for two clear objectives: to save the armed forces from the interference of the politicians, and to unify the provinces of West Pakistan into one unit. I pressed very hard for it and initiated the process of merger of the provinces.

I well remember one of the personal experiences which helped to convince me of the need for integrating West Pakistan. There was an occasion when we were putting up a manufacturing plant at the Wah Ordnance Factory. When I went there for inspection I found that the machinery was installed but could not be operated because power from Malakand hydroelectric station could not cross the Indus river. This appeared strange, but, on inquiry, I found that power transmission across the Indus was not possible because the Chief Minister of the North-West Frontier Province, Khan Abdul Qayyum Khan, and the Chief Minister of the Punjab, Mian Mumtaz Daultana, were not on good terms. It was a ridiculous state of affairs and most distressing. No one seemed to have any authority to control the provinces or to co-ordinate their working.

The basic weakness in the political system was that there was no focus of power. We had adopted a foreign system of parliamentary rule without understanding the requirements of the system or having the necessary conditions in which it could operate. I was not alone in recognizing the inadequacies of the parliamentary system applied to our circumstances. Professor Rushbrook Williams, who was closely associated with the Quaid-e-Azam when the latter was a member of the Indian Legislative Assembly in Delhi, recalled that the Quaid-e-Azam had told him time and again, 'This parliamentary system is not for us but we have to show allegiance to it to defeat the British, to get you out of the country. It is the only argument you will understand, but I doubt very much if we can work this system.'

During the brief period that the Quaid-e-Azam was Governor-General of Pakistan we had, in effect, a Presidential form of government in the country. The Quaid-e-Azam was Governor-General and he was also President of the Constituent Assembly. The Governor-General, and not the Prime Minister, presided at Cabinet meetings and this was done at the instance of the Cabinet itself. The Quaid-e-Azam was reluctant at first, for it was an unusual arrangement, but on reflection he said that he would attend the meetings; that he would take the Cabinet's advice but would not be overruled.

I remember an interesting meeting I had with the late Aga Khan soon after Liaquat Ali Khan's assassination. The Aga Khan used to write to me whenever I was in England for any conference. On this occasion I went to Nice and stayed with him at Yakimore, a very fine place, overlooking the sea. The Aga Khan was then suffering from heart trouble. He had a tremendous personality and I was deeply impressed by his knowledge of world affairs and his foresight. I can recall several of our conversations, and reconstruct them here from memory.

I said to him, 'Sir, if you had been a little younger, you would be a great asset to us.' He said, 'I wish I had been. Pakistan has been my dream. Now that it has become a reality I wish I could be of some assistance.' He went on to say, 'You have got Pakistan after great sacrifices. You do not want to lose it. But if the parliamentary system is the one you are going to follow then you will lose Pakistan. I have called you here to tell you that you will lose it this way, and that you are the one man who can save it.'

I asked, 'How do you think I can save it?' He said, 'This system has to be changed. Something has to be evolved which is akin to your history, your traditions and your way of thinking. And you are really the man concerned.' I said, 'Well, I understand, Aga'—I began to call him 'Aga' after a stage—'I know of your burning desire to see Pakistan prosper, but you must have patience. Things will work out all right.' He replied, 'No, you are a child. You do not understand. Things are not going to work out all right.'

Then, one day, the Aga Khan started talking about his association with the Quaid-e-Azam. He said: 'He and I never saw eye to eye, but I regarded him as a very great man indeed. I say this because you get one or two opportunities in life when you have to take major decisions. The Quaid-e-Azam had the choice of saying whether the Muslims of India should or should not have Pakistan, and he said: "They will have nothing but Pakistan." He took the right decision, at the right time. You can see his breadth of vision, how great he was, a man of tremendous determination and sense of purpose. Once he made up his mind he put everything into it. I wish he had lived.'

I devoutly wished that, too. The Quaid-e-Azam had the personality and the authority, if he had been spared by Providence, to produce a workable Constitution. People would have accepted anything from him. He was the undisputed leader and is still the idol of the people. Had he been able to give the country a Constitution things might have settled down well in time and the schisms which were later to divide the community might have been avoided.

III

By the time I became responsible for the affairs of the country in 1958 the mood of the people had undergone a certain change. The earlier enthusiasm had given place to lethargy and the first flush of robust optimism had turned into disillusionment. Many hidden tensions and conflicts had come to the surface and the worms of provincialism and parochialism had riddled the fine woodwork of national unity. Regional pulls and centrifugal forces were exercising great pressure and the nation seemed to be at war with itself.

We Pakistanis are a great mixture, of races and of types. Individualistic in our outlook in civil life, we do not easily make a team and yet when disciplined we make first-class soldiers. This offers every budding leader an opportunity to make a team of his own. We are apt to be emotional and do not always take a realistic view of things. No demagogue can resist the temptation of working on our emotions and misleading us. We criticize everybody except ourselves and as there is a dearth of people with knowledge and experience there is a scramble for offices. All this accounts for the distressing and dismal conditions in which the country found itself after the first few years of independence. Yet I was convinced that our people were willing and hard-working, capable of facing great difficulties cheerfully and making great sacrifices whenever called upon to do so. They can never fail in a crisis, blessed as they are with a faith which is a great force for unity and inspires them constantly with a sense of justice and feeling for mankind.

My task, as I saw it, was to set up institutions which should enable the people of Pakistan to develop their material, moral, and intellectual resources and capacities to the maximum extent. The essential prerequisite of this task was to analyse the national problems objectively. I could not convince myself that we had become a nation in the real sense of the word; the whole spectacle was one of disunity and disintegration. We were divided in two halves, each half dominated by a distinct linguistic and cultural pattern. The geographical distance between the two halves was in itself a divisive factor which could be exploited to create all kinds of doubts and suspicions among the people. We had inherited a deep antagonism which separated the people in the countryside from the urban classes. The latter represented a small minority in the total population, but it was a vocal minority and the

21 Addressing the
National Assembly
in Rawalpindi,
12 June 1965

22*a* With President
Gamal Nasser of the
United Arab Republic,
in Cairo, 5 November
1960

22*b* With President
Johnson in Washington,
14 December 1965

people in the villages suffered from a sense of domination and exploitation by the élite of the towns.

Then there were the regional identities which often asserted
themselves to the exclusion of the national identity. These identities
created new demands on national resources and since there was an
overall shortage of available funds, no region could secure all that it
wanted.

But more than anything else it was the irreconcilable nature of the
forces of science and reason and the forces of dogmatism and revivalism
which was operating against the unification of the people. A sharp cleav-
age had been created between the State and the Religion, and all the
old controversies—the temporal versus the spiritual, the secular versus
the religious—revived. In more precise terms the essential conflict was
between the *ulema* and the educated classes. All that was material,
temporal, and secular was identified with the educated and all that was
religious and spiritual became the monopoly of the *ulema*. The educated
classes were regarded as those who had been led astray by western
thought and influence. The *ulema*, who in some cases were versed in
Arabic and had made a special study of religious matters, were regarded
as the custodians of Islam. Among them were many who did not hesitate to convert the influence which they exercised over the minds of the
people into a political asset. They had gradually built up for themselves
a strong political position, opposed to that of the western-educated
groups in society. The conflict between these two classes has a long
history, which I shall have occasion to describe briefly later. What
surprised me was that the conflict should have assumed such grave
proportions in spite of the fact that there was complete agreement between the two groups in matters of principle. Both groups subscribed
wholeheartedly to Islam and both believed in building Pakistan into a
strong and dynamic nation. But the two had not been able to work out
a common and positive approach to national problems. Instead, the
educated regarded the *ulema* as relics of the past and the *ulema* treated
the educated as heretics and unworthy.

How were these conflicts to be reconciled? Islam visualizes life as a
unity and the Islamic code represents a complete cultural whole. How
can life be divided into separate compartments, religious and material,
each compartment governed by its own laws? In Islam all human
activity is determined by the same principle. Life is one and so are the
laws governing life. A man at home, at work, or at prayer is guided by
the same code of behaviour. The same rules which guide us in our
dealings with our own family apply to our dealings with others. There
are no special spiritual rules distinct from rules of conduct in everyday

life. Man is judged as a whole and his actions are determined by their moral content.

All this was true. But the picture of our society, as I saw it, did not conform to this. In practice, our life was broken up into two distinct spheres and in each sphere we followed a different set of principles. How were we to get out of this morass and adopt a unified approach to life? That was the crux of the problem. If we failed, we would stagnate and remain backward. And backwardness meant slavery: our own experience had proved that. Others had abandoned their religion in search of advancement. We were fortunate to have a religion which could serve as a vehicle of progress. But superstition and ritualism had given us a fatalistic outlook which was completely contrary to the teachings and message of Islam. Muslim society could not move forward unless Islam was relieved of all the inhibiting and alien influences which had distorted its real character.

It was this that was my great concern and I recorded the following note on 12 April 1959:

Ever since taking over the reins of government in the country, my main anxiety has been to unite the people and to resolve the internal and external problems of the country. The problems we are facing are enormous, but with God's grace it should be possible to resolve them at least partially, if not wholly. But how to unite the people is a matter which affects the realm of faith and spirit and to which I have not been able to find an effective answer so far. Yet it is imperative that an answer be found soonest possible, otherwise we run the risk of being overwhelmed by other forces and ceasing to exist as an independent people. In fact, then there is every possibility of losing Pakistan. This must not be allowed to happen under any circumstance. Hence the extreme urgency of finding an answer which is comprehensible, tangible, and which should rouse spontaneous and constant enthusiasm and prove workable in the light of the requirements of modern life. My feelings are:

Man as an animal is moved by basic instincts for preservation of life and continuance of race but as a being conscious of his power of thinking he has the power to control and modify his instincts. His greatest yearning is for an ideology for which he should be able to lay down his life. What it amounts to is that the more noble and eternal an ideology, the better the individual and the people professing it. Their lives will be much richer, more creative and they will have a tremendous power of cohesion and resistance. Such a society can conceivably be bent but never broken.

Such an ideology with us is obviously that of Islam. It was on that basis that we fought for and got Pakistan, but having got it, we failed to order our lives in accordance with it. The main reason is that we have failed to define that ideology in a simple and understandable form. Also in our ignorance we began to regard Islamic ideology as synonymous with bigotry and theocracy and subconsciously began to feel shy of it. The time has now come when we must get over this shyness, face the problem squarely and define this ideology in simple but modern terms and put it to the people, so that they can use it as a code of guidance.

In order to define the ideology of Islam and to apply it to present-day conditions of life and especially the conditions of life in Pakistan, it seems that the following broad outline will have to be elaborated:

(a) Singleness of God. Man's urge to love Him in thought and deed.

(b) All human beings are equal before God. Therefore the basic equality of man, without distinction of colour, race, or location, must be recognized.

(c) True that in such a society national territorialism has no place, yet those living in an area are responsible for its defence and security and development. Attachment to the country we live in and get our sustenance from is therefore paramount.

(d) If the above are the ingredients of religion, then religion has to have a say in matters both temporal and secular. Define how?

(e) This world is designed for us to live in constructively and fruitfully. It is not designed to be shunned. In order that creative power is developed modern education is absolutely vital.

(f) Define the duties of the State and those of the individual. What is the definition of a 'Momin' [believer]?

(g) State fundamental rights for the individual which are wholesome for the individual as well as for the State.

(h) What method should we adopt to acquaint the present generation and the future generations with this philosophy?

(i) Considering that the people of Pakistan are a collection of so many races with different backgrounds, how can they be welded into a unified whole whilst keeping intact their local pride, culture, and traditions?

The requirement is to express the above in a language which should be comprehensible to the largest number of people and capable of being put into practice.

Who should undertake this task? I could not possibly attempt it because I was conscious of my limitations. I could only emphasize the need for bringing about unity and balance in society. We had to reconcile the requirements of our faith with the requirements and compulsions of the time. No nation could live and survive in the glory of its past alone.

There was universal agreement that the country should have a democratic Constitution and a Constitution which should enable the community to organize itself according to the essential principles of Islam and to develop and progress with the times. The question was who should determine the democratic content of the Constitution and define the essential principles of Islam. There were two ways of doing this. We could determine these principles with or without the help of the *ulema* and then introduce them by decree. The other alternative was to let people determine these principles themselves with the assistance of specialized agencies acting in an advisory capacity. I chose the latter course. The Constitution Commission was later to recommend that we should set up an International Muslim Commission to advise us as to how our laws could be made to conform to the injunctions of the Holy Qur'an and the Sunnah. I doubted whether a Commission of this kind would serve any useful purpose. I sounded some Heads of States at that time but they showed no enthusiasm for the idea. It was obvious that we would have to address ourselves to our problems and work out our own solutions. The burden of thinking must rest on the community itself.

The essential decision that I made in dealing with the question of giving an Islamic content to the Constitution for the country was that the responsibility of determining the principles according to which the affairs of the nation should be organized and conducted should be entrusted to the community itself. The Constitution should provide a framework based on the experience and history of Islam and suited to the genius, temperament, and traditions of the people, but within that framework the community should be free to adopt principles derived from the Holy Qur'an and the Sunnah and evolve methods for the application of those principles to its own circumstances. This was the only way in which the principles of democracy could be reconciled with the principles of Islam.

The question arose as to how the community should discern and define the principles of Islam. There was no ready answer to this. No precedent of an Islamic Constitution was available. The Holy Qur'an contained the principles of guidance but did not prescribe a detailed Constitution for running a country. The example of the Holy Prophet (Peace be upon him) in organizing an Islamic State was, of course, available. After the Holy Prophet the four Caliphs organized and administered the State according to their understanding of Islamic principles. Each one of them had applied the principles of Islam and the teachings of the Holy Prophet in accordance with their circumstances. No specific pattern of government or even of the election of the Head of Government had been established. The conclusion was inescapable that Islam had not prescribed any particular pattern of government but had left it to the community to evolve its own pattern to suit its circumstances, provided that the principles of the Qur'an and the Sunnah were observed. In more recent times a number of Muslim countries had adopted constitutions to meet their requirements without claiming that they had produced an Islamic Constitution which could be adopted by all Islamic countries. It was clear to me that Pakistan must work out its own system of application of the principles of Islam to its conditions. It was equally clear to me that this exercise must be conducted within the accepted democratic norms, of which the most important is the participation of the people in the affairs of the State. The right of the people as a whole to organize and run their affairs could not be curtailed or compromised in any manner. And no person or group of persons, however knowledgeable, could be allowed to sit in judgement on the community expressing itself through its elected representatives. All this established the supremacy of the Legislature acting for and on behalf of the people. It also established that the people must have the freedom to choose their representatives and their leaders of government. To ensure that the Executive and the Legislature acted within the provisions of the Constitution there was need to set up an independent Judiciary. In this scheme of things there was obviously no place for a supra-body of religious experts exercising a power of veto over the Legislature and the Judiciary.

In all this, I was guided by my understanding of the institution of *ijma* (consensus) provided in Islam. According to one school of thought *ijma* represents the agreement, in a matter requiring opinion or decision, of the *mujtahids*, people who, by virtue of their knowledge of Islam, have a right to form their own judgement. Another school of thought interprets *ijma* as the opinion of the majority of all Muslims. There is yet another view that in modern times *ijma* means the opinion of the Legislature representing the elected representatives of the community and that the right to formulate independent judgement on matters affecting the life of the people vests in the Legislature and not in any body of scholars. I did not want to prejudge the issue and therefore in the constitutional arrangement I left it to the representatives of the people to decide how they would like to form their judgement in matters relating to the Qur'an and the Sunnah. I thought it necessary to provide an Islamic Advisory Council backed by an Islamic Research Institute to assist the Legislature in framing laws based on the concepts of Islam. The council was to have as members not only those persons who possessed a knowledge of Islam but also those who understood the economic, political, legal, and administrative problems of the country so that the requirements of Islam and the requirements of the time and circumstances could be harmonized.

I knew that the *ulema* would not be satisfied with this arrangement. They claimed the exclusive right to interpret and decide matters pertaining to Islam. While they maintained this claim they refrained from producing any detailed constitutional document, knowing that such an attempt would only expose their internal differences. Their demand was that the government should agree to adopt an Islamic Constitution, leaving it to the *ulema* to decide whether any law or measure was Islamic or not. I must pause here to discuss briefly the role of the *ulema* in the political life of Pakistan.

The history of the *ulema* in this sub-continent has been one of perpetual conflict with the educated classes. This conflict came to a head during the struggle for Pakistan. It is well known that a number of Muslim *ulema* openly opposed the Quaid-e-Azam and denounced the concept of Pakistan. Now I do not suggest that those among the *ulema* who opposed the creation of Pakistan were all men of easy conscience. Among them were people of ability and conviction, but there were also those who thought that Pakistan might mean the end of their authority. The best among them argued that the Indian freedom movement would be retarded if Hindus and Muslims did not act in union. Some also felt that Pakistan was essentially a territorial concept and thus alien to the philosophy of Islamic brotherhood, which was universal in character. Both these arguments were the result of confused thinking and revealed a lamentable ignorance of the problems which the Muslims of the sub-continent were facing. Freedom was coming; it could not be delayed. What worried the Muslims was not the pace of freedom but that when freedom came they should be able to order their lives according to their own lights. The end of British domination should not become for the Muslims the beginning of Hindu domination. They were not seeking to change masters. They knew through past experience that the Hindus would not agree to live with them on equal terms within the same political framework. Those of the *ulema* who were members of the Indian National Congress failed to realize the significance of this simple truth and eventually found themselves completely isolated from the mainstream of the Muslim struggle for emancipation.

Their opposition to Pakistan on grounds of territorial nationalism was again the result of their failure to grasp contemporary realities. How could the demand of a hundred million Muslims for a homeland of their own conflict with the concept of universal Islamic brotherhood? A homeland is an identity and surely the Muslims of the sub-continent could not have served the cause of universal brotherhood by losing their identity, which is what would have inevitably happened if they had been compelled to accept the political domination of the Hindus. The *ulema* thought in terms of a glorious though nebulous past and a vast but undefined future of Muslim brotherhood. And this more than anything else damaged the growth of Muslim nationalism and retarded the progress of Muslims in the sub-continent. Without a strong base of their own the Muslims of the sub-continent were no more than a bunch of busybodies dabbling and interfering in the affairs of others on the pretext of universal Islamic brotherhood. What use could they be to other Muslim countries when they did not have even a home of their own? Those who thought that a national outlook was incompatible with the concept of universal brotherhood were really suggesting that the Muslims of the sub-continent should not try to establish a homeland of their own because there were homelands enough of Muslims in other parts of the world. Why have a home of your own when there are so many Muslim homes in the Middle East? It was this kind of reasoning which led the Khilafat Movement, inspired by such noble ideals, into a blind-alley. Some of the ablest Muslim scholars in India argued that the western powers, especially the British, were destroying the Ottoman Empire. But they did not realize that the Arabs and the Turks were locked in a grim battle to establish their respective national identities. The Turks had started the Turkish nationalist movement and were strongly advocating the concept of Turkey for the Turks. Arab national sentiment demanded freedom from the Turks and a separate identity of its own. It suited the British to exploit these national sentiments. Our *ulema*, who led the movement for re-establishing the Khilafat in Turkey, never realized that the idea of Khilafat had been abandoned by the Turks themselves. Charmed by the vision of Islamic brotherhood, they embarked on a prolonged struggle, thinking that if the Khilafat was re-established, the Muslim world in the Middle East would be held together under the Turks and the Turks would, one day, become strong enough to come to India and drive out the British!

Now, the opposition offered by some of the *ulema* to Pakistan was not wholly the result of confused thinking or lack of awareness of the problems of Muslims. Behind it was the consciousness of power.

I wish to make it clear that here I am referring to that class of *ulema* who were openly engaged in politics and not those God-fearing people who have served the community by teaching the Qur'an and propagating the message of Islam in a selfless, humble, and devoted manner. The political *ulema* that I am talking of were those who claimed to be Indian nationalist Muslims as opposed to Muslim nationalists and were the members of the Indian National Congress or of other groups and organizations acting in collaboration with the Congress. These people exercised considerable power through their association with the Indian National Congress, which was the majority political party in the sub-continent. Even after the Quaid-e-Azam had demonstrated the representative character of the All-India Muslim League as the only political party entitled to speak on behalf of the Muslims of the sub-continent, Congress insisted on the inclusion of Muslim members of the Congress Party in any political set-up proposed by the British. These Muslim members of Congress believed that in undivided India, with Congress as the ruling party, the leadership of the Muslims would remain in their hands. The *ulema* knew that the leadership of the Muslims in the sub-continent was gradually passing to the modern educated classes who had found an eloquent and powerful spokesman in the Quaid-e-Azam. The determined fight which the Quaid-e-Azam was putting up against the British and the Hindus posed a serious threat to the authority of the *ulema*. The Quaid-e-Azam's advocacy of the cause of the Muslims, and his complete selflessness and devotion, transformed a mass of disorganized individuals into a powerful national reality. It was this new leadership that the *ulema* dreaded and against which they aligned themselves with the Indian National Congress.

The conflict between the educated Muslims and the *ulema* was not new. It started in the early years of British rule and reached its culmination during the struggle for Pakistan. For decades after the British had consolidated their position in India, the *ulema* kept the Muslims away from all sources of western knowledge. Not until the middle of the nineteenth century was this barrier of prejudice broken or did the Muslims begin to recover from this voluntary denial of knowledge. The Muslim renaissance in the sub-continent began with Shah Waliullah who started probing into the past and thinking in terms of the future. Then came Sir Syed Ahmad with his gospel that the Muslims could not progress without acquiring knowledge of modern sciences and technology. He asserted the simple truth that knowledge is not the preserve of any nation, it belongs to the whole of mankind. Quickly he was dubbed a *kafir* (non-believer) by a section of the *ulema*. But Sir Syed Ahmad, in spite of all the calumny that was heaped on him, refused to be browbeaten. He maintained a valiant posture and succeeded in releasing the intellectual energy of a nation. As more and more Muslims got educated in western sciences the hold of the *ulema* over the Muslim community began to weaken.

Pakistan was the greatest defeat of the nationalist *ulema*. But they are a tenacious tribe and power is an irresistible drug. Soon after the establishment of Pakistan this type of *ulema* reorganized its forces. Now that Pakistan had been established, these people asked, who indeed, except the *ulema*, could decide, how the new Muslim State should be run. Some of the nationalist *ulema* decided to stay in India; others hastened to Pakistan to lend a helping hand. If they had not been able to save the Muslims from Pakistan they must now save Pakistan from the Muslims. Among the migrants was Maulana Abul Aala Maudoodi, head of the Jama'at-e-Islami party, who had been bitterly opposed to Pakistan. He sought refuge there and forthwith launched a campaign for the 'Muslimization' of the hapless people of Pakistan. This venerable gentleman was appalled by what he saw in Pakistan: an un-Islamic country, un-Islamic government, and an un-Islamic people! How could any geniune Muslim owe allegiance to such a government! So he set about the task of convincing the people of their inadequacies, their failings, and their general unworthiness.

All this was really a façade. The true intention was to re-establish the supremacy of the *ulema* and to reassert their right to lead the community. Since the movement for Pakistan was guided by the enlightened classes under the leadership of a man who was the symbol of western education, the prestige of the *ulema* had been badly damaged. This damage had to be repaired. The political *ulema* had two courses open to them: either to re-examine their own position and to revise their attitudes so that the people might be able to gain from their knowledge in dealing with their problems; or to demolish the position of the educated classes in the eyes of God-fearing but uneducated masses. Not unnaturally, they adopted the latter course. A society which had just emerged from a century of foreign domination and was faced with the practical problems of building a new country suffered from many defects and weaknesses. The *ulema* concentrated on these. They spread throughout the length and breadth of the country to convince the people of the misery of their existence and the failings of their government. They succeeded in converting an optimistic and enthusiastic people into a cynical and frustrated community. The *ulema* claimed that they knew all the answers and could easily solve all the problems of the country, but that they were helpless as the country was in the control of the modern educated classes who had disowned Islam and taken to western ways. Since no leadership could provide an immediate solution to all the problems of the community, the *ulema* were able to build up a large following for their point of view.

It is in this context that the demand for an Islamic Constitution was so ardently advocated by the *ulema*. Since no one had defined the fundamental elements of an Islamic Constitution, no Constitution could be called Islamic unless it received the blessings of all the *ulema*. The only way of having an Islamic Constitution was to hand over the country to the *ulema* and beseech them, 'lead kindly light'. This is precisely what the *ulema* wanted. A Constitution could be regarded as Islamic only if it were drafted by the *ulema* and conceded them the authority to judge and govern the people. This was a position which neither the

people nor I was prepared to accept, opposed as it was to the fundamental democratic principle that all authority must vest in the people.

Gradually the outlines of the Constitution began to emerge. While
all sovereignty belongs to Allah the people of an Islamic State have the
authority to organize and administer their affairs in accordance with the
injunctions of the Holy Qur'an and the Sunnah. God had given them
access to sources of guidance and reason, and the intelligence to interpret and understand what was contained in those sources. They must
use these faculties and determine the principles of guidance, if necessary
with the assistance of experts. Having determined these principles,
they should find methods and procedures for their application to their
problems. They must be able to act in an organized manner through
their representatives to frame laws for the common good and they must
have a proper Executive to implement those laws and perform administrative duties on their behalf, and an independent Judiciary to
determine that the Legislature and the Executive conduct themselves
in accordance with the provisions of the Constitution.

After these basic questions had been decided I tried to determine
the form of government which would be best suited to the genius of the
people and would be in consonance with the teachings and history of
Islam. A thorough study of Islamic history and of the constitutions
adopted by different Muslim countries was undertaken. Two things
emerged clearly from this study: there was no place for kingship in
Islam and succession could not be determined on a hereditary basis.
The community as a whole must have the right to choose its leader and
the right to remove him. Another feature of Islamic history which had
found general acceptance was that the leader, once he is chosen by the
community, should have sufficient power to co-ordinate, supervise, and
control the activities of government. Delegation of authority was per-
missible but central control must remain in the hands of the chosen
leader who should provide unified direction to the country and its
administration. Such a central authority seemed all the more necessary
in our social and political circumstances. Without a strong central
authority the country could not be held together. Muslim rule in the
sub-continent started to decline and the community suffered after the
Moghul Emperor Aurangzeb mainly because of the weakening of the
central authority. And this was true of other periods of Islamic rule too.

The intelligentsia of Pakistan had become accustomed to a sort of
parliamentary democracy, but actual experience had shown that this
form of government, instead of serving the cause of the people, had
only encouraged divisive tendencies and brought the country to the
verge of collapse. We had suffered enough in the past on account of it

and could ill afford to repeat the same mistake. The alternative form, and the one which seemed to meet our requirements, was the Presidential form of government.

An elected President free to choose his Cabinet was the answer; and a legislature consisting of one or two houses, which should not be unduly large because of the paucity of the type of manpower required. The relationship between the President and his legislature must be so regulated as to give the President adequate powers to maintain stability and prevent frequent breakdowns: in other words, the type of executive and legislature that approximated as far as possible to those that existed at the time of the early Caliphs. We should provide reasonable checks and balances to ensure that both the President and the Legislature acted with propriety, good sense, and responsibility. And if either of them failed in their respective spheres of duty it should be possible to eliminate either one or both of them.

The Provincial Governors should be nominated by the President to ensure that his writ would prevail in the provinces. Without this the whole edifice would crumble. There should be a full measure of delegation of subjects to the provinces to give them adequate responsibility, autonomy, and flexibility.

To me these seemed the minimum basic requirements of the Constitution I visualized for the country. But people who had got used to the parliamentary form and knew how the form could be exploited, found it difficult to accept my thinking. I once invited some people in East Pakistan to meet me. The late Maulvi Tamizuddin Khan and Mr. Nurul Amin were among them. I discussed with them the whole range of constitutional problems.

Maulvi Tamizuddin said he was dead against the Presidential form of government and I asked what his objection was. He replied: 'My objection is that Muslim history as well as our political experience has been the rule of one man. My fear is that we will revert to it, even though we have got freedom and democracy.' I said: 'If this is in the Muslim blood, how are you going to take it out? In any case, don't you see the difference between an autocrat and an elected President? Does not the United States of America have a President and is the U.S. not democratic? And how do you propose to sustain the parliamentary form of democracy in this country, with ten or fifteen political parties, none with a national outlook or programme, except the Muslim League?' He thought that we should decree by law that there were to be only two parties, but I answered: 'Tamizuddin Sahib, if by law you can control people's conscience, then why don't you make all Muslims into one sect? In all, there are seventy-two sects in Islam, even though they all seek inspiration from the Qur'an. Let me tell you that you cannot control people's conscience by legal contrivances.' He said: 'Even then, I would like to have a parliamentary form of government.' In frustration and exhaustion I replied in strong terms. The old man took it well.

Mr. Nurul Amin remained quiet. I think he wanted to keep out of the controversy. But Maulvi Tamizuddin spoke with conviction, genuine conviction, however unrealistic. I always admired his courage.

So a great debate started as to the respective merits of the parliamentary and presidential systems of government. Some, like Maulvi Tamizuddin Khan, held that the parliamentary system in the country had been condemned without having been given enough time to establish itself. What they meant, perhaps, was that we had not given ourselves enough rope to hang ourselves with. Had we gone on for another five or ten years the way we were going, we should have been doomed.

The point is that a parliamentary system can only work when you have well-organized parties, and a limited number of parties, each working for a clear-cut social and economic programme. Some people say, 'What does it matter if we have five or ten parties? We can always have a coalition government?' Is that the best we can do for the country? Can coalition governments, in a developing country, take difficult and firm decisions, sometimes against tradition and the customary way of life? A responsible government cannot be a prisoner of wayward public opinion. You have to move ahead of public opinion and draw people in your direction. The objectives before me were the unification of the people and the development of the country. To attain these objectives we required a stable, representative government, continuity of administration, and well-planned programmes of economic growth. The nation had to move resolutely into the age of science and technology while maintaining a firm hold on the essential principles of its faith and ideology.

It is easy to talk about removing the inhibiting effects of history: it is a different thing dealing with them in practical life. How can you run a parliamentary democracy when you have big landlords in the country who can influence thousands of votes? How can you run a parliamentary democracy when you have *pirs* and *faqirs* who can influence the people indirectly? How can you have parliamentary democracy or stability when you have ten or fifteen or more political parties in the country without any programme whatsoever? How can you have parliamentary democracy when you have not even reached the level of universal primary education?

While trying to create institutions, the easiest thing to do is to get hold of some textbook, English or American or Russian, and say, 'This is how they did it. Why not follow their text?' The point is, will it work? Will people take it to heart? Will they regard it as their own? If not, then the whole exercise will end in futility.

IV

I was once asked, 'In which book did you come across the fundamentals of the Constitution?' 'In the book of Pakistan', I replied; 'it is based on my knowledge of the people and the soil of Pakistan.'

I do not know whether the term 'Basic Democracies' describes aptly or fully the system of local governments which I envisaged. It was basic in so far as the whole structure was to be built from the ground upwards, and it was democratic in the sense that the affairs of the country were to be entrusted to the people within a constitutional framework. I had two broad objectives in mind: one was to organize people to take care of the problems of their areas and to inculcate in them the spirit of self-help; the other, to find a meaningful electoral system for the election of the President and the members of Assemblies.

The democratic instrument, as worked by the politicians, had been warped beyond recognition. The Constitution which had been introduced in 1956 was no better than a bundle of unworkable compromises. My endeavour from 1958 on had been to restore the nation by introducing necessary reforms in various fields. All these reforms were devised and oriented to prepare the country and the people for a representative government in the shortest possible time. The object was not to impose any particular system from above, but to cause a system to grow from below in relation to the social, economic, educational, and moral realities of the situation. All changes and reforms that were introduced had only one purpose: to prepare the base on which the upward pyramid of a sound political system could be developed.

Past experience had shown that the western type of parliamentary democracy could not be imposed on the people of Pakistan. There were certain basic requirements in the western system which were lacking here: this system presupposed a high degree of social and political awareness, universal education, and an advanced system of mass communication for speedy and accurate dissemination of information on a wide variety of themes of individual and general interest. In the absence of these prerequisites, people could not be expected to exercise their right of vote in the context of broad national policies. It is too much to expect a man, sick and illiterate, and worried about his next meal, to think in terms of national policies.

Now, we could not wait for these conditions to come into existence before restoring democracy; we had to introduce a system which the people would be able to understand and work in spite of their handicaps. This meant going to the hard core of the nation. The large majority of our people lived in villages; they were mostly uneducated and illiterate. But they had the wisdom to understand their own problems. What was needed was to put the problems to them in a simple and straightforward manner to enable them to form a judgement. Again, in asking them to make a choice between individuals, they should be enabled to know them personally or by reputation.

These difficulties about the formulation of issues and providing knowledge about individuals could be largely overcome if there were well-organized political parties, supported by advanced media of communication, capable of explaining their programmes to the people. Unfortunately, we had no political parties worth the name; those that existed had no national programme. To ask people to join in a mass ritual of voting for candidates whom they had never seen or known really meant robbing them of their vote by inducement or intimidation. Such an arrangement suited only demagogues and charlatans. Since these had nothing concrete to offer, they vied with each other in arousing the passions of the people and working on their emotions. People engulfed by economic and social problems responded to their appeals. They were promised the moon and, for a moment, they allowed themselves to be deluded and duped. More often than not these appeals had a negative and disruptive character. All this tended to generate hysteria and created suspicion, distrust, and disunity among the people. Under this system people were really being used against themselves.

I was fully conscious of the opposition I would encounter on introducing any change in the system: first, from the intellectuals, a small but vocal minority fed on western ideas. These people, because they have had the advantage of education, form the élite and regard themselves as leaders of public opinion. They talk in terms of the people, often quite genuinely, but few among them have any real contact with the people and fewer still have given any serious thought to the problems of the people. It is enough for them to claim that all power should belong to the masses; they are not worried about how and in what form the power should be exercised. They claim to fight against illiteracy, poverty, hunger, and disease, but the fight is conducted through slogans not solutions. They react strongly against illiteracy but do little for the illiterate. They condemn poverty but have no sympathy for the poor. They blame hunger but offer no relief to the hungry.

Secondly, the opposition would come from the vested interests: the politicians and the landlords. They are accustomed to commanding the allegiance and loyalty of the people in their areas, and they will not allow the individual to exercise his judgement or question their authority. And finally, opposition would come from the orthodox classes, the obscurantists who frustrate all progress under cover of religion.

All these people would fight against any change in the electoral system which would make the common man the master of his own will. Yet one must do the right thing by the country, whatever the consequences.

I went down to the village level in the rural areas and the *mohalla* level in the cities. That was the level at which one could get to know the people directly and intimately; that was where the real problems existed. I realized that the masses in the village, however uneducated, were conscious of the immediacy and urgency of individual and community interests. It was at that level that they knew the people on whom they could depend to help and guide them and to work for them. A system of government which had its roots at that level would bear fruit.

I formulated the following principles to govern the future role of Basic Democracies: first, they should reflect the representation of the people obtained in the most direct manner; secondly, they should become the nerve centres of their areas where all local problems of development and civic responsibility could be studied at close range and their solutions discovered and applied with concentrated attention; thirdly, they should in course of time absorb the official agencies and begin to function as people's bodies; and, finally, they should be operated to generate vigour and enthusiasm and liberate those moral and intellectual forces which are essential to the development of a dynamic and dedicated leadership in the country.

Two days after Martial Law was promulgated, I told a Press conference, on 10 October 1958, that power would be handed back to the people. Three months later I went on record as saying that as soon as vital reforms had been carried out the country would have a Constitution based on the wishes of the people and capable of serving their interests. I had made it clear that Pakistan would not copy any other country's Constitution, but would have one entirely her own, in keeping with the country's social and economic conditions.

The creation of Basic Democracies was the first step towards fulfilling this objective. And as experience has subsequently proved, through the system of Basic Democracies we have been able to awaken and organize the masses into taking intimate and practical interest in their collective affairs and having a deep sense of self-help and participation. The gulf between the officials and the masses has been narrowed.

The decision to create Basic Democracies was taken at the Governors' Conference held in Karachi from 30 April to 1 May 1959. More detailed decisions on the new system were taken at the Governors' Conference at Nathiagali on 12–13 June that year. The formal Basic Democracies order was promulgated on 26 October, providing for the setting up of institutions ranging from local councils to provincial Development Advisory Councils.

Elections to the Basic Democracies units were completed early in January 1960. Martial Law regulations prohibiting the organization, convening, or attending of any political meetings organized by candidates, were relaxed for the forthcoming elections. Approximately, a unit of 1,000 voters (adults, male and female) was required to elect one representative. These single-member units, which numbered about 80,000 (approximately 40,000 in each Province), were then to be grouped together to form the tiers of the local administration system. There were to be about 4,000 of these first-stage groupings in each Province, and they were to be known as the Union Councils in the rural areas and the Town or Union Committees in the urban areas.

At this stage, I felt that I should have a mandate from the people to continue in my task. It was therefore decided that before the election results of Basic Democracies were announced, I should take the opportunity of seeking a vote of confidence from the 80,000 Basic Democrats so that I might be able to give the country a Constitution under a mandate from the people. The results of the vote of confidence, as announced by the Election Commission on 15 February 1960, were: 75,283 affirmative votes in my favour, representing 95·6 per cent of the approximately 80,000 votes cast.

After being sworn in as the first elected President of Pakistan, on 17 February 1960, I immediately announced the setting up of a Constitution Commission, under Mr. Justice Shahabuddin of the Supreme Court, with five members from each Province. The Commission's terms of reference were:

(1) To examine the 'progressive failure of parliamentary government in Pakistan leading to the abrogation of the Constitution of 1956, and to recommend how a recurrence of similar causes can be prevented'.

23 With His Majesty King Faisal of Saudi Arabia, in Rawalpindi, 21 April 1966

24　With his grandchildren at Murree, 11 June 1961

(2) To submit proposals for a Constitution, taking into consideration 'the genius of the people, the general standard of education and political judgement in the country, the present state of nationhood, the need for sustained development, and the effect of constitutional and administrative changes in recent months'.

(3) The proposals would embody recommendations as to how best the following ends could be achieved: (i) a democracy 'adaptable to changed circumstances and based on the Islamic principles of justice, equality, and tolerance'; (ii) consolidation of national unity; and (iii) a firm and stable system of government.

Many people thought at the time that I was moving too fast and that I should allow sufficient time for the reforms to take root. We had earned considerable respect and prestige in the world by bringing them about and achieving substantial results; much of this would be imperilled by too swift a return to a constitutional government. An English friend asked me, 'Why are you in such a hurry to bring in a Constitution?' I said, 'I thought you were a democratic people.' He replied, 'Yes, but you are running the country so well under the present system and you are making sound progress. You will land yourself in trouble again if you are not careful.'

At home, too, there were certain people, including some members of my Cabinet, who were convinced that the vested interests who had been badly hit by our reforms, such as landowners, politicians, and similar groups, would combine in an all-out attempt to unseat me and to destroy whatever had been achieved in the past few years.

I knew the feelings of the people at large also. Many thought I was throwing them back to the wolves and that, once again, there would be no respect for law, that corruption and jockeying for power would return, with all the other ugly features of our political life in the past. I realized that once the lid was off, the politicians would run amuck and try to demolish everything I had done. The Press would also lend a helping hand, because newspapers that advocate irresponsibility and opposition to government run up very high sales. I knew also that people who had benefited from the reforms were not strong or organized enough to defend their new positions. So it would be my task to defend them and the new laws against pressure-groups and vested interests.

Nevertheless, I came to the conclusion that it was better to take the risk, even if all our reforms had not yet taken root, and to let the people carry on from that point. They must assimilate and implement the reforms according to their capacity. I was not forced to this decision by any internal or external pressure, but I was deeply conscious of the grave responsibility which I had undertaken to give the country the right sort of Constitution. I thought I had the answer and I wanted to put it into effect.

I had announced in October 1958 that I intended to work 'as near as may be' to the 1956 Constitution. Though Martial Law had operated under the 1956 Constitution, it was effective because a focus of power was created by the Martial Law apparatus which was lacking in the 1956 Constitution itself. I had worked out definite ideas about the future Constitution. But I was fully prepared to 'accept the Commission's recommendations even if they are different from my ideas provided they are better than mine and good for the country'.[1] Further, the Commission 'enjoys full freedom and full powers to make such recommendations as it deems proper for the country. In this behalf it is not to be influenced by anything except its own conscience and its love for Pakistan.'[2]

After the establishment of the Commission there was nothing to do but wait for its Report, which was presented to me on 6 May 1961. The Commission found that the causes of the failure of the parliamentary form of government in Pakistan were 'mainly the lack of leadership resulting in the lack of well-organized and disciplined parties, the lack of character in the politicians and their undue interference in the administration'. Under the circumstances it recommended that Pakistan 'should have a form of government where there is only one person at the head of affairs, with an effective restraint exercised on him by an independent legislature, members of which, however, should not be in a position to seriously interfere with the administration by exercising political pressure for their personal ends'. The need for a strong centre with a quasi-federal structure was strongly advocated by the Commission.

Dealing with the minority view that the centre should be given only three subjects, defence, foreign affairs, and currency, the remaining powers being left with the Provinces, the Constitution Commission said,

One of the main grounds for this view was that the Lahore Resolution of 1940 speaks of independent states and that, therefore, the provinces should be autonomous. But the East Pakistan envisaged in the Lahore Resolution was the whole of Bengal and Assam which could have been an autonomous province as it would have had industries and large economic resources. It could not have been anticipated at that stage that the former Bengal and Punjab provinces would be divided and Pakistan would get, as its eastern half, the unindustrialized portion of Bengal. The partition of these provinces was a later development arising from the last-minute efforts of the majority community of undivided India to avoid partition of the sub-continent.

[1] Address to the Karachi High Court Bar Association, 15 January 1959.
[2] Constitution Commission Report (Karachi, 1961), pp. 2–3.

If, at the time of the Lahore Resolution, it could have been foreseen that ultimately a division would take place and that the present East Pakistan would be the only portion of Pakistan in the East, the Muslim League would not have thought of regarding it as an autonomous province because, without industrial development, it is impossible for East Pakistan to sustain itself as an independent unit. At the time the Lahore Resolution was passed, partition of the sub-continent into two independent countries was not within the pale of practical politics. It seems to us extremely unwise and unrealistic to insist on a literal following of the said Resolution regardless of whether the present units of Pakistan can develop themselves, and manage their own affairs, without a strong centre.[1]

The Commission advocated a bicameral legislature, a Vice-President, direct election on the basis of restricted adult franchise, and separate electorates.

I accepted the Commission's suggestions regarding the Presidential form of government, the federal structure, and its plea for a strong centre. However, I was unable to accept its recommendation for a bicameral legislature and a Vice-President. The franchise question was left to the legislature which decided in April 1964 in favour of Basic Democracies serving as an Electoral College for elections to the national and the provincial assemblies and to the office of President.

I must say I was impressed by the work of the Constitution Commission. It had produced a document worthy of the highest consideration and I remember I made detailed comments on its Report for the guidance of a Committee of the Cabinet which examined the Report.

My own analysis had led me to the conclusion that Pakistan needed a strong government capable of taking decisions which might not be popular but which were necessary for the safety, integrity and, in particular, development of the country. We could not afford the luxury of a system which would make the existence of the government subservient to the whims and operations of pressure-groups. On this I was not prepared to make any compromise.

A comparison is often sought between political conditions in India and Pakistan. How is it, it is asked, that the Indians have been working a parliamentary democracy while we have not been able to do so? Well, first of all national consciousness came to the Hindus much earlier than to the Muslims of the sub-continent; the Indian National Congress Party was formed much earlier. Among the Hindus there was no schism as among the Muslims. There were several Hindu parties, but they were united on the fundamentals. The Muslims were divided. Some wanted to try out living with the Hindus in the mistaken belief

[1] Ibid. pp. 40–41.

that they would have a place in Hindu nationalism. The majority of Muslims, however, knew that after the British they would be subjected to another form of domination, namely, that of the Hindu majority. Among the Hindus there may have been some who thought, 'let us tolerate the Muslims', but the majority wanted either to drive them out or keep them as serfs.

But the fact that the Hindus have been able so far to run a democratic State with a parliamentary form of government does not mean that this system has come to stay in India. I believe changes will occur and that the impetus and cohesion that the freedom movement generated is now dying out because of the emergence of personal wrangles, regional tensions, and linguistic identities. Disintegration of the Congress Party is inevitable. When that happens, India will face later what we faced earlier.

To come back to the Constitution Commission's Report, on the question of franchise and the mode of voting I differed with the views of the Commission. It recommended a system of direct elections based on restricted franchise. It suggested that the extension of franchise should go hand in hand with the spread of education and, in our present circumstances, the suffrage should be restricted to those citizens of Pakistan who either were educated enough to read the political debates, or had adequate property to give them 'a stake in the country'. For this purpose it recommended that a Franchise Committee be appointed which should submit, within one year, its report determining the required standards so that electoral rolls could be prepared in time for direct elections for the second term.

I could not see why Basic Democrats should not become an Electoral College. Here we had eighty thousand members elected directly by the people on the basis of adult franchise and they, in fact, formed the 'Grand Assembly of Pakistan'. Why should not they choose the President and members of the legislature? To condemn them because a small proportion of Basic Democrats were uneducated was nothing short of pedantry. Surely these eighty thousand members were better equipped and qualified to elect members of the assemblies than the previous eighty who used to make and unmake governments in the days of parliamentary governments? A case is sometimes made out against Basic Democrats acting as an Electoral College on the ground that, being limited in number, they are susceptible to bribery and corruption. I am afraid it is true that in some constituencies money does change hands, especially in big cities and places where there are moneyed people. But it is not entirely the fault of the Basic Democrats; it is the moneyed candidates who corrupt them and compete with each other in bribery. I have come to know that in a recent by-election in Karachi the opponents of a candidate thought of a simple formula for getting him defeated: they just went round and told voters to demand so much money per vote. Now, some voters cannot resist such a temptation. This would happen even if elections were held on the basis of direct adult franchise. In fact, far more money would then pass hands and only a millionaire would dare to contest. This, however, does not absolve us from doing all we can to eliminate or reduce chances of corruption in elections. The trouble is that unless people are politically conscious and realize their sacred duty of exercising the right of vote on principle, no amount of legal provision against corruption can help.

I was quite clear in my mind that until our educational and economic standards and the level of political responsibility improved considerably, the only course for us was to adopt indirect elections through Basic Democracies. Moreover, there would be terrible confusion and chaos in the country if the importance of Basic Democrats was belittled in any manner. It was the first time that representatives of the people had come to a position of equality with government officials at different levels of administration, and had acquired a direct say in the running of the country. If any attempt was made to by-pass them in building the final tiers of representative government, it would meet with strong resistance. The system was fast taking root in the country and an identification was being established between the official agencies of government and the representatives of the people.

I also could not agree with the Commission's recommendations for the creation of a post of Vice-President, to whom the President should delegate some of his functions. The Commission's view was that Vice-President should represent one wing and President the other wing. The idea that a Vice-President could relieve a President of his onerous duties is not correct. He could not have the total picture before him: major matters would always go up to the President, and a Vice-President should not be confined to routine work. The idea of a Vice-President as a running-mate was, in fact, unsound. The supreme need would always be to find the best man for President, because so much would depend on him. If he were to be bracketed with a second-rate man the focus of elective decision might be blurred.

Equally fallacious was the argument that a running-mate would help the President secure votes from the Province other than his own. A Presidential candidate should be a national figure enjoying the confidence of the people of all parts of the country. He would make a poor President if he depended on a Vice-President for political support in one part of the country. The representation of one wing of the country through a Vice-President would, inevitably, create east-west controversies and set up factions within the Presidential cabinet itself. What was needed was to provide for a stand-by to take over from the President in the event of his death or absence from the country. This could be done by establishing a convention that if the President was from one wing, the Speaker of the National Assembly should be from the other and that he should officiate in the absence of the President.

The Constitution Commission also recommended a complicated procedure relating to any disagreement between President and legislature over the budget and money bills. I agreed with its view that the President should have the right of partial veto, but I disagreed with the rest of the recommendation which required the President and members of the legislature to seek a fresh mandate from the people in the event of their failure to resolve the difference. I felt that we should have nothing but instability if we followed this procedure. To say, as the Commission had said, that the members of the legislature would be less inclined to act irresponsibly if they had to seek re-election in the event of any difference with the President, overlooked the fact that if we made Basic Democracies the electoral college, as we must, then re-election would hold no terror for an average legislator, whereas the President would have the formidable task of canvassing all over the country because his electorate would cover the entire strength of 80,000 electors.

The answer was to reduce to the minimum the causes of disagreement between the President and the legislature. The budget should be in two parts: one part should cover the expenditure required for the administration and the continuing expenditure on development programmes carried forward from the previous year; the other part should cover all new items of expenditure. Any reduction in expenditure in the first part should require the consent of the President and the second part should be voted by the legislature.

V

The proposals of the Constitution Commission were examined at a Governors' Conference in Rawalpindi from 24 to 31 October 1961. I announced the Constitution in a broadcast to the nation on 1 March 1962. I said that the new Constitution embodied 'a blending of democracy with discipline—the two prerequisites to running a free society with stable government and sound administration'.

The Constitution was generally well received though there was no lack of criticism in a certain section of the Press. Some of the old politicians thought that if the new constitutional scheme was allowed to get established, they would lose all importance. One of the bitterest critics was Chaudhri Mohammad Ali, author of the 1956 Constitution: he felt robbed of immortality. On the introduction of the Constitution the country started behaving like a wild horse that had been captured but not yet tamed. Every time you try to stroke it affectionately or feed it, it bites you and kicks you. That was the state in which things were at first. For a year or so, the going was hard, but then things began to calm down and the virtue of stability was recognized.

The whole object of the critics during the first year or so, inside the National Assembly, outside the Assembly, through the Press, through ex-politicians or Ebdoed politicians,[1] was to break my will. Once they had done that, they felt that I would have no option but to follow their dictates. They wanted to reassert their control and, once again, be the 'king-makers' if not the 'kings'. They wanted to bring about a situation where not so much my position (that would not have mattered) but the very existence of the country would depend on their sweet will. They wanted me to feel that I would not be able to run the country without them. That was their game.

At the height of the agitation against the Constitution I learnt the gist of a certain leading politician's thoughts: 'This President is a funny man. He knows that the whole lot of them are up against him and he also knows that I am the only man who can curb this agitation and produce some understanding between the people and him. Yet he has been back a fortnight from England and has made no overtures to me. There must be something seriously wrong with him.' They really thought I would go down on my knees and say: 'All right, I give up, you fellows win!'

Curiously enough, they also realized that they could not run the affairs of the country without me. They wanted to keep me on some pedestal so long as I left them free to do what they liked with the country. They said they were not after me personally but were after breaking my resolve and thereby putting me in a position where I could not prevent them from wrecking the country. All they wanted was an opportunity to get at the people through demagogy and empty slogans and to use them for selfish ends. I was bent upon preventing this—cost what it might. My faith in God and in the people sustained me. Our people are good, I knew, but they are simple-hearted, hence gullible, and they can be easily misled. It was this conviction which helped me, but there were moments when it was extremely difficult

[1] Those who chose to withdraw from political activity under the options offered by the Elective Bodies (Disqualification) Ordinance of 1959.

and trying. I would say to myself: 'This outburst of irresponsibility under a new Constitution is inevitable. Martial Law curbs have come to an end. The lid has been lifted. The steam has to be let off.' I knew that things would settle down in course of time, but it all depended on whether I remained firm or not. The final test of the Constitution would be the Presidential elections in 1965. For the first time the entire adult population in the country would choose the Head of State through their elected representatives. The results of that election would establish the support of the people for the Constitution. Until then the process of persuasion and education must go on.

People must learn to give and take; without this there can be no democratic system. After all, one cannot have it all one's own way; the minority must accept the verdict of the majority. They have the right to criticize, but not the right to destroy. My opponents sometimes say: 'This man is a dictator; he has all the power in his hands.' How? I do not know. After all, there always has to be someone finally in charge whatever the system, be it parliamentary or presidential, a monarchy or a dictatorship. There are many to assist but, in the ultimate analysis, one man has to take the final decision. This has been the case throughout history, and it is so even today all the world over. If the man is chosen by the people and if he is a good man, he has to be trusted and given full co-operation.

To my knowledge there has never been so much freedom in this country as there is today. On a number of occasions I have been accused, abused, and vilified, subjected to all kinds of rumours and slanders, all thoroughly unjustified and untrue, by some of the biggest blackguards in the country, and I have swallowed it. I have put up with it for the simple reason that I want to nurse and protect the system. I will not allow it to be demolished.

I also feel that if the man at the top commands respect, he does not have to be a dictator. The people will follow him in their own interest, because human nature demands and, indeed, cannot live without leadership. And whether one likes or dislikes the leader, nature compels one to support him because one knows subconsciously that one's safety and future depends on it. But to maintain a position of trust with the people, one must be sincere and selfless and have the fear of God in one's heart.

In the light of past experience, I had provided certain built-in safeguards in the Constitution to enable the executive to withstand home pressures without in any way hindering the working of the legislature. The opposition, conveniently forgetting the mandate which the people had given me, have continued to say that this Constitution has been thrust down their throats. Now, they can go to the people's representatives and ask them to change the Constitution: there is a clear provision in the Constitution that if there is anything which does not meet with the wishes of the people the members of the legislature can amend it. They have the powers even to impeach the President. But to ensure that these provisions are not frivolously used, they can be invoked only subject to certain restrictions.

The Constitution Commission had provided for the impeachment of President, Governors, Ministers, Chief Justice, and Judges of the Supreme Court. The President could be impeached for gross misconduct or wilful violation of the Constitution on a motion of one-fourth of the elected members of the legislature: we decided to make the motion admissible on a resolution signed by one-third of the total members of the National Assembly. The Commission had recommended that the President would vacate his office if he was found guilty by two-thirds of the total members of the legislature: in the Constitution, we made him removable by not less than three-fourths of the total members. In order to check irresponsible and vindictive moves against the President it has been provided that if the resolution for the removal of the President fails to obtain one-half of the total votes in the National Assembly, the movers of the impeachment resolution will cease to be members of the Assembly.

I felt that Governors and Ministers should be omitted from the list of those who could be impeached, because they were to be the appointees of the President. It was natural that if he sensed opposition to his Governors and Ministers in the legislature, the President would make it his business to remove them in order to carry the legislature with him. As nominees of the President, they did not have to be exposed to the legislature.

The Constitution Commission had made the amendment of the Constitution an easy process. It recommended that any amendment would be subject to the assent of the President in the same manner as any other piece of legislation, with the difference that the bill for the amendment should be supported by a two-thirds majority. If the President withheld his assent and referred the bill back to the legislature, the effect of his veto could be nullified by a three-fourths majority. We decided that before a bill for the amendment of the Constitution went to the President for assent, it should have a two-thirds majority support, but if he referred it back to the legislature, then it would have to be passed again by a three-fourths majority vote. However, when the bill went again to the President for assent, he would have the option to refer it back to the legislature once more, and if the legislature insisted he could submit the bill to a referendum by the entire Electoral College to decide whether it should or should not be assented to.

However, a bill to amend the Constitution that would have the effect of altering the limits of a Province, cannot be passed by the National Assembly unless it has been approved by a resolution of the assembly of the province concerned by two-thirds of the total number of members of the Provincial Assembly.

The structure of the Constitution has been raised on a number of pillars. These are: the Presidential system, the devolution of power to the Provinces to the maximum extent, the appointment of Provincial Governors by the President, the system of Basic Democracies serving as an Electoral College, the Advisory Council on Islamic Ideology for consultation in law making, and finally the relationship between the executive and the legislature and between the executive and the judiciary. If any of these pillars is shifted or removed, the whole structure would be weakened; the Constitution stands or falls as a whole. With the creation of the Electoral College all that has been done is to interpose an additional large assembly between the people, and the provincial and central assemblies and the President.

Now ideas need time to gather support. It is after the benefits begin to flow from those ideas that their defenders emerge. These defenders then become the protagonists and protectors of those ideas. In human affairs new concepts must produce new vested interests.

The reforms which I introduced have created powerful, though not yet organized, vested interests. There are millions of men and women who are tillers of the soil, deriving substantial benefits from the land reforms. Then there are the commercial and business classes and the educated classes who are getting more and more opportunities for education and employment. Today it is a problem to find suitable young men for government service, whereas some years ago to get into government service was regarded as the height of one's ambition. Now a new vista of life and opportunities is opening, new things are happening, new interests of a broad-based and popular character are developing, and a large new middle class is emerging. It is these people who will ultimately look after the new system given by the Constitution, though this will take time.

It has been my task to identify the new philosophy which would enable our people to lead a fuller and more progressive life. This philosophy has to be such as people believe in and are ready to defend and support. Weaning people away from an established system which they have long known, even if it is decadent and remote from their requirements, is a very difficult job. People tend to embrace the comforts of the old, rather than risk the hazards of the new. The most glaring example of this is the parliamentary form of government: the moment I offered a different and more practical system, some people started an agitation that I was trying to perpetuate myself in power. That is the last thing in the world that I desire. But I do want to perpetuate one thing, and that is a new tradition of progress and development. I do hope that I am creating some converts to my way of thinking and to this way of life. I also feel that this way of life can only really be sustained by young people. The older leadership must yield place to a new and younger leadership. My endeavour has been to create conditions for younger people to take over, for they alone will be able to develop this tradition and improve upon it.

That is the only vested interest I have: to save and protect the system for which I have sweated blood. I have had to work against very heavy odds and I will not see this system trifled with. Modify it, change it by all means, but in the light of experience, in a spirit of conviction and belief, and for the good of the people; not for any other reason. In a Presidential system, if one has a man as President who can stand up to pressure, the chances are that another five or ten years can be gained for new institutions to take deeper roots, for education to spread farther, and for a larger middle class to come into existence. There would then be enough people to defend these institutions. And that is what is at stake in Pakistan today.

The big change from the previous parliamentary system is that whereas the present National Assembly is sovereign in law-making, it cannot change the government. True, political bickering and mud-slinging by the Opposition goes on as in the past, but that is inevitable, especially since our new parliamentarians are inexperienced. But it is important that they should have full freedom of speech and expression.

I must confess to one miscalculation in respect of the Constitution. Having suffered through the perfidy of the so-called political parties, I was hoping that we would be able to run our politics without the party system. Therefore the Constitution was so framed that, in theory, it would function with or without political parties. After the introduction of the Constitution, I soon came to realize that one could not do without political parties. Within the legislature the members could only be organized on the basis of party rule and discipline. Outside, there had to be an organization to maintain contact with the people. There was also a need to explain government policies to the people in the countryside; this could only be done by a political party. So I came to the conclusion that under our conditions one could not really work the system without political parties. And I think a good deal of confusion in the first year after the announcement of the Constitution occurred because it took us time to build the Muslim League party, especially in the central and provincial legislatures.

This was not surprising since the legislators had been elected on individual merit and I knew very few of them. Before the elections I told the Provincial Governors and the officials that these elections must be completely free from influence or interference. I warned them that if I learnt that anybody had meddled with the elections in any way I would have serious cause for complaint. If we had decided to revive political parties before the elections, I have no doubt that the government would have had powerful support in the legislature. Revival of parties had been suggested to me, but in a hesitant and feeble manner. It is human to be wary of something from which you have suffered, and we had suffered greatly through the party system.

There was considerable surprise in the country when I joined the Pakistan Muslim League. This only showed how, like myself, many people felt that we should have run the Constitution without political parties. But the politicians, too, were dismayed at my decision to join a political party; they wanted me to remain isolated. The question was, could I remain outside the party system once parties had been allowed to come into being by the law?

People sometimes ask me to help organize an opposition party. Now that is really a most unusual demand. How do I do that when the ideology of most of our opposition parties is based on acute provincialism, religious exploitation, and extra-territorial loyalty. Let any opposition party work for Muslim nationalism in Pakistan and a strong centre, and it will have my support.

Unfortunately, even within the legislature, the opposition has been behaving in a way which has forced me to rely entirely on my own party. This need not be. The President should be free to pick men for his Cabinet, depending on merit and support, either inside or outside the legislature, regardless of party affiliations. A Presidential Cabinet, in our conditions, need not—indeed, should not—be a one-party Cabinet.

VI

Before concluding this discussion on the Constitution I must refer to a phenomenon which has been the cause of considerable tension and misunderstanding between the two Provinces. This is the slogan of 'disparity', which has assumed considerable social significance and usually refers to an assumed lack of equality between the two Provinces of the country. It is a much-abused word and covers a wide variety of complaints and grievances, very often of a personal character. If a candidate does not have the requisite qualifications and is, therefore, not selected for a job, he dubs it 'disparity'. So does a shopkeeper who cannot collect enough capital to set up a jute mill. The jute mill-owner, too, claims himself to be a victim of disparity because he cannot expand into synthetics and chemicals. The politician has seized on this general impatience for a personal advancement and turned it into a popular political slogan. He bases his whole campaign against the central government and West Pakistan on disparity.

Now disparity is recognized by all and so is the need to remove disparity. What is not realized is that 'disparity' is a phase in the process of development. Not all parts of Pakistan were equally developed or undeveloped at the time of independence. Certain parts of West Pakistan were relatively advanced industrially whereas in East Pakistan there was hardly any manufacturing capacity. During the early days of British administration in the central and eastern regions of the sub-continent, all commercial and industrial activity centred round Fort William in Calcutta. There was no significant shift when India came under the direct rule of the British Crown. East Pakistan remained a hinterland of Calcutta. Although the area produced 70 per cent of the world's jute not a single jute mill existed in the Province. The entire produce went to Calcutta in *katcha* bales to be processed and exported. Transport and communication facilities were of a rudimentary type, and no effort was made to exploit natural resources like coal, gas, oil, power, and water.

When the younger generation in East Pakistan is reminded of these facts they feel that past history is being used to explain away their present difficulties. They are encouraged to demand that progress in other parts of the country should be stopped till their Province comes up to the same level. Now they forget that the urge for advancement which inspires them is shared equally fervently by people in other parts of the country.

It is inconceivable that any government should be able to compel people in one region to work at less than their capacity till others build up an equal capacity. It should be the aim of a Welfare State to narrow down the gaps and eliminate imbalance, but the only way to do it is by providing greater incentives to less developed areas rather than by denying existing incentives to the relatively developed ones. It would be a futile and self-defeating policy to bring about uniformity by lowering levels of progress all round.

The problem of regional disparities in West Pakistan has been solved to a large extent by the integration of the former provinces into One

Unit. Resources are used to build up social overheads, the benefits of which are available to the whole of West Pakistan regardless of the former provincial boundaries.

The economic development of East Pakistan has been one of my major interests. I had said in the 1954 document that East Pakistan should be built up into an equal partner. That is the only way in which the province will be able to pull its weight in national affairs. Even though Suhrawardy as Prime Minister in 1957 had declared that East Pakistan had achieved parity with West Pakistan to the extent of 98 per cent, I thought it necessary to make a provision in the Constitution itself for the removal of inter-regional and intra-regional disparities. It has been provided as a principle of law-making in the Constitution that no law shall be enacted which may hinder the growth of any distinct language, script, or culture. And as a principle of policy, the Constitution enjoins on the government to take special care to promote the educational and economic interests of people of backward classes or in backward areas.

The Constitution also provides for special consideration to be given to people of a particular area to enter into the service of Pakistan to perform functions in relation to that area. This is intended to ensure that in relation to the central government, persons from all parts of Pakistan, and in relation to a provincial government, persons from all parts of the province, should have an opportunity of getting employment under the government.

Apart from these general considerations, the Constitution provides that parity should be achieved, as nearly as is practicable, between the provinces of East and West Pakistan in all spheres of central government. Similarly, the Constitution requires that persons from all parts of Pakistan be enabled to serve in the Defence Services of Pakistan.

To attend to the special economic needs of less developed areas, the National Economic Council is required, under Article 145 of the Constitution, to formulate plans to ensure that disparities between the Provinces and between the different areas within a Province in relation to per capita income are removed. It is the responsibility of the Council to ensure that the resources of Pakistan (including resources in foreign exchange) are used and allocated in such a manner as to remove inter-regional and intra-regional disparities in the shortest possible time. The National Economic Council is required to submit a report every year to the National Assembly on the results obtained and the progress made in removing disparities.

I decided to make these provisions in the Constitution to raise the problem of removal of disparity above the personal and parochial level.

In the political sphere, East Pakistan has equal representation with West Pakistan in the National Assembly and in the President's Council of Ministers. But parity in terms of uniform economic progress requires more than constitutional provisions. While the government recognizes the principle of parity, the people, too, have to discharge their responsibility. It is not enough to claim parity of resources and parity of opportunities; it is equally important to recognize parity of endeavour. Equality in progress can be guaranteed only by equality in effort. So the slogan of disparity should not be used as an excuse for personal inadequacies.

And I think we have achieved a considerable measure of success in building up economic capacity in East Pakistan to bring it to par with the more advanced areas of West Pakistan. Until 1957–8, East Pakistan was getting no more than 40 per cent of the total amount made available by the central government as assistance to the Provinces. According to the latest figures, in 1966–7, East Pakistan will receive from the central government 1,746·21 million rupees as against 1,200·7 million rupees assigned to West Pakistan. There is no truth in the claim that East Pakistan's earnings of foreign exchange are utilized by West Pakistan. The position in 1963–4 was that East Pakistan had a minus balance of foreign trade to the tune of 224·6 million rupees and a minus balance of 381·9 million rupees in inter-wing trade between East and West Pakistan. In 1964–5, the foreign trade balance of East Pakistan was minus 434·5 million rupees and the inter-wing balance minus 382·1 million rupees. These figures are conclusive proof that there is no transfer of capital from East to West Pakistan, nor is West Pakistan using the foreign exchange earnings of East Pakistan.

What needs to be recognized is that the whole country must participate fully in the national effort for development. This I have said requires not only making demands for parity but working for parity by contributing equal endeavour.

VII

You must always carry the people with you. You may have a first-class idea, but that idea can be useful and effective only if it is put into practice. And it is the people alone who can implement ideas. Unless the people are convinced of the validity of an idea, and are prepared to go along with it, the whole purpose is defeated. My attitude and approach has always been that I am a Pakistani, and I feel for my people and my country. Here are some of my ideas which have in them the fire of my heart; give them a trial for your own good. There has never been any attempt on my part to force anything on people against their interests.

The Constitution I have given is not an imported herb; it is a genuine home-grown plant. It suits the conditions, the requirements, and the genius of the people. It has all the elements of democracy and it will work and give stability to the country. I have full faith in the present system but it is for the people to give it a fair trial; it is for them to protect its integrity. There is no institution or system in the world that cannot be corrupted or brought into disrepute if the beneficiaries decide to exploit it to further their limited ends regardless of the larger interests of the community.

History will not go on giving us opportunities; we have to make use of those we have. If we fail to develop the system we have got, we shall be exposing ourselves to a bleak and chaotic future.

12

The Presidential Elections

The concept of Basic Democracies had been evolved and the scheme prepared in cut-and-dried form. Towards the end of 1959 the adult population of the country went to the polls to elect their representatives, who came to be known as Basic Democrats. Constituencies were delimited and Martial Law Regulations amended to allow candidates to organize public meetings. The results of this election were announced on 11 January 1960.

A few days before, I was advised by the Cabinet to seek a vote of confidence from the 80,000 members elected to the Basic Democracies Councils. I accepted this advice. I felt that I must have a clear mandate from the people to set up the necessary constitutional machinery in the country. I undertook an extensive tour of both Provinces. The mission was to meet the people and to explain my thinking to them and the lines on which I proposed to initiate the constitutional processes. I met millions of people during this tour and addressed innumerable public meetings. The Basic Democrats gave me an overwhelming vote of confidence. The ballot was held on 14 February and the results were announced on 15 February 1960. As I have mentioned earlier, I received confirmation in 95·6 per cent of the approximately 80,000 votes cast. I was sworn in at Rawalpindi on 17 February 1960, for a four-year term, as the first elected President and immediately thereafter I announced the setting up of a Commission to draw up a new Constitution for the country.

From February 1960 to March 1962 was the period during which the system of Basic Democracies was nursed and developed. Representatives of the people at various levels were enabled, in an organized manner, to familiarize themselves with the conditions and problems of their areas and a forum was provided for them to solve their problems in collaboration with the official agencies of the government. Schemes and projects were drawn up by the people themselves and implemented through voluntary effort supplementing official initiative and organization.

During these two years, people came to recognize the merit of electing representatives from among themselves and observing their work and watching their conduct at close range, in matters of immediate concern to the people. Simultaneously, institutions were set up to provide training to Basic Democrats in methods of government development work. The official machinery came in for close scrutiny by the people and gradually it began to identify itself with the needs and requirements of the common man. My whole effort was to build up the confidence of the people in their representatives so that they would be able to entrust them with more important political responsibilities in course of time. The mandate which I sought from the Basic Democrats in 1960 was the first step in this direction.

I gave considerable thought to the question whether Basic Democracies should be given political functions or be restricted to economic and social work. The theoreticians advised me that not only should the Basic Democrats be given no political responsibility, but that their association with government agencies should also be terminated. Now, I thought that if I were to agree to this I should be making the whole system ineffective. The association with the officials had produced two wholesome results: in the first instance, it was acting as a check on the working of the government; and secondly, and more important, it was providing the Basic Democrats with an opportunity not only to understand how government functioned but also to supervise and guide its functioning. If the ultimate aim was that all local government activities should become the direct responsibility of people's representatives, then this association between the Basic Democrats and the officials was unavoidable. I could foresee the time when officials would become the functionaries of the local councils and the representatives of the people would assume their legitimate role of administrators.

The idea that development and politics should be kept apart was equally unrealistic. I did not want the Basic Democrats to be reduced to the position of unwanted social workers without any authority or say in the political affairs of the country. We did not have enough men to provide parallel leadership, one for development activities and the other for political affairs. If the Basic Democrats were denied the right to represent their constituencies in political matters, they would lose all importance and become subservient either to the bureaucracy or to those who exercised influence because of their wealth or other tribal and sectarian considerations.

I was not unconscious of the fact that the Basic Democrats elected by the people in 1959 were not in all cases the best that the community could offer. The old politicians had carried on an insidious propaganda against the system, and all means were employed by them to prevent people of merit from assuming leadership in their areas. In certain cases they had their household servants elected as Basic Democrats. Their purpose was to disrupt the system and expose the 'village folks' to ridicule. In this they had the support of the urban 'élite' who often laughed at the regional costumes and 'native' manners of Basic Democrats. The big turban of one Basic Democrat was enough for the intellectual to distrust the whole system. How could anyone who did not converse in English become a representative of the people? These Basic Democrats, who had never read a Shakespearean play and could not quote a line from T. S. Eliot, appeared to them like some kind of barbarians who had been elevated to positions of leadership.

All this propaganda was aimed at the dignity of the common man and was the intellectuals' response to a system in which all people, regardless of wealth or education, had been provided with new avenues of progress. But inadvertently they helped to prove my point. Leadership was not the exclusive preserve of the few who had acquired proficiency in western sciences and humanities; leadership belonged to the people. A household servant might make a better leader than the master because he had more sympathy for the people and more time for the problems of the community. It was this attitude of the old politicians and certain sections of urban society that finally convinced me that if Basic Democrats were not given political responsibility they would be destroyed in no time and, along with them, the whole system would crumble.

By the beginning of 1962 people had begun to realize the utility and effectiveness of Basic Democracies and it was becoming obvious that I intended to give them political functions. The new Constitution was announced on 1 March 1962. The Basic Democrats then proceeded to elect the representatives of the people to the National Assembly in April 1962 and to the Provincial Assemblies in May 1962. Prior to these elections I issued an Order authorizing the Election Commission to take all necessary measures to ensure that the elections were conducted honestly, justly, and fairly, and that corrupt practices were eliminated. The old politicians thought that if they did not seek election they would find themselves excluded from political life. It was interesting to see many of those who had publicly criticized and discredited the system eating their words and approaching Basic Democrats for support. The masters were going to household servants and the élite to 'turbaned natives' for votes. It was a fitting nemesis!

The political parties had not yet been revived. I announced on

10 May 1962 that the whole question of political parties would be considered by the National Assembly 'after full and public discussion'.

The new National Assembly met in Rawalpindi on 8 June 1962. I was sworn in under the new Constitution of the Second Republic. Martial Law was lifted on that day and from then on the country was to be governed by the normal law of the land. I appealed to the Assembly and to the people to give a fair trial to the Constitution. As I saw it the main objectives before the National Assembly were:

(1) to ensure the integrity of Pakistan against external danger and internal disruption;

(2) to make Pakistan as strong as possible and to promote among its people a national outlook, removing all traces of distrust and suspicion between the two wings; and,

(3) to adopt measures for the moral and material happiness of the people, paving the way for a social welfare State.

These objectives could be achieved only through a strong and stable government capable of formulating and implementing long-term plans and policies. If the existence of government was subject to dishonest alliances and pressures of political parties, the country would not make any progress.

The next important thing was to bring about complete understanding and unity between East and West Pakistan. Because of the distance separating the two Provinces some differences and misunderstandings were inevitable, but it was of the utmost importance to realize that if these differences were carried too far in certain areas disaster would follow: we had to recognize that the unity, security, and progress of the country were matters of common concern. In my inaugural address to the National Assembly I said:

From today we are entering a new phase of our national life and activity. In a major change of this nature I hope people will act and react with a sense of maturity, wisdom, and discipline. It will give us great satisfaction if the blessings of the restoration of constitutional institutions are appreciated and recognized by people in all spheres in general, and by the members and the intelligentsia in particular. As leaders of public thinking, it devolves on them to give a lead in dignified behaviour and decorum. Confusion in thought and action is the last thing we as a nation can afford.

I would like to remind you that the recommencement of the constitutional process does not mean the re-start of political life from the stage where it stood on 8 October 1958. During the last three and a half years an enormous amount of thinking and planning has taken place at a fast pace. During this period, people have got used to expecting concrete results from the government. They will expect the same from you as well. This means that only constructive efforts and sound statesmanship will reawaken the discerning consciousness of the people and not mere emotional and fiery outbursts and speeches.

On the measure of success we attain in working the Constitution in the spirit in which it has been evolved depends the well-being of our future generations and also the vindication of the faith and belief of those who, under the leadership of Quaid-e-Azam, Mahomed Ali Jinnah, struggled so hard and suffered so much for the creation of Pakistan.

The great debate on the Constitution did not abate with the inauguration of the National Assembly; indeed, the whole thing continued to be discussed with great passion inside the Assembly. I made it clear that I would be prepared to accept any positive and constructive amendments in the Constitution; that was the whole purpose of providing a procedure within the Constitution itself to propose amendments. But if any attempt was made to tamper with any of the fundamental concepts, the whole constitutional framework would collapse. And I would not be a party to any process which would result in confusion and chaos.

The National Assembly had two important subjects to deal with: one related to the question of the revival of political parties, and the other to the mode of voting under the system of universal franchise provided in the Constitution. The Assembly came to the conclusion that political parties should be allowed to operate and I gave my assent to the Bill which was passed by the Assembly for this purpose. The Report of the Franchise Commission was also submitted to the Assembly and by a large majority the Assembly decided that people should elect the President of the country and their representatives to the National and the Provincial Assemblies through the Basic Democrats functioning as an Electoral College. The Assembly also decided that the Basic Democrats should first complete their functions as members of the Electoral College before they were vested with responsibilities in the sphere of social and development activities. I gave my assent to this also.

I would have thought that the National Assembly, having determined these two vital issues, would then get on with the work of nation-building. But political groups and organizations outside the Assembly maintained their pressure and kept the atmosphere charged with controversy. The opposition, which consisted of several groups, was severely divided on the question of revival of formal political parties. A section among them advocated that political parties should not be revived and a fight for what they called the 'democratization of the Constitution' should be waged under some kind of a united command. Others were more realistic. They decided to revive their respective political parties to prepare for the forthcoming general elections in 1965, under the Constitution. As far as I could understand, the former group wanted to avoid the general elections. In the days when they were in power they had always managed to retain control by frustrating all programmes of elections: they had rarely faced even a by-election, let alone general elections. About them I was not worried because I knew that the system had gained enough confidence among the people to be able to repel their designs.

The groups which proceeded to set up political parties were welcome to me. I knew that the Constitution would have to be submitted to a political test during the forthcoming general elections and I was determined that the country should have a full-fledged experience of elections on a national level. I would need, I realized, a political party to fight the final battle for the Constitution. The Pakistan Muslim League was revived and I accepted the Presidency of the League. My real anxiety about the opposition parties was that most of them had adopted political programmes which were basically negative in character and depended on emotionalism and agitation; no one among them had any national philosophy. There were some working for a virtual separation between the two Provinces in the name of autonomy. They also wanted to bring about the disintegration of West Pakistan. Others were working against all progress and development and wanted to establish some obscurantist type of dictatorship in the name of religion.

It was suggested to me at that time that I should not identify myself with any political party, and there was some advantage in that. But considering the agitational role to which opposition was committed, I decided to support the only political party which had presented to the people a positive and national programme reflecting the ideology of Pakistan and the people's urge for progress.

As 1964 approached, the opposition stepped up its activities and started looking for a presidential candidate. They knew that no single party was in a position to put up a candidate of its own. Some of them thought that, following their example, I might perhaps postpone the election on some pretext. But the scientific way in which electoral rolls were being prepared by the Election Commission and the whole programme of election was being formulated, convinced them that I was determined to submit myself to the will of the people. It was only thus that I could prove the Constitution was a real and dynamic institution and not a fake document devised to suit my personal ends. It was a people's institution designed to serve the people's ends.

I had a fair idea of the strength of the opposition. A number of elements were unhappy with the reforms I had introduced. Certain religious groups were making a song and dance about the Family Laws Ordinance. Those who had suffered as a result of the land reforms and lost authority were finding it difficult to adjust themselves to the changed conditions. Then there was an element in East Pakistan which wanted a weak and ineffective centre; its aim was to work up hatred against the central government and West Pakistan and thus undermine the solidarity of the country. I also knew that the opposition would lose no opportunity to blame me personally for all acts of omission and commission, major or minor, of the Administration. They would hold me responsible for what a foot-constable might have done in a remote village or a clerk in the court of some magistrate. Since the rule of law was not a part of their life, they would tend to attribute everything to an individual.

In September 1964 the Combined Opposition Parties (COP) agreed to nominate Miss Fatima Jinnah as their candidate for the office of President. Now Miss Jinnah had nothing in common with the various opposition parties yet she did not hesitate to come into the field, having obtained from them a unanimous pledge of support. To me, her acceptance of the Opposition offer did not come as a surprise. Since the entire Opposition campaign was to be based on emotionalism, her choice seemed logical: she was the sister of the Quaid-e-Azam and she was bound to attract considerable attention for sentimental reasons, if for nothing else. The Opposition also knew that after she had served their purpose they could easily get rid of her. In this they might have been mistaken, but it was their calculation at the time.

I do not know what considerations weighed with Miss Jinnah. She was leading a solitary life and had shown little interest in politics except for issuing periodical statements to the Press on days of national importance. Since the death of the Quaid-e-Azam she had maintained a consistent posture of opposition and criticism towards every government. Even during the days of Liaquat Ali Khan she was running an opposition of her own, never missing an opportunity of creating a sense of depression and distress among the people and undermining their confidence in the government of the day. In her seclusion and under the protection of the memory of the Quaid-e-Azam, she set herself up as an arbiter and a mentor. When Martial Law was promulgated she welcomed the change but soon after reverted to her customary role. On one occasion, I wrote to her that she might acquaint herself with the full facts of government policies before pronouncing judgement on them. I think she never forgave me for offering this advice.

Miss Jinnah might have reckoned that there was a good deal more opposition to me in the country than there really was, and that with the support of the old guard she would get to the position where she longed to be. In one respect I was happy about her nomination. The Opposition had brought into the field the strongest possible rival that they could find. The elections would be well contested and would establish the validity of my thesis based on reason and pragmatism against the Opposition's claim on people's sentiment and emotion.

The nomination of Presidential candidates was announced before the people chose their representatives for the Electoral College. Every adult member of society knew that the Basic Democrat whom he elected would be called upon to choose the future President of Pakistan. Under the Electoral College Act, passed on 17 April 1964, each of the two Provinces was divided into 40,000 territorial units and each one of these units was to elect one Basic Democrat to form the Electoral College for the office of President and for the members of the National and Provincial Legislatures. The Election Commission defined these units, 'having regard to territorial unity, distribution of population and administrative convenience'. The average population for each unit worked out at 1,073 persons on the basis of nearly 45 million registered voters out of a total population of 110 million. The work of delimitation and the settlement of objections was completed by 25 July 1964, and details of electoral units were published, along with the unit-wise registration of voters, by the middle of August. A large number of polling officers were required; they were drawn from the ranks of government officials, doctors, and teachers.

These elections to the positions of Basic Democrats generated far greater interest than the previous ones held in 1959. Everyone knew that the results would ultimately determine the pattern of democracy in the country. In East Pakistan more than 100,000 persons contested the elections. In West Pakistan over 128,000 persons filed nomination papers in 44 districts only. By and large, the elections proceeded smoothly though there were incidents of violence at some of the polling stations. A majority of the people elected as Basic Democrats belonged to the 30–40 age group. In East Pakistan more than 54 per cent of the elected members were educated up to the secondary standard; in West Pakistan 21 per cent of the elected members had received secondary education and over 27 per cent had received primary education. These percentages were higher than the provincial average of education.

None of the political parties was organized enough to issue party tickets for elections to 80,000 seats. The Opposition took advantage of this situation and claimed any candidate who had any prospect of winning as their candidate. The effect of this was that a most amusing situation developed after the results of elections were announced during

October and November 1964 in the two Provinces: every political party claimed to have won nearly all the seats. To support their claim they all started releasing lists of their candidates. It was not surprising that most of the names were common to all the lists.

II

Miss Jinnah launched her presidential election campaign in the third week of October well before the election of the Basic Democrats. She started from Karachi. In the very first public meeting she revealed her full hand: there would be no holds barred. Cool reasoning and argument were to have little place; it was going to be emotionalism all the way. She attracted a huge crowd in Karachi and there was a great deal of table-thumping and slogan-mongering.

I had a meeting with some of my political associates to review the results of her first public meeting. They looked depressed and worried. Their main concern was that the kind of attack she had launched would be difficult to meet because she was after all an old lady and widely respected as sister of the Quaid-e-Azam. I told them that she had to be treated as a presidential candidate—a rival—and that we had to fight her all the way, though decency and decorum must be maintained, regardless of the tactics which she and her associates might adopt. I also told them that the size of crowds should not cause any concern; the people were having the first-ever general elections and they must meet and hear both the candidates. The administration was firmly told not to interfere with Miss Jinnah's meetings in any way and to provide her with all facilities. She was given special consideration in the matter of travel and accommodation throughout the country.

There was a suggestion that I should follow her from place to place. I decided against this because I thought if meetings were held in the same town on the same day or on consecutive days it would inevitably lead to some clash among the supporters. She should have the first round in each Province. Let her first complete her tour of West Pakistan, and after she had gone to East Pakistan I should begin my campaign.

So Miss Jinnah travelled the whole of West Pakistan addressing public meetings in Karachi, Peshawar, Rawalpindi, Lahore, and a number of other major towns. Her theme was the same everywhere: the country had gone to the dogs; there had been no development; there was no liberty, no freedom of speech; government had no external or internal policy; I was a dictator who tolerated no opposition; and so on and so forth. She came out strongly in support of the old politicians, forgetting that when they were in office she used to be their bitterest critic. She now claimed that everything that had been done was either completed or initiated by the politicians. The Revolution was a big hoax and I was responsible for all the misdeeds of the politicians. I was to learn from her that cabinets had been made and unmade at my behest! That every Prime Minister and Governor-General had acted under my orders. The newspapers splashed her speeches on the front pages and soon the whole country was in the grip of the presidential election.

III

I opened my campaign with a public meeting in Peshawar. I talked mainly of the improvements that had taken place since the Revolution. It was an oppressive afternoon and a huge crowd had turned up. The Muslim League volunteer corps was ill-organized and there was constant pushing and pulling in the crowd. Suddenly I saw an old man squatting in the front row with a cage in his hand; inside the cage was a quail. In Peshawar quail-fights are very popular and it is common knowledge that a certain type of quail, however well you might nourish and look after him, deserts the field as soon as he sees his adversary. I pointed towards the cage and said that these COP leaders were no better than 'run-away quails'; in their whole political life none of them had ever stayed the course. This caused much amusement and the label 'run-away quails' stuck to the Opposition for the rest of the campaign. I avoided direct personal references, hoping to keep the campaign at a dignified level.

After Peshawar, I addressed a large public meeting in Rawalpindi. It was here that some of the Opposition speakers had indulged in downright slander and vilification, not only of the government but of myself personally. I think the Combined Opposition Parties wanted the whole campaign to degenerate into a vulgar exercise in mud-slinging. I was determined not to let this happen. I knew I would have to tell some home truths about my rival, but she must be shown the respect to which she was entitled.

From Rawalpindi I travelled by road to Lahore, addressing a number of wayside meetings. I have never pretended to be an orator and it took me a little time to improve the fluency of my Urdu. By the time I reached Lahore I found that I could speak for hours without having to refer to notes. This helped me to establish direct communication with the audience. The Lahore meeting was held in Mochi Gate—the famous political battleground. It was a tremendous audience full of enthusiasm. We had arranged to have a few poets and some local speakers to initiate the proceedings but the crowd was not prepared to listen to any one of them. They had come to hear me and wanted no poets, nor professional orators. As I came up to the rostrum the whole chaotic scene turned dramatically into a well-organized meeting. I spoke at length and explained the philosophy of the reforms and the Constitution in simple, straightforward language. That evening I felt that the West Pakistan battle had been won.

In the meantime, Miss Jinnah was having the run of East Pakistan. News of her meetings was creating quite an impression. While she scored some gains in East Pakistan, she also brought to the surface serious inner rivalries and tensions in the COP, particularly between the National Awami Party and the Awami League. One of the Awami League leaders had appointed himself Miss Jinnah's impresario, causing disappointment to leaders of other parties. And the rough and summary manner in which Miss Jinnah was inclined to treat her own workers was beginning to make them wonder whether they had been wise in nominating her.

The COP received a blow in the death of Khawaja Nazimuddin in the midst of the campaign. He was a veteran political leader and his presence lent considerable weight to the opposition. Worse still, Miss Jinnah left East Pakistan without waiting to attend Khawaja Nazimuddin's funeral. I was in Sukkur that evening. We passed a resolution of condolence on Khawaja Nazimuddin's death.

The COP had adopted a 9-point programme. Nothing exposed them more than the contents of this programme. With his customary shrewdness Chaudhri Mohammad Ali of the Nizam-e-Islam Party, who had been given the responsibility of drafting the programme, produced an ignoble bundle of compromises, keeping the language deliberately vague to accommodate all possible interpretations. When the programme was announced the National Awami Party, an avowedly leftist organization, found itself supporting a theocratic philosophy. All issues of fundamental importance were avoided. The programme gave no indication of the policy of the Opposition in foreign affairs. Nor did it explain what pattern of political relationship between East and West Pakistan was envisaged. Did the Opposition support One Unit or did it favour the disintegration of West Pakistan? Was the Opposition behind the system of Basic Democracies or opposed to it? Nothing was clear and people started asking 'What does COP stand for?' In one of my meetings I suggested that the COP stood for the 'Cult of Power'. They had nothing in common with each other except the urge to grab power at all costs, and were like so many wild cats with their tails tied together.

Now from our side we had provided all facilities to the Opposition to hold their meetings in an orderly and peaceful manner. They, on the other hand, were attempting to disturb my meetings. It was announced that some of the Awami League leaders had given a pledge to COP that they would not let me hold any public meeting in East Pakistan. The Awami League, more than any other political party in the opposition, wanted to create a situation of disorder and chaos in which the elections could not be held. Local toughs in some districts had been organized into a volunteer corps and they were going about intimidating the voters. The Awami League was fanning provincialism in East Pakistan and much of their political energy seemed directed towards creating distrust and hatred of West Pakistan.

My own political party, which was working on a national basis for a positive programme, was feeling distressed at the turn of events. We could not adopt agitational tactics, or meet hatred with hatred.

In East Pakistan I opened my campaign with a meeting in Dacca. The venue was Paltan Maidan, which is as famous as Lahore's Mochi Gate. The Opposition had apparently placed a number of people in the audience with the object of disturbing the proceedings, but they found themselves badly outnumbered. The place was overflowing with people and I received a patient hearing. I was convinced that whatever might be the strategy of the Opposition, the people at large were deeply interested in acquainting themselves, at first hand, with the political philosophy and programme of both sides.

I toured the whole of East Pakistan addressing large crowds; the biggest meeting was in Rangpur. All around me was a veritable ocean of humanity. In the countryside, wherever I went, I could point out signs of prosperity for the people to see. Roads had been built where there used to be cart-tracks, jungles infested with wild animals had been cleared and irrigation facilities provided. People had got electricity, better communications, and better marketing facilities. Their health had improved and they had better food and clothing. Innumerable projects of immediate benefit to the people had been completed under the Rural Works Programme. These were solid achievements of the régime which no amount of Opposition propaganda could belittle.

By the end of the first phase of the campaign, I think I had managed to put across to the people my basic thinking. Without unity between the two Provinces the country could not survive; their security and future depended on working together. It was vital for the country to have a strong centre to co-ordinate policies and to provide national guidelines. If the centre was weakened, the Provinces would fall apart and disintegrate. Seven years of stability had resulted in phenomenal progress in all spheres of life. Whatever assistance we had received had been put to good use. Pakistan was regarded in the world as a model of development. The prestige of the country had risen. We had succeeded in normalizing our relations with our big neighbours.

In the meantime, results of the elections of the Basic Democrats had been announced and Miss Jinnah undertook another round of West Pakistan. She was running into difficulties with her associates but her whole approach was now based on arousing provincial and sectarian feelings. Wherever she went she talked in terms of local grievances, ignoring the national perspective. The original curiosity of the people was also beginning to wane. It was pathetic to see her being driven from place to place by the COP leaders. They kept telling her that the whole country was behind her and that the Basic Democrats, who had been elected, all belonged to the Opposition.

I issued my Election Manifesto in which I set out my beliefs and my political programme. The Manifesto covered all aspects of national life and gave a clear picture of my thinking and my plans. The Opposition termed the Manifesto an election stunt but did not seem to specify any particular faults in it.

The elections were scheduled to be held some time in March 1965. The Opposition demanded that they should be held earlier. They thought that if there was a gap of three or four months between the election of the Basic Democrats and the general elections, the administration might try to influence the voters. I took the Opposition at their word and advanced the date of the elections by nearly three months. This took them completely by surprise and caused considerable disarray in their ranks.

The presidential election campaign now entered its final phase, when the candidates had to meet their electors, the Basic Democrats. These confrontation meetings were organized by the Election Commission and presided over by a Judge of the High Court. It was in these meetings that the voters came in direct contact with the candidates. The procedure was that the candidate would make his opening statement and this would be followed by questions from the voters. It was in these meetings that Miss Jinnah displayed the full range of her ignorance of national affairs: in spite of rigorous coaching and prompting by her associates, she could rarely find a precise answer to any question. The argument had finally reached the plane of reason and knowledge.

From Khyber to Cox's Bazar, people became intensely involved in the process of election. In every household there was only one subject of conversation and that was the presidential elections. The Press was divided into two distinct categories: one for the COP nominee and the other for the nominee of the Pakistan Muslim League. The election issues were discussed and thrashed out and, by and large, people knew what each candidate stood for.

The Awami League made one last bid to disrupt the elections. Their volunteers approached individual Basic Democrats and tried to threaten and frighten them. Miss Jinnah by then was saying in effect that if there was going to be chaos in the country, let there be chaos.

IV

Polling commenced at 8 o'clock in the morning on 2 January 1965, throughout the country. The first results started coming in towards midday. The Election Commission had arranged for the results to be announced over Radio Pakistan as they were received from each polling station. By about 4 p.m. the trend of public opinion had become evident: Miss Jinnah was losing almost everywhere. The Opposition strongholds in principal towns of the country were falling one by one. Chittagong, Khulna, Rajshahi, Sylhet, Hyderabad, Peshawar, Lahore, all returned a verdict against her. The only towns in which she got a majority were Dacca and Karachi. In West Pakistan I gained a substantial lead in all divisions and districts except Karachi. In East Pakistan I gained a majority in thirteen districts out of seventeen. The number of votes cast represented 99·62 per cent of the total electorate and I ended up with a 63 per cent majority against Miss Jinnah's 36 per cent.

The nation had given a clear and final verdict on the Constitution. Never before in the history of the country had general elections been held. The interest and response of the people was most gratifying. The country had chosen stability against chaos, security against disintegration, progress against stagnation.

Miss Jinnah's election strategy had been well-planned. I think some of the elements in it were provided by her associates who were old hands at the game. She knew that her main appeal was her relationship with the Quaid-e-Azam. She therefore thought that she should fight the entire campaign on the emotional plane. Her effort sometimes seemed to be to malign me personally and to present things out of context. She showed prodigious energy and went through a gruelling campaign, no mean achievement for a septuagenarian, and I give her full marks for that. I think she made a mistake in overestimating her personal appeal. People soon realized that she deserved all respect and consideration as the sister of the Quaid-e-Azam, but that did not necessarily mean that she could serve the people as their President. The final vote was between prejudice and reality and, I think, reality gained the edge.

I thanked the people who had supported me and also those who had differed with me: they too had served the cause of democracy. I wanted the moment of vindication to become a symbol of lasting unity. No trace of malice or of regret should inhibit anyone from rejoicing in the glory of the people. I appealed to the nation to work for the fulfilment of the ideology of Pakistan.

'Together let us build, together let us accomplish; so that Pakistan shall endure and prosper.'

PAKISTAN PAINDABAD

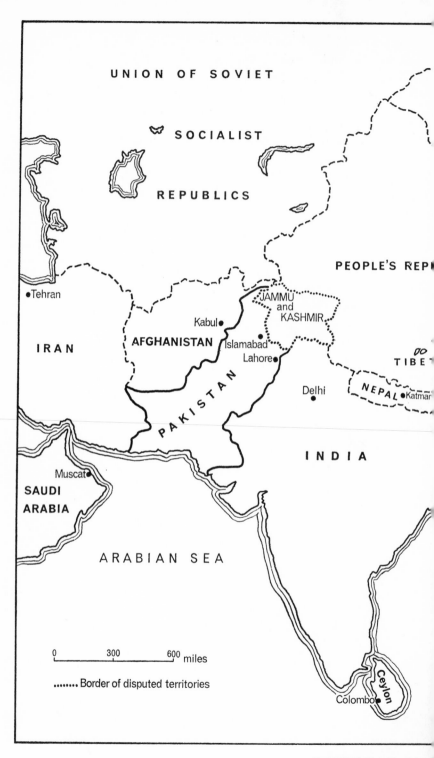

UNION OF SOVIET

SOCIALIST

REPUBLICS

PEOPLE'S REP

•Tehran

JAMMU
and
KASHMIR

Kabul•

IRAN   AFGHANISTAN Islamabad

Lahore•   TIBE

Delhi
•

P A K I S T A N

N E P A L •Katmar

Muscat•

SAUDI
ARABIA

I N D I A

ARABIAN SEA

0   300   600 miles

.... Border of disputed territories

Ceylon

Colombo•

PAKISTAN AN

MONGOLIA

MANCHURIA

North KOREA

Seoul

South

Peking

LIC OF CHINA

SINKIANG

Formosa

Sikkim

Bhutan

Hongkong

PAKISTAN

Dacca

N. VIET NAM

Hanoi

Hainan

BURMA

LAOS

SOUTH
CHINA
SEA

Rangoon

THAILAND

AY OF
ENGAL

Bangkok

CAMBODIA

Pnompenh

S. VIET NAM

Saigon

MALAYSIA
Sarawak

MALAYSIA

INDONESIA

BORNEO

Singapore

SUMATRA

HER NEIGHBOURS

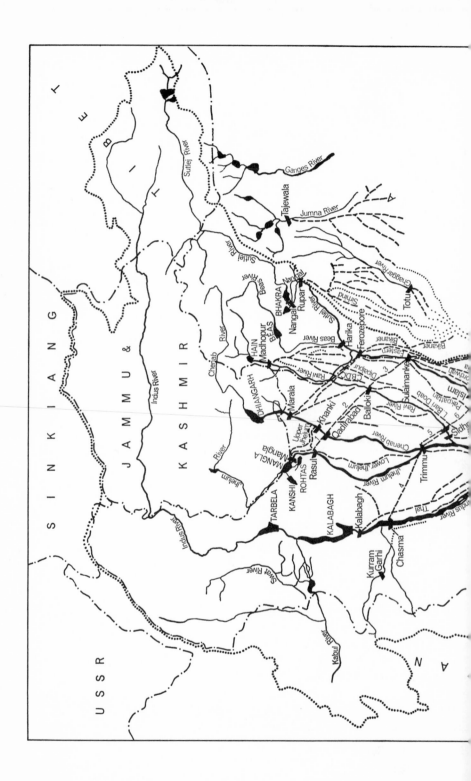

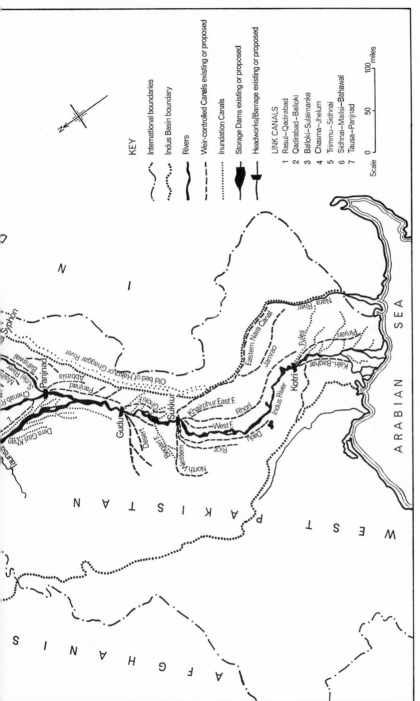

THE INDUS WATERS TREATY AREA

KEY

- International boundaries
- Indus Basin boundary
- Rivers
- Weir-controlled Canals existing or proposed
- Inundation Canals
- Storage Dams existing or proposed
- Headworks/Barrage existing or proposed

LINK CANALS

1 Rasul–Qadirabad
2 Qadirabad–Balloki
3 Balloki–Sulaimanke
4 Chasma–Jhelum
5 Trimmu–Sidhnai
6 Sidhnai–Mailsi–Bahawal
7 Tausa–Panjnad

Scale 0   50   100 miles

JAMMU AND KASHMIR: EXTRACTS FROM TELEGRAMS SENT BY THE INDIAN PRIME MINISTER

I must confess that my meetings with Pandit Nehru were a great disappointment. His whole attitude was characterized by a certain smugness based on the knowledge that possession is nine points of law—however illegal and immoral the possession. I could not imagine that the head of a country could violate agreements with such impunity. I am not referring to his personal assurances conveyed directly as well as through various channels, but to the solemn pledges which Pandit Nehru had formally conveyed to the Government of Pakistan on the subject of Jammu and Kashmir.

The following are a few extracts from telegrams sent from time to time by the Indian Prime Minister on the subject:

(i) *For Prime Minister, Pakistan, from Prime Minister, India, dated 27 October 1947:*

'I should like to make it clear that question of aiding Kashmir in this emergency is not designed in any way to influence the State to accede to India. Our view which we have repeatedly made public is that the question of accession in any disputed territory or State must be decided in accordance with wishes of people and we adhere to this view.'

(ii) *From Prime Minister, India, to Prime Minister, Pakistan, dated 31 October 1947:*

'Our assurance that we shall withdraw our troops from Kashmir as soon as peace and order are restored and leave the decision regarding the future of this State to the people of the State is not merely a pledge to your Government but also to the people of Kashmir and to the world.'

(iii) *For Liaquat Ali Khan, from Jawaharlal Nehru, dated 4 November 1947:*
'I wish to draw your attention to broadcast on Kashmir which I made last evening. I have stated our Government's policy and made it clear that we have no desire to impose our will on Kashmir. I further stated that we have agreed on impartial international agency like United Nations supervising any referendum.'

(iv) *From Jawaharlal Nehru, for Nawabzada Liaquat Ali Khan, dated 4 October 1948:*
'We have never resiled from our position that there should as soon as normal conditions return to Jammu and Kashmir be a fair and free Plebiscite.'

(v) *From Jawaharlal Nehru, for Nawabzada Liaquat Ali Khan, dated 4 October 1948:*

'I can only say that I share your desire to allow the will of people to prevail in finding a solution of Kashmir question, and that I shall always be ready to co-operate in finding a peaceful and honourable solution of this problem.'

APPENDIX II

PRESIDENTIAL ORDER OF THE DAY

PROCLAMATION

(Dated 7 October 1958 made by the President of Pakistan)

No. F. 81/Pres/58, 25th. October, 1958, Gazette, 31st. October, 1958—
The following PROCLAMATION made by the President at 10.30 p.m. on
the 7th. day of October, 1958, is published for general information:

'For the last two years, I have been watching, with the deepest anxiety,
the ruthless struggle for power, corruption, the shameful exploitation of our
simple, honest, patriotic and industrious masses, the lack of decorum, and
the prostitution of Islam for political ends. There have been a few honourable
exceptions. But being in a minority they have not been able to assert their
influence in the affairs of the country.

'These despicable activities have led to a dictatorship of the lowest
order. Adventurers and exploiters have flourished to the detriment of the
masses and are getting richer by their nefarious practices.

'Despite my repeated endeavours, no serious attempt has been made to
tackle the food crises. Food has been a problem of life and death for us in a
country which should be really surplus. Agriculture and land administration
have been made a handmaiden of politics so that in our present system of
government, no political party will be able to take any positive action to
increase production. In East Pakistan, on the other hand, there is a well
organized smuggling of food, medicines and other necessities of life. The
masses there suffer due to the shortages so caused in, and the consequent
high prices of, these commodities. Import of food has been a constant and
serious drain on our foreign exchange earnings in the last few years, with the
result that the Government is constrained to curtail the much needed
internal development projects.

'Some of our politicians have lately been talking of bloody revolution.
Another type of adventurer among them think it fit to go to foreign countries
and attempt direct alignment with them which can only be described as high
treason.

'The disgraceful scene enacted recently in the East Pakistan Assembly is
known to all. I am told that such episodes were common occurrences in pre-
partition Bengal. Whether they were or not, it is certainly not a civilized
mode of procedure. You do not raise the prestige of your country by beating
the Speaker, killing the Deputy Speaker and desecrating the National Flag.

'The mentality of the political parties has sunk so low that I am unable
any longer to believe that elections will improve the present chaotic internal
situation and enable us to form a strong and stable Government capable of
dealing with the innumerable and complex problems facing us today. We
cannot get men from the Moon. The same group of people who have brought

Pakistan on the verge of ruination will rig the elections for their own ends. They will come back more revengeful, because I am sure the elections will be contested, mainly, on personal, regional and sectarian basis. When they return, they will use the same methods which have made a tragic farce of democracy and are the main cause of the present widespread frustration in the country. However much the administration may try, I am convinced, judging by shifting loyalties and the ceaseless and unscrupulous scramble for office, that elections will be neither free nor fair. They will not solve our difficulties. On the contrary, they are likely to create greater unhappiness and disappointment leading ultimately to a really bloody revolution. Recently, we had elections for the Karachi Municipal Corporation. Twenty per cent of the electorate exercised their votes, and out of these, about fifty per cent were bogus votes.

'We hear threats and cries of civil disobedience in order to retain private volunteer organizations and to break up the One Unit. These disruptive tendencies are a good indication of their patriotism and the length to which politicians and adventurers are prepared to go to achieve their parochial aims.

'Our foreign policy is subjected to unintelligent and irresponsible criticism, not for patriotic motives, but from selfish view points often by the very people who were responsible for it. We desire to have friendly relations with all nations, but political adventurers try their best to create bad blood and misunderstandings between us and countries like the U.S.S.R., the U.A.R. and the People's Republic of China. Against India, of course, they scream for war, knowing full well that they will be nowhere near the firing line. In no country in the world, do political parties treat foreign policy in the manner it has been done in Pakistan. To dispel the confusion so caused, I categorically reiterate that we shall continue to follow a policy which our interests and geography demand and that we shall honour all our international commitments which, as is well known, we have undertaken to safeguard the security of Pakistan and, as a peace loving nation, to play our part in averting the danger of war from this troubled world.

'For the last three years, I have been doing my utmost to work the Constitution in a democratic way. I have laboured to bring about coalition after coalition, hoping that it would stabilize the administration and that the affairs of the country would be run in the interests of the masses. My detractors, in their dishonest ways, have on every opportunity, called these attempts Palace intrigues. It has become fashionable to put all the blame on the President. A wit said the other day, "If it rains too much it is the fault of the President and if it does not rain it is the fault of the President." If only I alone were concerned, I would go on taking these fulminations with the contempt they deserve. But the intention of these traitors and unpatriotic elements is to destroy the prestige of Pakistan and the Government by attacking the Head of the State. They have succeeded to a great extent, and, if this state of affairs is allowed to go on, they will achieve their ultimate purpose.

'My appraisal of the internal situation had led me to believe that a vast majority of the people no longer have any confidence in the present system of Government and are getting more and more disillusioned and disappointed and are becoming dangerously resentful of the manner in which they have been exploited. Their resentment and bitterness are justifiable. The leaders have not been able to render them the service they deserve and have failed to prove themselves worthy of the confidence the masses had reposed in them.

'The Constitution which was brought into being on 23rd. March. 1956, after so many tribulations, is unworkable. It is full of dangerous compromises so that Pakistan will disintegrate internally if the inherent malaise is not removed. To rectify them, the country must first be taken to sanity by a peaceful revolution. Then, it is my intention to collect a number of patriotic persons to examine our problems in the political field and devise a Constitution more suitable to the genius of the Muslim people. When it is ready, and at the appropriate time, it will be submitted to the referendum of the people.

'It is said that the Constitution is sacred. But more sacred than the Constitution or anything else is the country and the welfare and happiness of its people. As Head of the State, my foremost duty before my God and the people is the integrity of Pakistan. It is seriously threatened by the ruthlessness of traitors and political adventurers whose selfishness, thirst for power and unpatriotic conduct cannot be restrained by a government set up under the present system. Nor can I any longer remain a spectator of activities designed to destroy the country. After deep and anxious thought, I have come to the regrettable conclusion that I would be failing in my duty if I did not take steps, which in my opinion, are inescapable in present conditions, to save Pakistan from complete disruption. I have, therefore, decided that:—

(a) The Constitution of the 23rd. March, 1956 will be abrogated.
(b) The Central and Provincial Governments will be dismissed with immediate effect.
(c) The National Parliament and Provincial Assemblies will be dissolved.
(d) All political parties will be abolished.
(e) Until alternative arrangements are made, Pakistan will come under Martial Law. I hereby appoint General Mohammad Ayub Khan, Commander-in-Chief, Pakistan Army, as the Chief Martial Law Administrator and place all the Armed Forces of Pakistan under his command.

'To the valiant Armed Forces of Pakistan, I have to say that having been closely associated with them since the very inception of Pakistan, I have learned to admire their patriotism and loyalty. I am putting a great strain on them. I fully realize this, but I ask you, Officers and men of the Armed Forces, on your service depends the future existence of Pakistan as an independent nation and a bastion in these parts of the Free World. Do your job without fear or favour and may God help you.

'To the people of Pakistan I talk as a brother and a fellow compatriot. Present action has been taken with the utmost regret but I have had to do it in the interests of the country and the masses, finer men than whom it is difficult to imagine. To the patriots and the law abiding, I promise you will be happier and freer. The political adventurers, the smugglers, the black-marketeers, the hoarders, will be unhappy and their activities will be severely restricted. As for the traitors, they had better flee the country if they can and while the going is good.'

APPENDIX III

PROCLAMATION OF MARTIAL LAW

(Government of Pakistan Notification No. 977/58 dated 7 October 1958.
Gazette Extraordinary, 15 October 1958)

1. Whereas I adjudge it essential for national requirements to exercise jurisdiction within the international boundaries of PAKISTAN, I, the Supreme Commander of the Armed Forces of PAKISTAN, do hereby give notice as follows.
2. Martial Law Regulations and Orders will be published in such manner as is conveniently possible. Any person contravening the said Regulations and Orders shall be liable under Martial Law to the penalties stated in the Regulations.
3. The said Regulations may prescribe special penalties for offences under the ordinary law.
4. The said Regulations may appoint special Courts for the trial and punishment of contravention of the said Regulations and Orders and of offences under the ordinary law.

Mohammad Ayub Khan, HP, HJ,
General,
Supreme Commander and Chief Martial Law
Administrator in PAKISTAN.

APPENDIX IV

STRUCTURE OF BASIC DEMOCRACIES

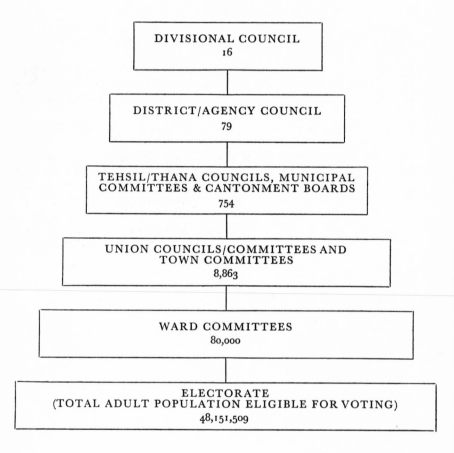

DIVISIONAL COUNCIL
16

DISTRICT/AGENCY COUNCIL
79

TEHSIL/THANA COUNCILS, MUNICIPAL
COMMITTEES & CANTONMENT BOARDS
754

UNION COUNCILS/COMMITTEES AND
TOWN COMMITTEES
8,863

WARD COMMITTEES
80,000

ELECTORATE
(TOTAL ADULT POPULATION ELIGIBLE FOR VOTING)
48,151,509

REFORM COMMISSIONS

NAME	APPOINTMENT	SUBMISSION OF REPORT
1. Land Reforms Commission	31.10.58	20.1.59
2. Maritime Commission	19.11.58	8.4.59
3. Law Reform Commission	23.11.58	27.12.61
4. Administrative Re-organization Committee	2.12.58	25.4.62
5. Commission on National Education	30.12.58	26.8.59
6. Location of Federal Capital	21.1.59	12.6.59
7. Credit Enquiry Commission	24.2.59	10.9.59
8. Food and Agriculture Commission	8.7.59	29.11.60
9. Scientific Commission	15.7.59	8.9.60
10. Pay and Service Commission	31.8.59	1.6.62
11. Company Law Commission	15.10.59	27.12.61
12. Medical Reforms Commission	19.11.59	16.4.60
13. Sports, Culture, and Youth Committees	10.12.59	6.8.60
14. Police Commission	2.1.60	19.5.61
15. Constitution Commission	17.2.60	6.5.61
16. Commission on Price Structure	18.2.60	3.7.60
17. Film Fact-finding Committee	10.3.60	28.4.61
18. Surplus Manpower Commission	18.10.60	7.7.61
19. The Commission for Social Evils	13.1.61	18.6.63
20. Power Commission	12.5.61	8.8.62
21. Finance Commission	12.12.61	15.1.62
22. Credit Committee	10.5.62	7.11.62
23. Franchise Committee	4.8.62	18.2.63
24. National Income Commission	4.4.63	13.11.64
25. National Finance Commission	25.3.64	4.5.66
26. Commission on Minorities	4.5.65	Not yet out
27. Broadcasting Committee	29.7.65	Not yet finalized
28. Press Commission*	5.9.58	4.5.59
29. Sugar Commission*	30.9.57	4.8.59
30. Marriage and Family Law Commission*	4.8.54	1.6.56 Report implemented, 2.3.61

* Commission set up earlier, but report submitted or implemented after October 1958.

PRESIDENT'S MANIFESTO

*(issued on the eve of President Mohammad Ayub Khan's Election
to his second term of office and published at the inauguration ceremony on 23 March 1965)*

I BELIEVE

1. that Allah, in His infinite mercy, created Pakistan to give the Muslims of these regions a homeland in which to mould their lives in accordance with the fundamental principles and the spirit of Islam.
2. that Pakistan is destined to play a glorious role in the history of mankind and in particular in the advancement and progress of Muslims all over the world.
3. that the will of the people is supreme in all matters of the State.
4. that democracy provides the surest means of securing the fullest participation of the people in the affairs of their country.
5. that whatever the institutional form democracy may take in Pakistan, it must be based on pragmatism rather than dogmatism and must safeguard the basic right of the people to freedom of speech, freedom of association and freedom of assembly under the rule of law.
6. that the people of Pakistan must themselves determine the form of government which should be established consistent with the ideological basis of the country and the fundamental need for preserving the sovereignty, security and unity of the country.
7. that the people of Pakistan must move, as fast as possible, into the age of science and technology, while steadfastly preserving the basic tenets of their faith, in order to attain a higher standard of living.
8. that all class distinctions should disappear and Pakistanis should live and prosper as a model community symbolising Islamic brotherhood and equality of man.
9. that there must be complete equality of opportunities available to all citizens of Pakistan.
10. that Pakistan should develop into a Welfare State where basic necessities are available to all.

I MAINTAIN

1. that the reforms such as the land reforms, educational reforms, constitutional reforms and administrative reforms introduced during the last six years are aimed at freeing the society from the shackles of past domination, and elimination of class tensions and conflicts.
2. that further progress, in pursuit of the beliefs I have enunciated, would be possible only if we develop sufficient self-reliance to study our own problems and to solve them in our own way.
3. that only an enlightened approach based on practical realism rather than

dominated by theorization, will help us to shed retrograde and antiquated traditionalism and usher in an era of true liberation: political, cultural, social, economic and intellectual.

4. that in all material and economic matters our attitude should not be doctrinaire but one dictated by the basic requirements of the situation.

5. that Pakistan's sovereignty and unity as a nation can be guaranteed only by a strong Centre capable of providing full provincial autonomy without allowing centrifugal forces to re-assert themselves.

6. that in our dealings with other countries the determining factor must always be the interest of Pakistan and that we must always endeavour to enlarge the areas of understanding and friendship with other countries particularly those who are our neighbours.

7. that we must work toward the establishment of world peace and human happiness and strive in all possible ways to save mankind from the horrors of war.

I UNDERTAKE

1. to maximize the utilization of national resources.

2. to provide for the widest possible and most equitable distribution of wealth.

3. to adopt all practical means to raise the income of the common man so as to reduce the disparity between the rich and the poor.

4. to ensure that the burden of taxation is distributed in a fair and equitable manner.

5. to eliminate cartels and monopolies.

6. to rationalize the land revenue system so as to give a fair deal especially to the small land-holder.

7. to adopt all practical measures to prevent the recurrence of floods in East Pakistan and to provide, as far as possible, adequate facilities for the rehabilitation of those affected by this menace.

8. to adopt all such measures as may be necessary to control waterlogging and salinity in West Pakistan and to reclaim affected areas as far as possible.

9. to ensure the stability of the prices of goods used by the common man and to prevent inflation to the extent possible.

10. to take steps for the rehabilitation of homeless people and to provide better housing facilities.

11. to ensure that improvement in the standard of living of the people is not neutralized by unbalanced increase in population.

12. to associate local people in the administration of their affairs and to transfer gradually such functions as may be possible to the Basic Democracies.

13. to expand further the scope of rural works programme, in financial as well as functional terms.

14. to build up a strong rural community capable of looking after its own needs.

15. to provide greater educational facilities as envisaged in the Outline of the Third Five-Year Plan.
16. to work out a code of ethics for the press and to establish a voluntary machinery within the press itself to regulate effectively its conduct according to the code.
17. to take further measures to root out corruption in all branches of the Administration and to raise the standard of efficiency in the public services.
18. to take expeditious steps to achieve parity between the two wings of the country in the light of the constitutional provisions and to ensure that the pace of progress of the various regions of West Pakistan, as a single indivisible Unit, is increased further to bring about a balanced pattern of growth throughout the country.
19. to provide growing facilities for cultural integration and for the promotion of original and creative thinking.
20. to advance the ideology of Muslim nationalism which will enable Pakistan to serve as a strong base for collaboration with other Muslim countries of the world.
21. to support all liberal causes and to provide whatever assistance may be possible to such people or communities as may be in bondage or under the yoke of colonialism, imperialism or any other form of domination.
22. to continue to strive for the right of self-determination for the people of Jammu and Kashmir, and for its exercise in accordance with the UNCIP resolutions and to provide all moral support to the freedom fighters of Kashmir.
23. to provide full protection and safeguards to minorities in Pakistan and to ensure for them equal opportunities, rights and privileges.

I URGE

1. for Patience. Growth and development need time and not all the benefits can be secured by one generation. We have to work not only for ourselves but also for those who will follow us, and the thought that most of the benefits of our efforts may be reaped by the coming generations should be the mainstay of our effort.
2. for Faith. We must have faith in ourselves and in our destiny, and whatever the community might embark upon should be a source of pride and satisfaction to all of us.
3. for Moderation. Reforms should be undertaken in a missionary and not in a vainglorious spirit. The objective should be to produce a better arrangement rather than to destroy an existing arrangement.
4. for National Outlook. We cannot afford to think in terms of provinces or regions. The economic advancement which we have already achieved has taken us to a stage where further progress will depend on our ability to evolve a national outlook, a national vision and to secure national unity.
5. for Hard Work. Empty slogans and fond hopes will get us nowhere. It is only through hard work undertaken in a selfless spirit and in the service of the community that we can achieve results.

It is in an endeavour to reach the objectives which I have outlined above that I am seeking re-election to the office of the President of Pakistan. My sole aim is to establish the sovereignty of the people and to work for the progress of Pakistan and the happiness and prosperity of the people of Pakistan.

PAKISTAN PAINDABAD

APPENDIX VII
ELECTION RETURNS, 1965

Required to be submitted by the Returning Officer to the Election Commission

Province	S. No.	Names of contesting candidates	No. of valid votes polled	No. of invalid votes	Total No. of votes cast both valid and invalid	Percentage of votes secured by each candidate
Total for East Pakistan	1.	Field Marshal Mohammad Ayub Khan	21,012			53·12
	2.	Mr. K. M. Kamal	93			·23
	3.	Mian Bashir Ahmad	11	274	39,824	·02
	4.	Miss Fatima Jinnah	18,434			46·60
			39,550	274	39,824	
Total for West Pakistan	1.	Field Marshal Mohammad Ayub Khan	28,939			73·56
	2.	Mr. K. M. Kamal	90			·23
	3.	Mian Bashir Ahmad	54	536	39,876	·14
	4.	Miss Fatima Jinnah	10,257			26·07
			39,340	536	39,876	
Grand Total for whole of Pakistan	1.	Field Marshal Mohammad Ayub Khan	49,951			63·31
	2.	Mr. K. M. Kamal	183			·23
	3.	Mian Bashir Ahmad	65	810	79,700	·08
	4.	Miss Fatima Jinnah	28,691			36·36
			78,890	810	79,700	

I hereby declare, under section 38(1) of the Presidential Election Act, 1964, Field Marshal Mohammad Ayub Khan, who has secured the highest number of votes, to be elected to the office of the President of the Islamic Republic of Pakistan. This return of the election is hereby submitted to the Election Commission.

Place: Rawalpindi.

Date: January 8, 1965.

Sd/-G. Mueemuddin,
Returning Officer

BIOGRAPHICAL NOTES

Nurul Amin (1897–   ) In 1948 became Prime Minister of East Bengal. In 1954 a landslide victory of the opposition United Front cost him his seat in the Legislature. In 1965 elected Member of the National Assembly of Pakistan and Leader of the Opposition.

Maulana Abdul Hamid Khan Bhashani (1885–   ) Known for his championship of peasant causes in Bengal and Assam. In 1954 election in East Pakistan, formed United Front with other opposition parties on the basis of a 21-Point Programme. After Martial Law was withdrawn in 1962, revived the National Awami Party of which he is the President.

Mohammad Ali Bogra (1901–1963) In 1953 became Prime Minister of Pakistan, which office he held till October 1954. In April 1955 led Pakistan delegation to Afro-Asian Conference in Bandung. In 1962 was elected Member of the National Assembly of Pakistan, Leader of the Opposition, and later Leader of the House and Foreign Minister, which office he held till his death in January 1963.

Chaudhri Mohammad Ali (1905–   ) After Partition, in August 1947, appointed Secretary-General, Government of Pakistan, and continued up to 1951. Succeeded Mohammad Ali Bogra as Prime Minister of Pakistan in August 1955, holding office until September 1956. Is at present Chief of the opposition Nizam-e-Islam Party.

Hamidul Haq Choudhry (1903–   ) Joined Khawaja Nazimuddin's Cabinet as Minister in East Bengal in 1948. Deputy Leader of the Pakistan delegation to U.N. General Assembly in 1949. Became Foreign Minister of Pakistan (26 September 1955 to 12 September 1956). Proprietor of the English daily paper, *Pakistan Observer*, Dacca.

Choudhri Khaliquzzaman (1889–   ) Leader of the Muslim League Party in United Provinces for ten years (1937–47). Appointed Governor of East Pakistan in 1953. In November 1954 was appointed Pakistan Ambassador in Indonesia and the Philippines.

I. I. Chundrigar (1899–1960) On Partition in 1947 joined first Pakistan Cabinet under Liaquat Ali Khan. When Suhrawardy succeeded Chaudri Mohammad Ali as Prime Minister, Chundrigar became Leader of the Opposition. With Suhrawardy's fall, he became Prime Minister of Pakistan for three months (Oct.-Dec. 1957).

Mian Mumtaz Muhammad Khan Daultana (1916–   ) After Partition joined the first Punjab Cabinet as Finance Minister under

Mamdot. In April 1951 became Chief Minister of Punjab and resigned in April 1953 following anti-Ahmadiyya communal disturbances. In October 1957 joined Pakistan Cabinet under Chundrigar.

A. K. FAZLUL HAQ (1873–1962) In 1937 became Prime Minister of Bengal. He moved the famous Lahore Resolution in 1940. In April 1954 became Chief Minister of East Pakistan heading the United Front Cabinet. Was a Minister for the Interior in the Central Cabinet under Chaudri Mohammad Ali in 1955. In 1956 became Governor of East Pakistan and continued till 1958. For his championing of the cause of the Muslims of Bengal, he was called 'Sher-i-Bangla' (Lion of Bengal).

H.R.H. AGA KHAN (1877–1957) The spiritual leader of the Ismaili Sect, H.R.H. Aga Khan in 1906 led historic Simla Deputation which included outstanding Muslim leaders from all parts of India to demand special safeguards for Muslim rights. As President of the General Assembly of the League of Nations, welcomed Egypt, Iraq, Turkey, and other Muslim nations into the fold of the League.

ATAUR RAHMAN KHAN (1907–   ) In September 1956 became Chief Minister of Awami League Cabinet in East Pakistan. In April 1958 was again appointed Chief Minister in Awami League Cabinet and held office for two months. In August 1958 became Chief Minister of East Pakistan and held office till the promulgation of Martial Law on 7 October 1958.

KHAN ABDUL GHAFFAR KHAN (1891–   ) Known as the 'Frontier Gandhi'. In 1946 played host to Pandit Nehru during his visit to N.W.F.P. In 1965 went to London for medical treatment and on the way back stopped in Afghanistan where he has been campaigning for so-called 'Pakhtoonistan' ever since.

KHAN ABDUL QAYYUM KHAN (1901–   ) In August 1947, when Partition took place, he was appointed Chief Minister, N.W.F.P. In 1953 joined Mohammad Ali Bogra's Cabinet as Minister for Food, Agriculture and Industries.

LIAQUAT ALI KHAN (1895–1951) Finance Minister in Interim Coalition Government of India in 1946. In 1947 became Pakistan's first Prime Minister. Was assassinated in Rawalpindi on 16 October 1951.

MAULVI TAMIZUDDIN KHAN (1889–1963) In 1938 became Minister for Agriculture, Health, Industries and Commerce in Bengal Cabinet. In 1947 elected Deputy President, Pakistan Constituent Assembly, of which Quaid-e-Azam was President. After the death of Quaid-e-Azam he was elected President of the Constituent Assembly. On the dissolution of the Constituent Assembly by Governor-General Ghulam Mohammad, he filed a suit in the Sind High Court and won the case, but lost it in the Supreme Court. In 1962 elected Member of the National Assembly and elected unanimously Speaker of Assembly under 1962 Constitution.

DR. KHAN SAHIB (1882–1958) On 14 October 1955 became the first Chief Minister of unified West Pakistan under One Unit scheme. In April 1956 founded Republican Party of which he was leader. Assassinated in May 1958.

KHAWAJA NAZIMUDDIN (1894–1964) Before Partition, was Home Minister in Bengal Cabinet and later Prime Minister of Bengal. In 1947 became Chief Minister of East Pakistan. In 1948, on the death of Quaid-e-Azam Mohammad Ali Jinnah, Nazimuddin became Governor-General of Pakistan. In October 1951 he became Prime Minister. Was dismissed by Governor-General Ghulam Mohammad, on 17 April 1953.

M. A. KHUHRO (1901–) In 1947, after Partition, became First Chief Minister of Sind. In 1957 appointed Defence Minister in Pakistan Cabinet under Noon.

MIAN IFTIKHAR HUSSAIN OF MAMDOT (1906–) In 1947, after Partition, became first Chief Minister of Punjab. After the 1951 election became Leader of Opposition in Punjab Assembly. In April 1954 was appointed Governor of Sind.

MAULANA ABUL AALA MAUDOODI (1903–) Started public life as Editor of the daily paper Al-Jamiat. In 1954, during the anti-Ahmadi disturbances in Lahore, was sentenced to death by a Martial Law Court, but later the sentence was commuted to imprisonment. Author of several books on Islam and Islamic History. A right-wing Opposition leader.

MIAN IFTIKHARUDDIN (1908–1962) Before Partition started an English daily, Pakistan Times, at Lahore. After Partition became Minister for Refugees and Rehabilitation in Punjab Cabinet under Mamdot. In 1956–7 joined with Bhashani and Abdul Ghaffar Khan to form opposition National Awami Party.

ISKANDER MIRZA (1890–) In 1954 appointed Governor of East Pakistan. Joined the Pakistan Cabinet as Minister for the Interior and Frontier Regions under Mohammad Ali Bogra. Took over from Ghulam Mohammad as Governor-General of Pakistan in 1955. In 1956, when first Constitution was passed, was elected President of Islamic Republic of Pakistan. On 7 October 1958 promulgated Martial Law, and on 27 October 1958 handed over powers to Field-Marshal Mohammad Ayub Khan.

MALIK FIROZ KHAN NOON (1893–) In December 1957 became Prime Minister of Pakistan and was removed from office on promulgation of Martial Law on 7 October 1958.

ABDUS SATTAR PIRZADA (1907–) Was Minister in Sind Cabinet (1941–3). Became Minister for Food, Agriculture and Health in the first Pakistan Cabinet headed by Liaquat Ali Khan. Became Chief Minister of Sind which office he held till November 1954.

FAZLUR RAHMAN (1905–1966) In 1947 appointed Minister for Commerce and Industries in the first Cabinet of Pakistan headed by the late Quaid-e-Millat, Liaquat Ali Khan, and continued up to 16 October 1951. Again he was Minister for Commerce and Education from 19 October 1951 to 17 April 1953 under the late Khawaja Nazimuddin.

ABU HUSSAIN SARKAR (1894–) In June 1955 appointed Chief Minister of East Pakistan in the United Front Cabinet and held office up to August 1956. Again, in June 1958, became Chief Minister for two days. A leader of the National Democratic Front.

SHEIKH MUJIBUR RAHMAN (1920–) In 1954 became a Minister in the United Front Ministry in East Pakistan under A. K. Fazlul Haq. In 1955 again became a member of the Awami League Cabinet under Ataur Rahman Khan. He is now President of the East Pakistan Awami League in which capacity he launched the Six Point Movement for wider regional autonomy for provinces.

H. S. SUHRAWARDY (1893–1963) In 1946 became Prime Minister of Bengal. Elected Secretary, Bengal Provincial Muslim League, which organized election campaign in 1945 resulting in overwhelming Muslim vote in favour of Pakistan. In September 1956 became Prime Minister of Pakistan, heading Awami League–Republican Coalition Government, and continued up to 17 October 1957.

GLOSSARY

adalat, a court of justice.

advaan, the section of string which holds the woven part of the bed to the wooden frame of the *charpoy.* If the *advaan* is missing, the bed both sags and has a gap towards one end.

a'lim, religious scholar, one who possesses knowledge.

Ansar, Civil Armed Guards.

auqaf, charitable endowment, trust.

basha, a thatched hut.

charpoy, simple bed, of woven string on a wooden frame.

chowkidar, watchman.

darbar, court, or audience or levee.

darul harb, the area of war. This is used to define areas where Muslims may not practise their religion freely, and is contrasted with *darul Islam.*

Eidul Fitr, Muslim festival at the end of Ramadhan, the month of fasting.

faqir, a beggar.

gulli danda, see *kabaddi.*

Hafiz-e-Qur'an, one who knows the Qur'an by heart.

ijma, consensus.

jagir, a landed estate (from a type of land tenure common under the Mughals).

jawan, soldier.

kabaddi; gulli danda, both are children's games, widely played in the Indo-Pakistan sub-continent.

kafir, unbeliever.

katcha, clay-built; literally 'uncooked'.

malik, tribal leader.

Marwaris, people from Marwar in India, widely known as a community assiduous in trade.

Maulvi, informal title, denoting some degree of religious standing in the community.

mela, fair.

mohalla, a street, or a reasonably self-contained neighbourhood in a town.

Momin, true Muslim; literally a believer in God, one who has faith (*iman*).

panchayat, local court of arbitration.

pir, a spiritual guide.

Qazi courts, a court (presided over by a Qazi) which concerns itself with matters of Muslim religious and family law.

Quaid-e-Azam, the great leader. The title conferred by the Muslims of the sub-continent on Mahomed Ali Jinnah.

Risaldar, commander of a cavalry unit.

sherdal, herd of lions.

sherdil, lion-hearted.

tahajjud, particular Muslim prayer said after midnight.

ulema, religious scholars (the plural of *a'lim*).

waqf, charitable endowment, usually of land.

zakat, a sort of alms, a tax on the annual savings of Muslims.

zamindar, landowner.

INDEX